Mr & Mrs Smith
Hotel Collection

South-East Asia

FOR TW

Rice paddies, palaces, high-rises and hammocks: the Smiths have explored south-east Asia from every angle to bring you the slickest city pads, hippest heritage hangouts and most blissful beachside boltholes. And this time, hotel lovers, we've really spiced things up: our latest guide flaunts 34 of our favourite escapes in Thailand, Indonesia, Cambodia, Vietnam, Laos, Malaysia, Singapore and the Philippines. However, that's just the beginning: you'll find hundreds more handpicked on our award-winning website www.mrandmrssmith.com.

We don't just reveal vital tips on each glamorous getaway; we also provide the inside track on these inspiring destinations – all so you don't waste a moment planning your travels. Browse up-to-date restaurant and bar recommendations, get advice on when to visit and what to see, discover the most inspiring viewpoints and even get the lowdown on how to get around and fit in like a local.

To ensure each stylish stay meets our romantic requirements, our intrepid tastemakers (together with their own Mr and Mrs Smiths) bed-tested these hotels incognito, and shared with us their uncensored tales. Enjoy the escapades of world-renowned chef David Thompson, broadcaster Nadya Hutagalung, filmmaker Tony Ayres and actor and rock star Kriss 'Noi' Clapp – just a few of our discerning reviewers from the worlds of fashion, food, media, music and the arts.

And don't forget to take advantage of the BlackSmith membership card over the page: it's our little gift to you. Once registered, it opens up a world of on-arrival goodies, extra perks and special member offers – we wouldn't want you missing out.

So, pack up those sunglasses and sarongs, pick out that perfect hotel, and prepare yourself for an extra-special journey to the East…

Best wishes and bon voyage,

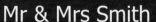

Mr & Mrs Smith

(take)

advantage of us

This is your own personal BlackSmith card, which entitles you to six months' free membership. The moment you register it at www.mrandmrssmith.com, you can access the members' area of our website, take advantage of exclusive last-minute offers from our hotels, and get money back on every booking. The card also provides members-only privileges – such as free bottles of champagne on arrival, spa treats, late check-out and more – when you book hotels and self-catering properties through us. Look out for the Smith icon at the end of each hotel review.

REGISTER NOW
To start getting money back every time you book, hotel offers
and exclusive travel benefits, activate your BlackSmith card by
registering online at www.mrandmrssmith.com/register-card
or by ringing one of the numbers below (it only takes a minute).

ROOM SERVICE
Activate your membership today and you will receive our fantastic monthly e-newsletter Room Service.
It's packed with news, travel tips, even more offers, and great competitions. We promise not to bombard
you with communications, or pass on your details to third parties – this is strictly between you and us.

LOYALTY COUNTS
Book with us and we'll deposit up to five per cent (depending on your membership tier) of the total room
cost into your loyalty account. You can use this money against any future bookings made on our website
through the Smith Travel Team.

AND THERE'S MORE?
As if all this wasn't enough, you can even get access to VIP airport lounges, automatic room upgrades,
flight and car-hire offers, as well as your own dedicated travel consultant, simply by upgrading your
membership to SilverSmith or GoldSmith. Go to www.mrandmrssmith.com for more details.

ON CALL
Thanks to our global Travel Team, Mr & Mrs Smith operates a 24-hour travel service five days a week.
The numbers to ring:

From the UK 0845 034 0700
From Australia 1300 896627
From New Zealand 0800 896671
From the US and Canada 1 866 610 3867 (toll-free)
From anywhere else outside Asia +44 20 8987 4312

From Singapore 800 321 1098 (toll-free)
From Hong Kong 800 905 326 (toll-free)
From Thailand 0018 003 2102
From Indonesia 0018 033 216 0149
From Malaysia 1800 815 256
From anywhere else within Asia +61 3 8648 8871

(contents)

(at a glance)

CAPITAL CITY SLICKERS
Capella Singapore	160
Ma Du Zi Hotel	178
Maison d'Hanoi Hanova Hotel	288
Naumi	166
The Sukhothai	184

RUSTIC ESCAPES
Como Shambhala Estate	90
Kirimaya	226
The Purist Villas & Spa	96

TEMPLE-HOPPING HAVENS
Amantaka	110
The Apsara Rive Droite	116
Heritage Suites Hotel	26
Rachamankha	200
Satri House	122
Viroth's Hotel	32

BLISSFUL BEACH IN REACH
Aleenta Hua Hin	210
Aleenta Phuket-Phang Nga	252
Alila Cha-Am	216
Alila Villas Soori	68
The Amala	74
Anantara Phuket Resort & Spa	262
Karma Kandara	58
The Legian & The Club	80
The Library	236
The Nam Hai	298
The Racha	268
Six Senses Ninh Van Bay	308
Trisara	274
YL Residence No. 17	242

GOURMET GETAWAYS
Abacá Boutique Resort	146
Aleenta Phuket-Phang Nga	252
Alila Villas Uluwatu	46
The Amala	74
Anantara Phuket Resort & Spa	262
The Apsara Rive Droite	116
The Balé	52
Bon Ton Restaurant & Resort	134
The Library	236
The Nam Hai	298
The Sukhothai	184
Trisara	274
YL Residence No. 17	242

DESIGN-CONSCIOUS COOL
Alila Cha-Am	216
Alila Villas Soori	68
Alila Villas Uluwatu	46
Capella Singapore	160
Knai Bang Chatt	16
The Library	236
Ma Du Zi Hotel	178
Maison d'Hanoi Hanova Hotel	288
Naumi	166
The Purist Villas & Spa	96
The Racha	268
Rachamankha	200
Viroth's Hotel	32
YL Residence No. 17	242

HERITAGE HIDEAWAYS
Amantaka	110
Bon Ton Restaurant & Resort	134
Heritage Suites Hotel	26
Puripunn	194
Satri House	122

SUPER SPAS
Abacá Boutique Resort	146
Aleenta Hua Hin	210
Alila Cha-Am	216
Alila Villas Soori	68
Alila Villas Uluwatu	46
Amantaka	110
Anantara Phuket Resort & Spa	262
The Balé	52
Capella Singapore	160
Como Shambhala Estate	90
Karma Kandara	58
The Legian & The Club	80
The Nam Hai	298
The Racha	268
Six Senses Ninh Van Bay	308
Trisara	274

GREAT FOR KIDS
Anantara Phuket Resort & Spa	262
Karma Kandara	58
Kirimaya	226
Knai Bang Chatt	16
Puripunn	194
Six Senses Ninh Van Bay	308
Trisara	274

Time zone GMT +7 hours.
Dialling codes Country code for Cambodia +855:
Kampot (0)33; Kep (0)36; Phnom Penh (0)23; Siem
Reap (0)63 – drop the zero if calling from overseas.
Language Khmer (Cambodian), French and English.
Currency Cambodian riel (KHR) or US dollar (US$).
Tipping culture Locals may not be generous tippers,
but if you find the service is good then it is worth
dropping some coin (not that you'll find any in
Cambodia). Five to 10 per cent is fair.

KEP

1 Knai Bang Chatt

SIEM REAP

2 Heritage Suites Hotel

3 Viroth's Hotel

KEP

COASTLINE **Cambodia-on-Sea**
COAST LIFE **Cat-sailing and crab-snacking**

Playground to princes, politicians and pleasure-seekers, the palm-fringed headland formerly known as Kep-sur-Mer was Cambodia's most glamorous beach resort for the first half of the 20th century. Residents and tourists abandoned Kep's smart villas and grand mansions while civil war, the Khmer Rouge and Vietnamese occupation took their toll, but since the 1990s, this raffishly charming seaside outpost has been re-emerging from its shell. The sandy stretches aren't the country's finest, or the jungle the most extensive, but anyone with a hankering for adventure, a taste for seafood and an eye for architecture will discover a pearl on sleepy shores, far from the tide of mass tourism. Cambodia's 'riviera' could be the unexpected highlight of your trip.

GETTING THERE

Planes Phnom Penh is the closest airport (www.cambodia-airports.com), 164km north of Kep, with good regional connections. International travellers are likely to fly in via Bangkok, Ho Chi Minh City, Hong Kong, Kuala Lumpur or Singapore. Transfer in style – arrange a helicopter to Kampot (+855 (0)23 213 706; www.helicopterscambodia.com).

Trains After four decades of neglect, the railway link from Phnom Penh to Kep is closed for repairs.

Automobiles Kep lies three hours south of Phnom Penh by road. Forget self-drive: ask your hotel to charter a car with a driver – you can pay the driver to stay on so you have wheels to explore or hire a local driver once you arrive. If you're travelling overland from the Mekong Delta in Vietnam, arrange a hotel pick-up from the border at Prek Chak, near Ha Tien.

LOCAL KNOWLEDGE

Taxis There are no metered taxis in Kep, so smart Smiths may opt to visit with their own chauffeured car. Hotels can arrange vehicles or local options include remorque-motos (a Cambodian tuk tuk) or motorbike taxis – a fun way to get around if it's not raining.

Siesta and fiesta Kep is seriously snoozy, with local restaurants winding down by 9pm. There aren't really any stores in Kep, but the banks in nearby Kampot are open 8am–3.30pm weekdays, plus there is now an ATM.

Do go/don't go Weather-wise, November to March is the perfect time to visit; book ahead, as hotel beds will be in short supply. Beaches will also be busy with off-duty locals at weekends. Kep is best avoided during the height of the wet season (July to October): nobody likes sunbathing in the rain.

Packing tips Snorkelling gear for down-under adventures; sailing shoes for working the yachty look.

Recommended reads *First They Killed My Father* by Luong Ung is a poignant account of life (and all too often, death) under the Khmer Rouge, and is one of the best-written survivor accounts. Robert Philpotts' travelogue *The Coast of Cambodia* sees the author journey south-east from Koh Kong Island near the Thai border to Kep.

Local specialities The coast here provides seafood at its unpretentious best, with seaside shacks cooking up squid with green peppercorns, spicy clams and fresh shrimp, as well as fish from the Gulf of Thailand. Best of all are Kep's famous crabs, landed daily and sold live at the town's Crab Market – wander down among the fishermen's huts for freshly grilled crab, squid skewers and sticky rice. Kep's predominantly Khmer cuisine harbours Chinese and Vietnamese influences, but thanks to French colonisation, baguettes are also a familiar sight. The nearby town of Kampot is famous for its fine pepper, de rigueur on Parisian dining tables before Cambodia's long civil war.

Also Local fishing boats can take you on a scenic tour of any of the neighbouring islets, such as Koh Tonsay (Rabbit Island).

WORTH GETTING OUT OF BED FOR

Viewpoint For commanding vistas blending jungle into coastline, give the legs a little workout with a climb up to 'sunset rock', located a few hundred metres behind the town's big antennae (locals can guide you there). Pack a tipple or two and enjoy a sundowner as the light works its magic.

Arts and culture Kep is all about lazing around shore-side, but for die-hard culture vultures, forays further afield are well rewarded. Before the kings of Angkor set to work on the architectural masterpieces that dot the Siem Reap region, their ancestors were building temples across the pre-Angkorian kingdoms Funan and Chenla, south and east of modern-day Phnom Penh. Seek out pagodas perched on hilltops with commanding views, and secret temples hidden inside limestone caves: at Phnom Chhnork, about 8km from Kampot, you'll find a 7th-century cave temple so perfectly preserved it looks like a restoration gift from the Chinese. Don't miss Wat Kirisan at the foot of Phnom Soor mountain in Kompong Trach: its Buddhist shrines are tucked away in a hollow karst cave formation, with a sunroof to the sky.

Activities For action on surf and turf, head to Knai Bang Chatt's Sailing Club (+855 (0)12 349 742). Get nautical on a Hobie Cat, learn to fish with a seafaring local or ride the waves aboard a windsurfer. If terra firma is more your thing, go native on a 110cc motorbike and tour the countryside; borrow a helmet before you zoom off though – roads can be ropey.

Best beach Several of the area's best beaches are actually on Koh Tonsay, an island just off the coast; you will need to commandeer a local boat to take you there. If Kep whets your appetite for the Cambodian coast, continue west to the beach capital of Sihanoukville where the sands are squeaky soft and the islands still surprisingly undeveloped. For something a bit more sophisticated, switch countries and cruise to Phu Quoc, a Vietnamese island ringed by shimmering beaches.

Daytripper The French colonial elite escaped the heat by carving retreats out of the jungle wherever they found high ground: in the 1920s, Bokor Hill Station was Cambodia's coolest spot before air-con. Set a lofty 1,000m up in the heart of Preah Monivong National Park, this hilly area boasts sweeping views down to the coast and ramshackle ruins of the town that time forgot, including the ghostly Bokor Palace Hotel and a crumbling Catholic church. Catch it open on public holidays or talk to your hotel about arranging exclusive access.

Children Swimmers will be splash-happy in these tropical waters: older kids can play *Swallows and Amazons* with sailing lessons, while you give the smalls a high-seas adventure on the hop across to Koh Tonsay. Once they've recreated Angkor Wat in sand, budding explorers will also enjoy cave clambering at Wat Kirisan or discovering hidden pagodas at Phnom Chhnork.

Walks The rolling hills that loom up behind town are home to Bokor National Park. There are a few trails looping through this remnant primary forest, offering glimpses of Kampot or Phu Quoc Island. Your hotel can organise a ramble or a hike to the Popokvil Waterfalls with an experienced guide. With luck, you might spot hornbills, monkeys, rare orchids and pitcher plants.

Perfect picnic Pack champagne and canapés (or sparkling wine and spring rolls) from your lodgings and travel by boat to Koh Tonsay Island. Ask to be dropped at a secluded strip of sand and await a sumptuous seafood lunch, freshly grilled on the beach for you by hotel staff.

Shopping Unless you happen to be a crab collector or pepper importer, save your shopping for Phnom Penh or Siem Reap. Lili Perles (+855 (0)12 634 214) near the Crab Market is the only shop in town, producing home-made necklaces, earrings and bracelets. Mr Smith, before you breathe a sigh of relief, we've already briefed Mrs Smith on the whereabouts of Siem Reap's designer boutiques.

Something for nothing Take a seat on the creaky wooden veranda of Kep's Sailing Club for soothing views of tropical islands on the horizon and the sound of gently lapping waves.

Don't go home without... paying a visit (and a donation) to the Kampot Traditional Music School (+855 (0)33 932 992; www.kampot-music-school.com). This charitable centre offers free education to orphans from the Kampot and Kep area, including classical Khmer music and folk dance training. Watch a lesson or rehearsal by appointment on any weekday afternoon.

KEENLY KEP

Design buffs will enjoy exploring the abandoned villas and residences dating back to the New Khmer Architecture movement of the 1950s and 1960s. Some are squatted and others under redevelopment, but ask the friendly locals to let you have a sniff around.

DIARY

January–February Chinese New Year is the second of three new years in Cambodia; look out for colourful dragon dances and festive parades in Kampot. **March** Time your trip to coincide with the Kep Trio Charity Event, which includes a 10km run and 10km bike ride. That's only two-thirds of a triathlon guys – surely you're game?

Mid-April Khmer New Year (Chaul Chnam Khmer) is the big one. Three days of celebrations include lots of water splashing and talc throwing. Kep's beaches throng with exuberant picnickers as Phnom Penh and Kampot residents descend on the coast.

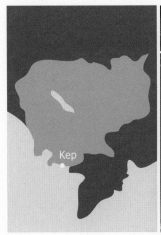

Kep

Knai Bang Chatt

STYLE Bauhaus goes tropical
SETTING Frond-fringed south coast

'Commitment-phobes should approach the starlit, seaside dining area with caution: you could so easily be undone'

Things get retro even before we reach Knai Bang Chatt. My extended Smith family has spent two hours watching unseasonal drizzle through the windscreen wipers on the drive down from Phnom Penh, fighting off nausea and pesky siblings. So far, so reminiscent of the great British holidays of my childhood. But when we find explode-in-your-mouth Space Dust for sale at the petrol station en route I'm really back there. The sticky powder does nothing for the car's upholstery, but makes the snoozing dogs and ambling buffaloes on the road funny again. By the time we spy the sea between the coconut palms and casuarina trees we are almost perky.

Knai Bang Chatt is hidden behind a secret-garden wall, down a small, bumpy track off Kep's main drag. As we shake off the Space Dust and say goodbye to our long-suffering driver, I suspect my suggestion that we might need his services during the weekend is even less than half-hearted. Yes, the Le Corbusier-style mid-20th-century villas are lovely – genuinely retro and rather chic too – but the reason I won't be going far is that I want

to wallow in the illusion that this weekend's reunion with our visiting friends is happening in the beach house I would have inherited if only my parents hadn't been busy having the great British holiday experience.

While the junior Smiths are perturbed by the passionfruit juice at reception, I'm excited to find that I'm rewarded for sharing with two children by getting what appears to be the star room (Mr Smith is, unfortunately, back in the city doing business). Wall-length windows overlook the infinity pool and the sea, and there's also a private outdoor seating area. The futon-style bed has been supplemented with an extra mattress right by the window and, for the first time in their lives, the junior Smiths fight about who gets to sleep alone there.

Our explorations throughout the weekend are pretty much limited to the charmed spaces within the walls of the property. Breakfast at the driftwood table facing the ocean, flat and glassy after the storm, is long and discursive. Much time is spent on the curtained day-beds under the frangipani trees considering our next move. We eventually make it to the end of the wooden jetty where we hear boys in a passing fishing boat singing in time to the rhythm of the oars. Their catch provides our lunch at the neighbouring Sailing Club, a converted traditional fisherman's house built on stilts over the sea.

To appreciate Knai Bang Chatt properly, you really do need to venture out to see what has become of the rest of the bourgeois 1960s resort town of Kep. Following the shady corniche road around the town's headlands and beaches, we trace the partially dismembered remains of colonial and modernist villas. Forlorn washing lines strung between surviving sections of wall mark out those that are being squatted by families; the skeletons of others have been reclaimed by the tropical vegetation. These ruined holiday homes are an arresting reminder of Khmer Rouge rule in the 1970s (while I was enjoying the damp British seaside). Parked SUVs and pristine walls enclosing tracts of sea-view land, however, proclaim that the bourgeoisie are back and this is once again prime real estate.

After taking in kitsch cement statues (a giant rampant crab and unfeasibly buxom bathing belle that mark the two ends of the seafront), we stop at the Crab Market. This is where the Phnom Penh daytrippers select seafood straight from the fishing boats. It's a lively scene and if you've ever wondered why fishwives get such a bad rap this is the place to come and see some in action. We stroll around trying to look as if we too know how to size up the produce – flattened dried squid, shockingly pink preserved prawns, bottles of fish sauce, buckets of viscous palm sugar, heaped fragrant green mangoes and several varieties of Kampot pepper.

Tonight we've chosen to have dinner inside Knai Bang Chatt, where there is a tempting daily-changing set menu. Flexibility being next to godliness in Cambodia, I'm not surprised to find that negotiation with the kitchen staff is possible and we arrange a vegetarian dish built around tangy green peppercorns as well as some child-friendly options.

We eat on a terrace jutting out into the sea. At this time of year it's too hot to sit here by day, but at night this spot catches whatever air is stirring. Surrounded by tea-lights, it feels as if we are floating and it takes some time for our eyes to adjust to the different darknesses of sea and sky and pick out the horizon. Mr Smith is far away up the Mekong this weekend, so I can't claim to have exploited the romantic possibilities of Knai Bang Chatt, but commitment-phobes should approach the starlit, seaside dining area with caution: you could so easily be undone.

The hotel has a small spa — if the curtains are looped open the therapist is free — and I finish my stay with a massage. Like so much I experience in Cambodia, it is not quite what I expected but turns out to have been just what I needed. Stepping out of the spa I am pleasantly bedazzled by the sunlight and the recent attention to my pressure points, ready for as much Space Dust as the journey home can throw at me.

Reviewed by Mr & Mrs Smith

NEED TO KNOW

Rooms 11 rooms.

Rates US$155–US$325, including breakfast.

Check-out Noon, but flexible subject to availability, and a 50 per cent charge after 1pm. Earliest check-in, 2pm.

Facilities Computer, library and video room with movie projector, small spa, beachfront chill-out area, ping-pong table, free WiFi throughout, sailing club with Hobie Cats, kayaks and a speedboat. In rooms: fruit plate, free bottled water.

Poolside Infinity pool with views over the Gulf of Thailand. Day-beds and sofas formed from tropical driftwood abound.

Children Welcome: baby cots and mattresses for older children are provided free, or an extra bed is available for US$30 a night. Babysitting can be arranged for US$5 an hour with 24 hours' notice.

Also Knai Bang Chatt's three renovated modernist villas were built in the Seventies by protégés of acclaimed Khmer architect Vann Molyvann. Founded by a pair of stylish Belgian expats, its name means 'a rainbow encircling the sun'.

IN THE KNOW

Our favourite rooms The resort's 11 rooms are spread over three villas. Each has its own character, but we loved the (mostly first floor) Sea View Doubles. Room 4 has spectacular views and a large terrace that more than makes up for a smaller bathroom. Rooms 7 and 9 are in the newest building, with a bold sense of space and designer bathrooms.

Hotel bar The bar and restaurant are one and the same, with rooftop gatherings not unheard of on a busy night. There's an intimate mood as the bar is only open to Knai Bang Chatt guests. Head to the allied Sailing Club next door for signature cocktail, the Kep Sunset. An old fisherman's house, it also serves Khmer and Western food until 10pm.

Hotel restaurant At this informal alfresco pavilion near the seafront, the accent is on seafood, with Khmer-style set lunches and Western dinners, plus occasional fusion dishes.

Top table Enjoy a lazy lunch on the driftwood bench down by the ocean, which offers a snippet of shade. For dinner and the best sea views, bag a table on the promontory.

Room service Available from 8am to 10pm, but smart Smiths will prefer to soak up the outdoor setting by the sea.

Dress code Did you pack anything retro? The Seventies architecture of the place will make you wish you had.

Local knowledge Kep itself is less about blissful beaches and more about seaside adventure, so get active at the Sailing Club for nautical larks. Hobie Cats, a speedboat and kayaks are up for grabs. Afterwards, enjoy a trad Khmer massage or book a pampering beauty session back at the hotel's spa, or outdoors by the pool or beach.

LOCAL EATING AND DRINKING

On Route 33, Breezes (+855 (0)976 759 072) is the only restaurant of real repute in Kep. Gloriously set on a headland jutting into the sea, it's the perfect place to dine. Part of a boutique resort perched beneath a backdrop of jungle, Veranda (+855 (0)33 399 035), on the Kep Hillside Road, offers panoramic views of coastal Kep. Play home or away with a mixed menu of Khmer, Asian and international dishes, but save space for the exquisite home-made patisseries and sorbets. Rikitikitavi (+855 (0)12 235 102) restaurant is not strictly local, being 24kms down the road in neighbouring town Kampot, but it is worth the detour. Epic Arts Café (+855 (0)33 932 247) is a small café in Kampot's Old Market area that offers delightful home-made cakes and shakes.

GET A ROOM!

For more information, or to book this hotel, go to www.mrandmrssmith.com – our expert team can take care of all your travel arrangements. Register your Smith membership card to enjoy exclusive offers and privileges.

 SMITH MEMBER OFFER A 30-minute massage or a discovery hour on a sailing boat for each guest.

Knai Bang Chatt Phum Thmey, Sangkat Prey Thom, Khan Kep, Kep City 989, Cambodia (+855 (0)12 349 742; www.knaibangchatt.com)

SIEM REAP

CITYSCAPE Colonial streets, sacred sites
CITY LIFE Market shopping, temple hopping

Thronged by adventurers and travellers since the 1900s, this once-sleepy Khmer village is now a bustling tourist hotspot. Dark years under Pol Pot may have taken Cambodia to the brink of collapse, but the green shoots of recovery are nowhere stronger than in Siem Reap, where a fresh crop of boutique hotels, trendy French bistros and lavish spas breathe new life into the town. Siem Reap has never needed fancy trimmings to draw visitors: its star attraction is the architectural marvel Angkor Wat. Rescued from their jungle embrace, the Angkor temples have the grand scale of the Great Wall, the iconic beauty of the Taj Mahal and the powerful symbolism of the pyramids. With its laid-back pace and good-time vibe, Siem Reap feels like a happy grin barely hidden by a shy hand.

GETTING THERE

Planes Touch down at Siem Reap International Airport (www.cambodia-airports.com) from regional gateways including Bangkok, Ho Chi Minh City, Hong Kong, Kuala Lumpur or Singapore. For good connections, try Singapore Airlines (www.singaporeairlines.com) or Thai Air (www.thaiairways.com). It's about a 40-minute flight from Cambodian capital Phnom Penh.

Boats Fast boats connect Phnom Penh and Siem Reap via the undulating Tonlé Sap river and lake (it's still a five- to six-hour ride). Luxury cruise operators also run between Ho Chi Minh City, Phnom Penh and Siem Reap, if aquatic action floats your boat.

Automobiles Self-drive is not permitted – thank goodness – because a lack of road rules makes the traffic chaotic at best. Buses ply the streets to Phnom Penh from US$6 and take six hours. If you want to explore, ask your hotel to hook you up with a reliable driver. Incurable romantics might prefer the local remorques (tuk tuks) which start at just US$15 a day.

LOCAL KNOWLEDGE

Taxis You can take a taxi from the airport for a flat rate of US$7 to any destination in Siem Reap. There are no metered taxis as such, but the tuk tuk drivers more than make up for it by offering their services every 10 seconds or so. Motorbikes are a cheap way to get around the temples, starting at just US$8 a day. Short hops around town are US$1 or less.

Siesta and fiesta Banks are open 8am–3.30pm weekdays, and ATMs are pretty common. Shops vary widely, but core hours are 8am–8pm. Cambodians like to eat just after sunset, so truly local places close early. Night spots warm up around 9pm, but the bassline doesn't fully kick in until around midnight.

Do go/don't go The cooler, drier months from November to February make rambles in the jungle more enjoyable, but the world and his wife will be there, too. The wet season, which peaks from June to October, need not put a dampener on your trip, as the landscape is lush and the showers short.

Packing tips A scarf, T-shirt and guidebook – so you have something to wave at temple touts when they shout 'You buy scarf, T-shirt, guidebook?'

Recommended reads Of the often-dry temple guides, *Ancient Angkor* by Claude Jacques is the least likely to make you nod off, partly thanks to beautiful photography by Michael Freeman. *River of Time* by Jon Swain is a trip back to old Indochina and includes a gripping account of the French embassy stand-off after the Khmer Rouge takeover of Phnom Penh.

Local specialities Thailand and Vietnam may be the region's gourmet heavyweights, but Cambodia is no slouch when it comes to going a few rounds in the kitchen. Angkor has put Cambodia on the tourist map, and *amoc* (baked fish with coconut, lemongrass and chilli) may yet put the country on the culinary map. Siem Reap has it all, from shabby street stalls for sampling fresh local Khmer flavours to designer dining rooms offering fusion cuisine. Try street favourite *nam ben chok* (light noodles with chicken curry) at Psar Chaa, in the Old Market, or enjoy a blue steak at a French bistro with the atmosphere of old Indochine.

Also You can hire a private car to take you round the temples from US$30 a day. Tour guides are available from US$25 per day. Hanuman (www.hanumantourism.com) offers local reliable guides.

WORTH GETTING OUT OF BED FOR

Viewpoint Despite the ungodly hour, Angkor Wat is busier than a rush-hour Tube station at sunrise. Dodge the crowds with a dawn visit to the enigmatic faces of the nearby Bayon or seek solace amid the ruins of Ta Prohm. If the morning sounds uncivilised, try a sundowner on the shores of the Western Mebon, an island temple in the middle of the immense Western Baray reservoir.

Arts and culture Any stay in Siem Reap will mostly focus on temple trawling, but there's modern history as well: learn about the culture of survival at the Cambodia Landmine Museum (www.cambodialandminemuseum.org). The museum includes deactivated civil war mines and serves as a chilling reminder of the effects of war.

Activities Cooks 'n' Tuk Tuks fires up the wok at 10am daily with a visit to a local market, then returns to the RiverGarden resort for a masterclass in Cambodian cuisine – lessons cost US$25 a head (+855 (0)63 963 400; www.therivergarden.info). Channel your inner cowboy (or girl) at the Happy Ranch (+855 (0)12 920 002; www.thehappyranch.com), where you can saddle up to survey Siem Reap on horseback. Helicopters Cambodia (www.helicopterscambodia.com) and Helistar (www.helistarcambodia.com) both operate short scenic flights over Angkor starting at US$90 for eight minutes.

Daytripper Go beyond Angkor and you'll rediscover remote temples lost in the wilderness. Beng Mealea has a similar architectural footprint to Angkor Wat, but has been almost entirely swallowed by the jungle. Continuing west, hike through the dense forest to Kbal Spean, or the River of a Thousand Lingas. Sacred to the ancient Khmers, this romantically cascading series of streams has been venerated with hundreds of phallic symbols, symbolically rendering the waters fertile as they descend to the rice paddies below. Guides can be booked through Beyond (http://beyonduniqueescapes.com).

Children Little Smiths will love clambering about the spiritual adventure playground that is tree-entwined Ta Prohm; and you can expect inquisitive infants to test your natural storytelling ability to its limits after visiting the Bayon's giant carved-stone faces. Calm things down at the Angkor Butterfly Centre (www.angkorbutterfly.com/abchome.html), where more than 30 species of Cambodian butterflies flutter by in lush tropical gardens.

Walks The ancient Khmer capital Angkor Thom offers a tantalising trek thanks to a carpet of forest and rewarding temples. Starting out at the spectacular south gate, make your way along the top of the massive walls to the west gate with nary a visitor in sight. Check out Baphuon, the 'world's largest jigsaw puzzle', and the Terrace of Elephants. Finish at Bayon, one of Angkor's most mysterious treasures.

Perfect picnic Pack a picnic breakfast from the hotel and arrive in Angkor Wat through the secluded back door (eastern entrance) around 7am, almost exactly the hour the sunrise crowd heads back to their hotels. The mother of all temples almost to yourself – that's worthy of a wow.

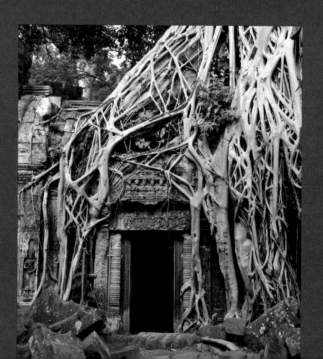

Shopping The Angkor Night Market is a smart stop for a taster of everything you can buy in Siem Reap, but practise your best bargaining banter. Artisans d'Angkor (+855 (0)63 963 330; www.artisansdangkor.com) in the Chantiers Ecoles compound just off Sivutha Street is the place to get Khmer-style sculptures, or pick up pretty modern silks by French-Madagascan fashion designer Eric Raisina at his Wat Thmei workshop (+855 (0)63 963 207). Mrs Smiths should check out Wanderlust, which sells clothes, jewellery and interiors pieces made by local Cambodian women, and is located in Alley West in the Old Market area (+855 (0)63 955 980; www.wanderlustcambodia.com).
Something for nothing Deep down, Siem Reap is a spiritual place, and strolling through the backstreets reveals a serene side to local life. Wander the pagoda district, setting off from the ancient, pre-Angkor brick temple of Wat Preah Inkosei. Follow the sleepy riverside road south to Wat Bo, complete with its traditional frescoes, and meander on to Wat Dam Nak, a former royal palace.
Don't go home without exploring the watery world of the Tonlé Sap lake, *Tintin*-style, in a dugout canoe. Terre Cambodge (www.terrecambodge.com) offers a day cruise of the lake for US$60 a person. Teetering on soaring bamboo stilts, over-water skyscraper village Kompong Pluk resembles something from a film set.

SUPERBLY SIEM REAP

Browse Banteay Srei, the art gallery of Angkor also known as 'the temple of the women'; this jewel in the crown of Angkorian artisanship is a Hindu temple dedicated to Shiva. The petite proportions of its architecture and the delicacy of the sculptural reliefs has led to speculation that the temple was built by and for women only.

DIARY

January–February Chinese New Year, which falls between mid-January and mid-February each year, heralds the second new year of three in Cambodia. Some businesses shut but you'll see dragon dances aplenty. **Mid-April** Khmer New Year (or Chaul Chnam Khmer) is the big one: three days of celebrations include lots of water splashing and talc throwing. Avoid Angkor unless you like sharing it with one million visitors. **October–November** Bon Om Tuk is the Water Festival celebrating King Jayavarman VII's victory over the upstart Chams. The Siem Reap River hosts frenetic long-boat races and the town heaves at the hinges; by night revellers sleep where they fall, so mind your step.

• Siem Reap

Heritage Suites Hotel

STYLE Come-hither Khmer classic
SETTING Pretty pagoda district

'The overall effect is of a private pocket
of tranquillity, where simple elegance
and a slower pace of life prevail'

I guess everyone else must be at the temples,' says Mr Smith wryly as we stroll into the deserted dining room for breakfast. It is Saturday morning, our first in the elegant confines of Heritage Suites after escaping from Bangkok the night before. Having arrived late, and after a casual dinner in the clubby, colonial Lantern restaurant (perhaps named for its stately hurricane lamps), we'd spent the night cocooned from the world we'd left behind in 'Orchid', one of the hotel's Bungalow Suites, with its gargantuan bed and pod-like bath tub. The absence of any distractions or interruptions quickly eased our souls and we awoke bright-eyed and eager to explore Angkor.

The fact is, we aren't particularly late for breakfast. It is a very civilised 9am, but in hot and dusty Siem Reap people rise early to make the most of the cooler morning hours. Since Mr Smith and I have visited the multi-temple Angkor site before, we choose a gentler pace – one where indulgent lie-ins and leisurely meals take priority. After breakfasting on perfectly cooked eggs Benedict, and quite possibly the best coffee to be found in Cambodia, we embark upon a personal tour of the complex.

Nothing quite prepares you for the first glimpse of hero temple Angkor Wat – its sheer majesty cannot fail to inspire awe. Even the second time around, it is absolutely, undeniably, breathtaking. It being mid-morning by the time we arrive (it's only about eight kilometres from the hotel, but we did manage to linger over breakfast), it is ridiculously hot, so we spend our time cowering in the lower galleries, admiring the intricate murals and admitting we probably should have got out of bed just that little bit earlier.

If Angkor Wat is the emperor of the Khmer kingdom, then neighbouring temple the Bayon is its spiritual adviser; its brooding stone faces watch on wisely from all angles. Stumbling through its corridors, we resist the urge to touch, take dozens of photos and then hot-foot it to the last stop on our tour: Ta Prohm. Sprawling, a little decrepit and embraced by the searching, skirting roots of banyan, fig and kapok trees, Ta Prohm might have sunk into obscurity if it weren't for a certain film starring Angelina Jolie. Thanks to its cameo role it's become the second most popular attraction on the circuit and previous experience has prepared us for an encounter

with dozens of tourists chiming 'Angelina' as they snap their very own *Tomb Raider* moment. This time, an almighty storm breaks out, sending the tour coaches scurrying back to town – it means we have the unique opportunity to experience Ta Prohm on our own. Mr Smith, as insightful as ever, remarks that it is one of those rare 'in the moment' occasions that will remain with us for life.

After such a magical morning, I am feeling slightly weary. It is hot and I'm hungry and longing for a lazy afternoon sprawled in a cool corner. There's something rather special about a hotel with such romantic appeal – Heritage Suites is so peaceful and secluded that it is very easy to relax and completely be ourselves. Its cream-walled layout creates an intimate compound and, as the name suggests, it has a traditionally styled decor that manages to avoid colonial clichés by mixing in vibrant splashes of colour and sleek leather furniture. Genuine, gentle service makes us feel like we are staying with friends, all the more so because we barely glimpse any other guests all weekend. The overall effect is of a private pocket of tranquillity, where simple elegance and a slower pace of life prevail. Needless to say, it doesn't take much to persuade Mr Smith to join me for a light lunch of *dim sum* and fresh spring rolls. This is our first

taste of Asian food – having opted for gourmet Western dishes last night – and it is the perfect reminder that when in Siem Reap you should eat as the Khmers do. The local food tastes far better than anything made from imported ingredients. Our appetites sated, we collapse by the divine saltwater pool.

As evening approaches, the poolside sun-deck takes on a sexy, clubby persona with seductive lighting, an open fire and a backing soundtrack to match. It would be very easy to settle here for the night, but revived by a glass of champagne, we give in to our curiosity and venture into Siem Reap.

The city has expanded almost beyond recognition since we last visited five years ago, but it's still small enough to stroll around and has, thankfully, retained its easy, laid-back ambience. First stop: G&Ts at the art deco-inspired Foreign Correspondents Club bar, after which we head for dinner at Hôtel de la Paix's fashionable in-town eatery AHA. After the mellow, colonial-esque vibe of FCC, AHA seems a little too try-hard, but the tapas-style, mod-Khmer food reinforces us for an adventure to Pub Street, Siem Reap's equivalent of Bangkok's Khao San Road. Often dismissed by the city's more high-minded guides, there's still no better, livelier place for people-watching – especially for fellow Smiths who can dip in and out again – and it is fun to share traveller tales over a few Angkor beers.

All too soon, midnight strikes and this bar fly yearns for her bed. Feeling rather smug to escape Backpackerville, we hop a moto back to the serene luxury of Heritage Suites. As my head hits the downy pillow, Mr Smith suggests setting an early alarm so we can explore more of the temples in the morning and tap into our inner Angelinas. I don't even indulge him with a reply.

Reviewed by Liz Weselby

NEED TO KNOW

Rooms 26, including 20 suites.

Rates US$150–US$528, including breakfast.

Check-out Noon, but flexible subject to availability, and a charge of 50 per cent up to 6pm. Check-in, 9am when available.

Facilities Bodia Spa, gardens, free WiFi throughout. In rooms: iPod dock, incense, goodnight gift, free bottled water.

Poolside Chill out in the spacious saltwater pool surrounded by verdant foliage.

Children Plans are afoot for a child-free policy, so think romantic retreat more than family-friendly fun. Kids are welcome for now; the hotel supplies free cots, extra beds (US$25 a night) and babysitters (US$5 an hour, with three hours' notice).

Also Guests enjoy in-room check-in, which includes a personalised selection of tropical fruit. Smoking is allowed.

IN THE KNOW

Our favourite rooms Suites are named after flowers and include courtyard gardens, steam rooms and alfresco showers. Hibiscus is our favoured bloom – a bold bungalow with Cambodian and Indian touches. Go for an Executive or Royal Suite for an outdoor, private Jacuzzi.

Hotel bar The Lobby Bar is a smart, ivory-mahogany space that's elegant from its tiled floors to its dark-wood rafters. A small, thatched bar by the pool is ideal for cocktails outdoors.

Hotel restaurant The Lantern, above the Lobby Bar, looks both East and West for its influences, serving dishes such as French-accented seafood and Cambodian spiders. If 'tarantula nest' is too scary, try the grilled Mekong lobster with star anise. Better still, the tasting menu is a great-value feast of seven dishes.

Top table Book a seat on the balcony for intimate dining with views over the Lobby Bar below.

Room service Available between 6am and 11pm, including everything on the Lantern menu: order pasta for home comfort or *longan* and *rambutan pannacotta* for a taste of the exotic.

Dress code Colonial-esque couture: print dresses and creamy linens will complement the plantation-style furniture.

Local knowledge You're only 10 minutes from the temples at Angkor Wat. For a more off-the-beaten-track tour, such as trips to see the overgrown shrines of Beng Mealea and Phnom Khulen, contact Heritage Adventures for temple dinners, jungle camping and bike rides (www.heritage-adventures.com). Templed out? The hotel's Bodia Spa is a small sanctuary for the body and soul. Indulge in the Escape Angkor experience, a five-hour journey to heaven and back.

LOCAL EATING AND DRINKING

L'Oasi Italiana (+855 (0)92 418 917) is tucked away on East Bank, shrouded by trees, near Wat Preah Inkosei. Gnocchi with white truffles and risotto with porcini prove this is not just another pizza joint. **FCC Angkor** (+855 (0)63 760 280) on Pokombor Avenue is an art deco masterpiece of a bar with a decorative pool and torchlit garden that makes a romantic spot for cocktails alfresco. A backstreet hideaway for caffeine fiends, **Common Grounds** (+855 (0)63 965 687) is the hotel's neighbourhood café, at 719 Street 14. **Le Café** in Wat Bo (+855 (0)92 271 392) is part of the French Cultural Centre, offering a superb menu of breakfasts, pastries, salads and sandwiches. In the old market area **AHA** (+855 (0)63 965 501), on the Alley, serves Khmer-fusion tapas in smartly designed surrounds.

GET A ROOM!

For more information, or to book this hotel, go to www.mrandmrssmith.com – our expert team can take care of all your travel arrangements. Register your Smith membership card to enjoy exclusive offers and privileges.

 SMITH MEMBER OFFER A tour of the Angkor Wat temples in the hotel's vintage Mercedes.

Heritage Suites Hotel Wat Polangka, Siem Reap, Cambodia (+855 (0)63 969 100; www.heritagesuiteshotel.com)

Viroth's Hotel

STYLE Dinky designer den
SETTING Lush Wat Bo quarter

'The crisp functional minimalism
is softened by warm colours and
splashes of red'

'm sorry, we don't have your booking,' says the smiling receptionist, flicking through the reservation book. It's late, we've caught the last plane into Siem Reap and, after a long day, all I want to do is slip into our room and turn off the light. My eyes dart from the receptionist to Mr Smith and back as I splutter plaintively.

Normally, when tired and emotional, I take such things rather badly, but this time I can't. Viroth's affable front-of-house manager makes the problem seem easy to fix. It's that kind of hotel – the staff members are genial, helpful and genuinely friendly. It is then that Mr Smith confesses he may have forgotten to make the booking, but in the face of such grace there is little I can do but smile. Within a few minutes we are settled in a large, cool, slate-floored room. The initial hiccup of our arrival is immediately forgotten as we Smiths retire early, promptly tucking ourselves up and resting peacefully in our very comfortable bed: you see we have come to Cambodia on a mission.

The real point of coming to Siem Reap is to see the magnificent temples. There are so many architectural wonders that it's a good idea to start your research and planning a couple of weeks before you arrive. Once in town, the best time to go is at dawn, before the torrid heat builds, or in the late afternoon as it abates. Explore one or two for a few hours at a time so you're not overwhelmed by the grandeur or fatigued by the sun's biting rays – that's our plan anyway. Having arranged a car with the hotel, we stumble down the stairs well before daybreak to find our guide already waiting for us.

We walk through the portal of iconic Angkor Wat, the area's best-known temple, and onto the causeway to see the sun rise. However clichéd it sounds, the sight inspires awe and wonder. Around the outer galleries, the crowd thins out and there is some shade. I find the bas-reliefs mesmerising – their deep, elegant carvings depict the Khmer universe, its gods, wars, myths and beliefs. We walk silently along the arcades, trying to comprehend a world so different from our own.

Once back in this world, we return to Viroth's just in time for a late breakfast. All is quiet as we climb the stairs to the broad, shaded terrace. We are alone, a blessing after contending with the masses at the temple. Breakfast is simple, a small menu but with some surprisingly good croissants. Afterwards, walking downstairs, we see the hotel in daylight for the first time. Its cool grey floors, white walls and lush green trees create a relaxed yet urbane feel. Viroth's is a place to feel at ease. A lap or two in the turquoise mosaic pool is a good way to feel even better in this bijou bolthole. The wise escape the mounting heat – and recover from early temple trips – by heading off for a nap. We Smiths retire too.

There are only seven rooms here, all generously sized, and most have a terrace, albeit *très petite*. The crisp, functional minimalism is softened by warm colours and splashes of red. I sleep well, but Mr Smith has other plans. I awake to find he's

retreated to Viroth's rooftop spa, where he has a massage, a soak in the Jacuzzi and, I suspect, a little additional spa treatment.

Viroth's is an easy stroll – 10 minutes or so – across the small river and into the centre of the old town, where we wander for a spot of shopping. Most of Siem Reap's markets are at their best in the morning, although the main market continues into the late afternoon. We dive into its dark, shaded alleyways, finding the bundles of smoked fish, pots of freshly made palm sugar and piles of excellent pepper far more enticing than the glittering Angkor souvenirs, the fake antiques and the kitsch that litters the outer rim. We push our way past the frivolous fringe hawkers into the market proper, sit down at one of the stalls and have a local lunch of *nom banchok namya*, silken white noodles topped with a mild green curry made with ground fish and lemongrass.

Up for more Angkor culture, we take in another temple. The Bayon is extraordinary – countless towers ringed with the face of the Buddha smiling serenely at the passing world and surveying the clamouring tourists passing through the galleries. We manage to find some shade and a bit of tranquillity on one of the upper levels and sit there for a while. It's magnificent – the colour of the faces change as time passes and the shadows stretch into the late afternoon.

About an hour out of town is Banteay Srei, an outlying temple of remarkable beauty, and possibly the most perfect jewel in the whole Angkor complex. Many of the pink sandstone carvings, more than a thousand years old, are still so precise, delicate and in flawless condition. The scale of this sanctuary is small, and its distance from town means it's less crowded, making it much easier to appreciate the shrine in peace. We stay until the sun sets before driving back to Viroth's.

Siem Reap has some seductive eateries too. Do, however, ensure you book at the hotel's restaurant, a few minutes' walk away. Its marvellous open courtyard is surrounded by wooden decks, sectioned off by wafting orange screens, underneath the span of some ancient trees. The Khmer menu offers something for everyone and we decide it has some of the best food in town. I like the local fish stewed in coconut cream, while Mr Smith is partial to the grilled pork wrapped in betel leaves. Afterwards, we walk into town, crossing over a small bridge to the night market, where beer, Westerners, spruikers and even flesh-nibbling fish thrive each evening.

Viroth's may not be as plush as some of the bigger hotels in large cities, but its wonderful charm lies in the sincerely sweet staff who chat and advise (not because it's their job but because they want to). They bring life to the hotel and ensure that those who stay return. Mr Smith and I have already made another booking – this time for sure.

Reviewed by David Thompson

NEED TO KNOW

Rooms 7 rooms.

Rates US$90–US$130, including à la carte breakfast.

Check-out Noon, but if the room is available late check-out can be arranged for 50 per cent of the day rate. Check-in, 2pm.

Facilities Rooftop spa and Jacuzzi, free WiFi throughout, gardens. In rooms: cable TV, minibar.

Poolside Given its celebrated status as a small, intimate hotel, the pool is suitably small and intimate. Overshadowed by deliciously verdant vegetation, it is great for a cool plunge on a hot day.

Children Viroth's is something of a grown-ups paradise, but that doesn't mean smaller Smiths aren't welcome. Extra beds can be added to rooms for older children for US$20 a night, but the hotel doesn't supply baby cots.

Also The mobile rooftop spa is an innovation. The massage comes to you. Dip into the Jacuzzi afterwards to wind down after a long day tramping around the temples. Smoking is allowed in designated areas only.

IN THE KNOW

Our favourite rooms All follow the same contemporary blueprint, with sensual rain showers, but ground-floor Room number 1 lives up to its name with a delightful private garden area. Upstairs, Room 7 takes top billing thanks to the best pool view in the pad.

Hotel bar The rooftop bar is all about stylish sofas that suck you in. Settle down with a bottle of wine and let the evening slip by. Rooftop usually equals breeze and that can be priceless in the hot season.

Hotel restaurant Viroth's is a rooftop re-creation of the nearby signature restaurant on Wat Bo Road. The menu is traditional Khmer with the emphasis on inspired presentation and delicate flavours. Try fish *amoc* for the essence of Cambodia in a banana leaf.

Top table No one particularly stands out, but try to live life on the edge (of the rooftop) for views of the cityscape.

Room service Available from 7am to 11pm, room service includes all the dishes on the menu during restaurant hours and selected snacks at other times.

Dress code Bring your glad rags, as this stylish spot should put you in the mood for a night out (or two). Owners Viroth and Fabien can point you towards some happening venues.

Local knowledge Go local with a wander through the pretty grounds of Wat Bo, the most important pagoda in the Siem Reap area. Some of the best Buddhist frescoes from the 19th century adorn the ceilings of this charming place and there is a small collection of Angkorian pottery, regalia and weaponry. Several of the 'DJ monks' on Wat Bo Radio speak English if you want to learn more.

LOCAL EATING AND DRINKING

For fine French dining, look no further than the art deco-inspired *Le Malraux* (+855 (0)63 966 041; Sivutha Street). The menu includes a succulent salmon tartare, as well as Armagnac to put hairs on your chest. Continuing the minimalist design theme perfected by Viroth's, Nest (+855 (0)63 966 381; Sivutha Street) is a garden bar with soaring sail-like canopies and snug rattan day-beds. The cocktail list is worthy of a very thorough investigation. For a creative caffeine fix, wander down to the Old Market and into Joe-To-Go (+855 (0)63 969 050), a small café brewing up gourmet coffee. All profits support a school for disadvantaged local children.

GET A ROOM!

For more information, or to book this hotel, go to www.mrandmrssmith.com – our expert team can take care of all your travel arrangements. Register your Smith membership card to enjoy exclusive offers and privileges.

SMITH MEMBER OFFER A hand-woven cotton scarf for each room.

Viroth's Hotel 0658, Street 23, Wat Bo Village, Siem Reap, Cambodia (+855 (0)12 778 096; www.viroth-hotel.com)

HOW TO... FIT IN LIKE A LOCAL

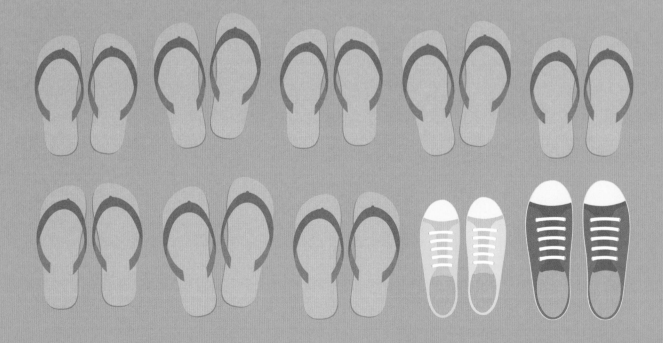

SALUTATIONS

Forget any Euro-style cheek kissing: in Thailand, Cambodia and Laos, people greet each other with steepled palms, as though in prayer. To pull off this move – known as the *wai* – it should be teamed with a respectful bow. As the manoeuvre is intended to reflect social hierarchy, the person of lower rank (or age) should *wai* first – but we say err on the safe side and wade in first. If you haven't mastered it and you're unsure when to *wai*, don't fret: handshakes will do the job just as well.

SAVOIR-FAIRE

Never bare your sole: feet are regarded as impure and touching or pointing with your trotters is taboo. Follow in locals' footsteps and remove your shoes when you enter private homes, temples and family-run shops. In the Buddhist Mekong region and parts of Indonesia and Malaysia, the head is the most sacred part of the body, so never pat someone on their bonce. Resist holiday urges to flash your flesh: bikinis and board shorts should be banished to the beach – and going topless is a total no-no. When visiting holy or royal sites, cover up completely. A final tip for the ladies: monks must never make contact with a woman, even indirectly, so place any offerings in a bowl or on the receiving cloth.

SENTIMENTALITY

Throughout south-east Asia – even in liberal Thailand, where most city types are pretty open-minded about sexuality – PDAs, aka public displays of affection, are considered impolite and embarrassing. While we at Smith wholeheartedly encourage romance (as you know), decorum dictates that passions are best played out in the privacy of your pool villa.

SERENITY

The Chinese custom of keeping your personal pressure gauge out of the red sector prevails. Where emotions are concerned, the etiquette in this populous region is to keep them firmly in check and avoid confrontation at all costs. It's all about maintaining composure, peace and harmony, harking back to the days when the hippie trail turned south-east Asia into a travel destination. Lose your cool, and things could quickly go *Patpong* (rhyming slang for wrong).

SOVEREIGNTY

Thailand's king has semi-divine status and most of his countrymen hold him in utmost respect. This includes images as well, so no stepping on pictures of him or even money (which bears his visage). Although the level of adoration might seem astounding, be careful never to disrespect the monarch: denouncing the royal family is an arrestable offence.

SUPPING

South-east Asians live for food and the rhythm of the day is dictated by meal times, with a steady procession of snacks in between. To get properly stuck into a region's cuisine, order an array of contrasting dishes – and be adventurous. Fingers may have been the tradition, but fork and spoon are now the tools of choice, with knives rarely employed outside the kitchen. Chopsticks are commonplace, but think before you leave them sticking out of your bowl: it's considered bad luck (as they'd resemble the incense sticks used to honour the dead), so use a chopstick rest or lay them neatly across the rim of the bowl.

SIPPING

A pot of green tea appears in most restaurants on the house, but if you like your beverages to pack a punch, rest assured that beer and spirits are the preferred poisons here – both are served on the rocks. To make like a serious player, order a bottle of liquor with mixers to share at your table. Wine lovers will also find their tipple of choice widely available: it's cheerfully cheap in Cambodia and Laos but surprisingly expensive in Indonesia, Malaysia and Thailand. Coffee connoisseurs should seek out the Indonesian delicacy *kopi luwak* (*ca phe chon* in Vietnam). The beans for this fine brew are only roasted for use once they have been consumed by a civet and, erm, 'passed' by the critter.

SHOPPING

Haggling, negotiating – call it what you will – remember it's all a game, even if it does seem to be treated as though a matter of life and death. Barter away with market hawkers and individual boutique owners, but drop the debating skills in large shops. If something has a fixed price, don't even think about bargaining. Feigning disinterest or working the classic 'walk away' move can help prices to plummet.

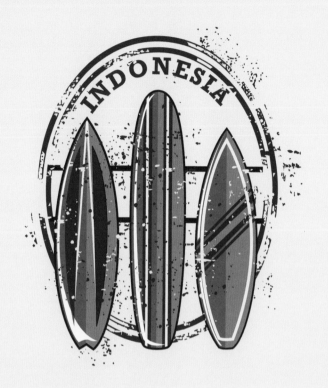

Time zone GMT +8 hours.

Dialling codes Country code for Indonesia +62:
Bali (0)361 – drop the zero if calling from overseas.

Language The official language is Bahasa Indonesia,
although, confusingly, most people speak Bahasa Bali,
which is further complicated by local dialects. In main
tourist areas, English is widely understood, and those
working in the hospitality industry may have a few
words of Italian, French, German and even Dutch.

Currency The rupiah (RP), although big resorts may
accept US dollars ($US) and euros (€).

Tipping culture Not expected, but adding 10 per cent
for good service is appreciated.

Java

Bali

Lombok

Denpasar

BUKIT PENINSULA, BALI

4   Alila Villas Uluwatu

5   The Balé

6   Karma Kandara

SEMINYAK & TABANAN, BALI

7   Alila Villas Soori

8   The Amala

9   The Legian & The Club

UBUD, BALI

10   Como Shambhala Estate

11   The Purist Villas & Spa

BUKIT PENINSULA, BALI

COASTLINE Craggy cliffs, southern sands
COAST LIFE Crest of a wave

Fishing boat–flocked Jimbaran Bay and secluded enclave Nusa Dua may be the best-known destinations on Bali's southern peninsula, but Bukit's other secrets are slowly spreading. Magnificent cliffs and white-sand beaches dot the coastline of this palm-covered promontory. Surfers long ago discovered the epic breaks at Uluwatu and Padang Padang, and now it's your turn. With exceptional oceanside resorts springing up along the Bukit's dramatic southernmost shores, it's the ideal location for swimming, sailing and diving. Funiculars, or steep staircases for the more adventurous, deliver pampered campers straight onto bijou beaches, while sybarites enjoy massages in sleek villas that cling to the craggy overhang.

GETTING THERE

Planes Fly into Denpasar's Ngurah Rai International Airport (www.baliairport.com), a 30-minute drive north of Jimbaran Bay and the Bukit Peninsula.
Boats High-speed ferries from neighbouring Lombok and the Gili islands connect to Benoa Harbour, just north of Nusa Dua on the Bukit Peninsula.
Automobiles You can rent a car at the airport for around US$25 a day, but rustic Bukit roads can be rough, and rules non-existent. By far the easiest way to get to your hotel is to organise a transfer with the concierge.

LOCAL KNOWLEDGE

Taxis While common in busy areas like Jimbaran and Nusa Dua, you'll need to book pick-ups further afield; try Blue Bird taxis (+62 (0)361 701 111). Ask for the meter to be turned on or negotiate a price *before* you set off. For long journeys or exploring, hiring a driver is a cheaper way to go.
Siesta and fiesta The Balinese rise early to fish and farm, and retire not long after the sun goes down. Restaurants and bars in the main tourist hubs – including Jimbaran Bay and Nusa Dua – stay open to the wee hours. In quieter areas, such as more rustic parts of Uluwatu and the Bukit Peninsula, don't be surprised to see the lights off in a shop in the middle of the day, and options for eating beyond the resorts may fade fast after 9pm.
Do go/don't go The days are bright and beautiful from July to September, but August is Bali's peak holiday season, so best avoided if you value peace and solitude.
Packing tips Mr Zogs Sex Wax and graphic-print board shorts for budding surfers. Mrs Smith might like to air that one-shoulder Norma Kamali swimsuit and have at hand a stylish straw hat for the day; Tory Burch tunic and Jimmy Choo sandals for the evening.
Recommended reads The three-volume *Bali Today* by Jean Couteau is a timeless collection of short stories about Balinese culture and the highly entertaining interactions between locals and transplanted expats.
Local specialities Jimbaran is renowned for the local catch brought in by fishermen each morning. Sample some at one of the beach *warungs*, informal open-air eateries right on the sand. Have a go at whipping up a Bukit banquet at Bumbu Bali, the respected Nusa Dua cookery school (www.balifoods.com).
Also This is your chance to perfect your board-riding technique. Remember: during dry season (April to September) the surf's best on the island's west side; in wet season (October to March) hit the east side.

WORTH GETTING OUT OF BED FOR

Viewpoint Even if you're not getting married – but especially if you are – the glass Tirtha Chapel (www.tirthabridal.com) on the cliffs at Uluwatu offers astonishing views of the Indian Ocean.

Arts and culture If you're particularly interested in European artists who've made the island their home and inspiration, Museum Pasifika (http://museum-pasifika.com) in Nusa Dua is worth visiting for its collection of Balinese art. Further north at Sanur, the Museum Le Mayeur (+62 (0)361 286 201) displays the work of Belgian artist Adrien Jean Le Mayeur de Merpes. Between the years 1932 and 1958, he worked on Gauguin-influenced tableaux of the Balinese countryside and particularly of his wife, Legong dancer Ni Pollok.

Activities Surf's up all over the Bukit Peninsula, but both novice and serious surfers might like to team up with one of the wave experts at Tropicsurf (www.tropicsurf.net) who'll take you to the best breaks. Other water action – jet skiing, diving, parasailing and the like – can be found at Tanjung Benoa. Close by at Nusa Dua, swingers (ahem) can also get some action at a series of great golf courses. The Bali Golf and Country Club (www.baligolfandcountryclub.com) is popular.

Best beach Follow the signs to Geger Beach on the southern tip of Nusa Dua, then head along the track that turns off a sharp bend in the road and you'll find a postcard-perfect stretch of white sand. There are sunloungers for hire to soak up the rays.

Daytripper After the street hawkers and traffic of the mainland, you'll appreciate the empty spaces and vibrant underwater life of Nusa Lembongan, just north-east of the Bukit Peninsula. From Benoa Harbour, jump aboard the *Aristocrat* (www.balihaicruises.com), a luxurious 64-foot catamaran, for the leisurely journey to this beautiful island. A barbecue lunch and a visit to these deserted beaches will make it memorable.

Children Glass-bottom boats are the most fun way to get from Nusa Dua and Tanjung Benoa to Serangan (aka Turtle) Island. Your little ones can learn how the reptiles' eggs are kept in conservation huts to hatch and how the babies are nurtured and then released back into the sea. Entrance is free, but carry small notes so you can buy food to feed the animals.

Walks Power walkers won't work up a sweat, but the seaside path at Nusa Dua takes you past all the area's big resorts, which is perfect if you fancy sampling their wares – an icy cocktail or three, perhaps?

Perfect picnic Stock up on baguettes, cold cuts and truffles, if you please, at Dijon Food Specialties (+62 (0)361 759 636) in Kuta, or nip into Bali Buddha in Ungason (+62 (0)361 701 980) for organic breads, fruit and chocolate, before descending the steps to Padang Padang. One of Bukit's nicest beaches, the water is usually calm enough for a leisurely paddle.

Shopping Collectors come from across the island to acquire original ceramics from Jenggala Keramik (+62 (0)361 703 311; www.jenggala.com) in Jimbaran – there are also regular showings of work by local artists. Also in Jimbaran is Paul Ropp (+62 (0)361 701 202; www.paulropp.com), where you'll find unique frocks, men's shirts and trousers made from antique sari material.

Something for nothing The only price you'll pay visiting the traditional fish market at the north end of Jimbaran Bay is having to rise by 6am to see the action. Watch and listen as customers, among them Bali's finest restaurants, drive a hard bargain for a kaleidoscopic selection of fish and shellfish.

Don't go home without... visiting the revered 11th-century Hindu temple Pura Luhur Uluwatu, a popular pilgrimage for followers who believe the black coral monument guards the island from evil spirits. Keep a tight grip on your camera and sunglasses though, because the resident monkeys are cheeky thieves. The temple's regular *kecak* dance shows at sunset are touristy but atmospheric.

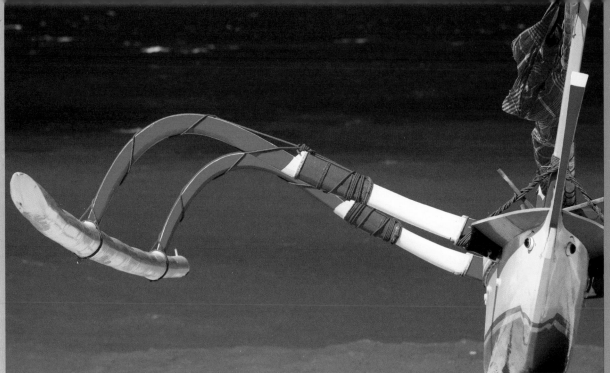

BEAUTIFULLY BUKIT PENINSULA

Although increasing numbers of sun worshippers and surfers are discovering the azure waters and soft, powdery beaches of the Bukit Peninsula, don't be at all surprised if you arrive at Padang Padang, Dreamland or Pura Masuka and find that there's no one else there.

DIARY

February In the last week of February, locals across the island celebrate Saraswati Day to honour the goddess of knowledge. Blessing ceremonies are held to protect books and even computers. **March** Nyepi celebrations begin with noisy parades of giant papier-mâché monster dolls, called *ogoh-ogoh*, which are burnt at temples to exorcise evil spirits. From sunrise the next day, the whole island closes down with people staying indoors to trick those same malicious spirits into believing the island is deserted so they'll leave for another year. **June** Swimmers, runners and cyclists do their thing along, up and around Jimbaran Bay for the Bali International Triathlon (www.balitriathlon.com). Competitors start with a 1,500m swim, followed by a long run up the beach, and a 40km bike ride to Nusa Dua, where you can watch weary, wobbling contenders wheel across the finish line. **August** Head north of Bukit to participate in the street bazaars, art exhibitions and performances at the Sanur Festival. Traditional singers and dancers gather for the week-long Nusa Dua Festival, which is also a glutton's dream come true.

Uluwatu

Alila Villas Uluwatu

STYLE Minimalist eco-glam
SETTING Indian Ocean edge

'Beautiful young people waft about in
white outfits spritzing face mist, smiling
– always smiling'

Oh. My. Giddy. Aunt. That is the only possible reaction to an arrival at Alila Villas Uluwatu. Although you could squeal like the Japanese lady.

It's as if you've stepped onto another planet in another solar system in another time – not just one giant leap, but three. All at once. It's like the Pond's Institute has landed on a cliff in Bali. Beautiful young people waft about in white outfits spritzing face mist, smiling – always smiling – and moving without a sound. If it wasn't so *nice* it might be just a little bit creepy.

All this has been observed from the lobby, which is, of course, to lobbies what Tiger Woods is to golf – and the ladies – a whole different league. The 'lobby' has the most perfect sight lines to the 50 metre infinity pool and the Indian Ocean beyond. It is one of the smartest pieces of architectural design you will ever see, simple as that.

Once you re-gather your senses, retrieve your jaw from the floor and stop mouthing profanities, you are

escorted around the property by one of the beautiful quiet people. But when you walk into the oft-photographed 'stick' pavilion jutting out over the ocean, your breath is sucked away again. If first impressions count most, this has been quite the start. And we're not even close to our room yet.

And so to our one-bedroom Pool Villa. Maybe the stats can give you a rough idea: a 300-square-metre footprint, larger than average plunge pool surrounded by decking and two enormous day-beds, indoor/outdoor shower, iPod dock, flatscreen TV, espresso machine... You get the picture. But until you are there it's just a picture. In real life it is *soooo* much better.

The room is stunningly modern with lots of white (something of a recurring motif), dark timber and quite a few large mirrors – perhaps beautiful people like admiring themselves more than us fatties do. 'Product' abounds: product for him, just for her, for face, for hair, for shower, for mosquitoes, for after shaving, before sleeping and post sunbathing. And everything is just so beautiful. Begrudgingly I have to admit that the soap 'especially for him' knocks even the great Cussons Imperial Leather for a metaphorical six. Never have I smelled so sweet as I did for those two days.

More great design is evident in the shape and placement of the rooms to best catch the local zephyrs and reduce the need for air-con. Oh, yes, this place is green, the greenest ever built in Bali, and while not strictly a health resort there are daily yoga classes and lots of literature on 'life journeys' and 'holistic wellbeing' for your quiet contemplation. There is no alcohol in the minibar, but you have a butler at all times to answer your late-night whisky and Bintang calls. Thanks, Wayan. The overall mood is one of 'young' and 'now' and 'of its time'. This is new-age luxury at its very best.

Mrs Smith and I settle in for the afternoon and find ourselves the only guests by the infinity pool. With villas as enticing as the ones on offer here, replete with pool

and butler, I imagine more than a few guests never actually emerge into a public space after check-in. It's their loss.

Our favourite encounter of the trip occurs when we inquire, quite sheepishly, if there might be a game of Scrabble we could borrow. The beautiful, smiling young man we ask looks thoroughly bemused and replies, verbatim: 'We have Wii and Nintendo DS for your room if you like.' We have arrived in the future. About four hours later the same white-clad, smiling, beautiful boy glides over as we leave dinner clutching the freshest, newest Scrabble box and claiming he 'found it in another villa'. His exuberance and service standards are world class, although I suspect that someone was sent into Denpasar, the capital, to buy it. Which only makes us love the place even more.

On either side of the pool are the resort's two restaurants. There's the Warung, a casual, elegantly designed Indonesian, and Cire, the more upmarket

international offering. For us, the hands-down choice was the Warung, where the food is fresh, local, indigenous and fantastic. For all its charms we think Cire might need to try a little less hard. The food is most certainly ambitious and the service is first rate, but, as the adage goes, sometimes less is more. If I want crazy French meets Indonesian cuisine adorned with every zeitgeisty ingredient under the sun, I have Sydney for that.

Alila is about a 15-minute drive from Uluwatu Temple, which is worth a visit at sunset for gorgeous dancers and thieving monkeys. Otherwise, there is not much nearby in the realm of Bali life as such. Seriously, though, you probably won't think about leaving the grounds once you're there. If you need something to do, you can always indulge at the rather special Spa Alila. The therapists are wonderful (and beautiful and quiet) and the products they use, as explained by Mrs Smith in language I would understand, are like the Macallan compared to your standard Johnnie Walker Red Label. Ergo, they are good.

The Alila group is still young and things might not be quite as polished as at, say, an Aman, but you just know they will get there sooner rather than later. Early evening drinks in the sunset cabana (ie, the stick pavilion) are almost fantastical — just expect the soundtrack to be more Ministry of Sound chill-out than Balinese bamboo xylophone.

And be prepared to be the least attractive person in the place. Unless you are beautiful, of course. Which you probably are, so you'll feel right at home. In the best home you ever had.

Reviewed by Stuart Gregor

NEED TO KNOW

Rooms 61 pool villas, with a choice of one to three bedrooms.

Rates US$560–US$1,080 (one-bedroom); US$1,400–US$5,340 (two- to three-bedrooms). Excludes à la carte breakfast at US$25 a person and 11 per cent tax and 10 per cent service charge.

Check-out Noon. Late check-out costs half a night's tariff up to 6pm; after 6pm, a full extra night. Check-in, 2pm.

Facilities Free WiFi throughout, library with books, DVDs and computers, spa, gym, yoga, gift shop, gardens. In rooms: personal butler service, flatscreen TV with satellite channels, CD/DVD players, preloaded iPod, Spa Alila toiletries, minibar, espresso machine, TWG Tea, private pool.

Poolside Feel like you're floating above the world in the 50m infinity pool perched along the cliff edge.

Children Very welcome, although you may need the staff's knowledge of the local area to keep them entertained. The hotel can supply free baby cots and extra beds for older kids for US$30 a child a night, and babysitters for a fee.

Also Are daily spa treatments an extravagance? Nothing beats the classic Balinese Massage at Spa Alila – except, of course, the Journey to You, a full day's pampering from yoga at sunrise to massage under the stars.

IN THE KNOW

Our favourite rooms Villa 409 commands the highest point of the resort, so it's the pick for couples in pursuit of total privacy with a 180-degree ocean vista. Sleek modern design, care of Singaporean architects WOHA, embraces the outdoors, harnessing natural stone, wood, rattan and water.

Hotel bar The striking wood-slatted cabana lounge bar juts from the dramatic Bukit cliffs, overhanging the pounding waves below. Get your bearings with signature cocktails such as the Alila Gin Mojito, then settle in to enjoy the salmon-pink sunset.

Hotel restaurant Open throughout the day, the contemporary Western-style Cire has cuisine inspired by the nautical surroundings. Across the pool, the more mellow Warung offers authentic Indonesian fare.

Top table Romantics should reserve a cliff-hanging open-air cabana for two, for idling above the Indian Ocean.

Room service Available 24 hours a day, serving dishes from the restaurant menus and craved-for comfort foods.

Dress code Asian clientele sport tailored beach frocks; European guests extend the style spectrum to barefoot chic.

Local knowledge Bali's Bukit Peninsula is famous for its legendary breaks, so surfers will be in blue-water heaven (watching them from Uluwatu Beach's boho bars is fun too). Also nearby is the sacred Pura Luhur Uluwatu, a romantic cliff-side temple swarming with monkeys, which stages local dance performances at sunset.

LOCAL EATING AND DRINKING

Popular with surfers and backpackers is the simple yet welcoming Yeye's Warung (+62 (0)361 742 4761), between Uluwatu and Padang Padang beaches, where you can get Indonesian, Thai and Indian food, along with pizza and burgers (retro surf videos add to the vibe). Just a 15-minute drive away is Jimbaran Bay and its famous beachfront seafood warungs, where freshly grilled fish, prawns, lobster and squid are served at tables on the sand at lunch or under the stars. Nammos Beach Club is part of Smith-approved resort Karma Kandara (+62 (0)361 848 2200), east of Alila Villas Uluwatu. Take the inclinator down to a protected beach, where you'll find a club that wouldn't be out of place on the Aegean. Dip in the ocean, order signature cocktails and wood-fired pizzas, and listen to the cool Café del Mar-style tunes.

GET A ROOM!

For more information, or to book this hotel, go to www.mrandmrssmith.com – our expert team can take care of all your travel arrangements. Register your Smith membership card to enjoy exclusive offers and privileges.

 SMITH MEMBER OFFER A 90-minute Balinese massage for each guest.

Alila Villas Uluwatu Jalan Belimbing Sari, Banjar Tambiyak, Desa Pecatu, Bali 80364, Indonesia (+62 (0)361 848 2166; www.alilahotels.com)

Nusa Dua

The Balé

STYLE Zen and sensibility
SETTING Nusa Dua brow

'Mr Smith has plunged into the nearest body of cool water. Naked. Thankfully, our villa has a private pool'

Is it possible for the Island of the Gods to transform a tired mama and papa into a hip and happening Mr and Mrs Smith? In my head, at least, it doesn't seem an incredible stretch, especially since our ultimate destination is the Balé, a child-free retreat on the eastern side of Bali's Bukit Peninsula at Nusa Dua.

We are ushered in from the sweltering tropical heat to our Deluxe Single Pavilion – minimal, chic and deliciously secluded – and our first mission becomes food. Even before our *gado-gado* arrives the smell of the *alang-alang* roof and the plinking chords of the *gamelan* have lulled me into a midday trance. Mr Smith, on the other hand, has plunged into the nearest body of cool water. Naked. Thankfully, our villa has a private pool or the resort's other guests may have had a rude shock. *Gado-gado* devoured we take to skinny-dipping interspersed with competitive bouts of Scrabble. When we've had enough triple word score seeking, Mr Smith, who is something of a Zen master, indulges in a spot of yoga in the buff; my mind, however, turns once again

to food and I peruse the menu, contemplating our next meal. This is already proving such a luxury: we have barely arrived and already we've had time for each other *and* for ourselves.

For those who want to explore the more – how can I put this? – rustic side of Bali, there is always popular Geger beach, which is across the road and down a side lane, as are most things on the island. (The Balé runs a complimentary shuttle service here, as it does to many local places of interest.) We last less than five minutes among the European tourists, mangy stray mutts and deckchairs before deciding that nice though it is a meal by the main pool at the Balé seems like a far more civilised way to pass the time.

The restaurants at the Balé are helmed by chef Brandon Huisman who has done an amazing culinary leap from preparing yak at his previous post in a Bhutanese resort to offering up delicious raw food options for his guests in Bali. We order a raw coconut *pad thai* made using chilled slices of young coconut as a substitute for the rice noodles traditionally found in the dish. In the mid-afternoon heat this sour, spicy, slippery version of a Thai classic is exactly the cooling diversion we need after our failed beach outing. Mr Smith is so taken with the meal and the whole concept of living raw that he is soon suggesting enthusiastically that we should convert to uncooked at home, too. I have visions of myself clasping a coconut between my knees, struggling to scoop out the succulent flesh.

As good as the food is at the Balé, the local in me begins to hanker for some tasty Indonesian fare. Not knowing the area at all, we ask the hotel staff for a neighbourhood recommendation. Initially sceptical and convinced we would be served a Westernised version of Indonesian food, the grumpy foodie in me is quickly pacified at Bumbu Bali. All the traditional Balinese dishes are on the menu and we decide on the vegetarian *rijsttafel* – a Dutch word translating as rice feast – and it almost knocks the

two of us off our chairs. Each course is an exquisite sampling of flavours that in itself seems like an entire meal. A vegetarian spread of such a high standard is a real treat and if you're ever in Bali we highly recommend trekking here from wherever you are staying.

The following day, we decide it is time to take relaxation to the next level and so book in for two hours of pummelling at the resort's spa. The hot stone therapy using crystals looks promising, since I fancy myself as something of a modern-day hippie chick and have indulged before in crystal healing. Our spa room is, like the rest of the property, somewhat overly spacious. Personally, I prefer things a little more intimate – nesty and cosy – but that doesn't stop me from falling asleep almost as soon as the therapist places her hands on my back. I wake when the aromatherapy massage ends and the crystal healing begins. By now, I'm eagerly awaiting some words of ancient wisdom

passed down through the elders – what magical crystals might open which chakras, for example – but the therapist simply proceeds, without a word, to give me what feels like a hot stone massage (she's a junior, it turns out, so the experience may be more revealing with a more experienced practitioner). While incredibly relaxing, it could be more personalised, with an analysis of what types of healing crystals are used to suit each individual.

Back at our villa, my head clear and body nourished, I start making up a little ditty: 'This little piggy went to Bali / this little piggy ate dessert naked in the pool / this little piggy has been rubbed and loved...' And, at that moment, it dawns on me that the only parts of my body that have been on duty since arriving at the Balé are those used for eating, sleeping or playing Scrabble. Sure, by this point, I am feeling a little like a sloth, but I'm also enjoying every sun-kissed minute. The mind is a magical device and, teamed with our private paradise at the Balé, I've forgotten about anything beyond the wooden gate. This is exactly what we needed. It's only taken a couple of days but a tired and testy mama and papa are indeed transformed. Meet the young, revived and relaxed Mr and Mrs Smith.

Reviewed by Nadya Hutagalung

NEED TO KNOW

Rooms 29 private villas, including three two-bedroom Double Pavilions.

Rates US$500–US$750 for a one-bedroom pavilion; US$800–US$950 for a two-bedroom pavilion, including à la carte breakfast, local area transfers and a 15-minute welcome massage. A 21 per cent tax and service charge applies.

Check-out Noon, but flexible subject to availability. Earliest check-in, 2pm.

Facilities Gym, spa, library, yoga room, beach club, free WiFi throughout. In pavilions: private pool, minibar, CD/DVD player, flatscreen TV, indoor and outdoor showers.

Poolside Stone-clad walls separate the two tiers of the main swimming pool and rise into plant beds for the greenery shrouding the upper pool, where sunloungers shaded by parasols await.

Children This hotel is better suited to couples – leave little Smiths with the grandparents.

Also The Balé Wellness Spa offers tantalising treatments including crystal healing hot stone therapy, steamed-rice facials, and a 90-minute coffee ritual for men. Rather than booking several treatments separately, check out the packaged rituals.

IN THE KNOW

Our favourite rooms At 240 square metres each, the Single Pavilions offer more than enough space, but our favourite is definitely the enormous 480-square-metre Deluxe Single (number 38), which comes with an L-shaped private pool. Double Pavilions 19 and 20 offer stunning views of the ocean. All villas have light, airy interiors with double-height rooms that soar up to the rafters, white walls, pale wooden furnishings and an arsenal of gadgets.

Hotel bar Fluid, situated beside the main pool, is a laid-back lounge where guests can chill out with a cocktail. With its soft lighting and Café del Mar-style soundtrack, its atmosphere is more relaxed than a cat stretched out in sunlight.

Hotel restaurant Faces, an open-sided space beside the main pool, specialises in modern Mediterranean and Indonesian cuisine. If you'd prefer to order off-menu, dishes can be tailormade to suit your individual tastes. Healing herbs and regional fruits pepper the selection of healthy snacks and meals on offer at Bliss, the bijou spa-restaurant.

Top table Ask the staff at Faces to set up a private table for you in a pavilion away from the main dining room.

Room service Western and Asian dishes are available 24 hours. The emphasis is on in-room dining with private barbecues and candlelit dinners practically encouraged.

Dress code Faces is casual during the day, smarter in the evening. Bathrobes and slippers are acceptable dining attire at spa-restaurant Bliss, which seats only six people.

Local knowledge Learn to cook Balinese food with a two-hour masterclass at Faces restaurant – then feast for lunch.

LOCAL EATING AND DRINKING

Right in front of the resort, Nusa Dua Beach Grill, on Geger Beach, serves fabulous pizzas and salads. For a more traditional meal, Waroeng Kampoeng (+62 (0)361 744 0913), on Jalan Pamelisan Agung, Jimbaran, is a smaller local restaurant offering genuine Balinese and Indonesian dishes. Ironically, the best Balinese food on the island is cooked by a Swiss-born chef who is undoubtedly Bali's favourite adopted son: Heinz von Holzen's authentic menu at Bumbu Bali (+62 (0)361 772 299), on Jalan Pratama, Tanjung Benoa, has inspired several cookbooks. The 15-minute drive across the peninsula to Jimbaran Bay is worth it, especially if you track down Bagus Cafe (+62 (0)812 390 7681).

GET A ROOM!

For more information, or to book this hotel, go to www.mrandmrssmith.com – our expert team can take care of all your travel arrangements. Register your Smith membership card to enjoy exclusive offers and privileges.

 SMITH MEMBER OFFER A bottle of wine and canapés on arrival and late check-out at 3pm.

The Balé Jalan Raya, Nusa Dua, Selatan, Bali 80363, Indonesia (+62 (0)361 775 111; www.thebale.com; www.lifestyleretreats.com)

Ungasan

Karma Kandara

STYLE Supersized villas
SETTING Dramatic cliffhanger

'This isn't just the sea. It's an epic, eye-popping, mind-drenching, soul-serenading expanse of big blue'

How good is that moment at the start of a beach holiday when you spot the ocean for the first time? It doesn't matter if it's the Bahamas or Bognor – that initial glimpse of blue always makes me grin. So, as our golf buggy winds its way from reception through a pretty maze of walled limestone lanes, over little humpback bridges and past splashes of hibiscus and bougainvillea, I'm craning for a look at the Indian Ocean.

At a sunshine-yellow door we descend stone steps into our Luxury Pool Villa. I'm absorbing its vast proportions when Mr Smith emits a squeak of astonishment. I spin round – there, at last, is the sea. I squeak too, because this isn't just the sea. It's an epic, eye-popping, mind-drenching, soul-serenading expanse of big blue. It is the ocean and the sky and the gleaming infinity pool that flows to the cliff's edge and seemingly beyond. It's up and down and side to side and forever. It's blue without frontiers.

This is Bali's southernmost tip, at the end of a limestone peninsula that extends over the ocean like a ship's prow, providing the all-embracing blue view. A vertiginous 150 metres below is Ungasan Beach, site of a sacred cave temple. This spot, uncommonly gorgeous even on an island that excels at gorgeous, was identified by a feng shui master as Bali's most powerful location. Energy apparently flows inland from the ocean through a deep green ravine around which 46 villas, all with private pools, are dotted. A sceptic might say that whatever the energy, you simply couldn't go wrong with a setting like this. Staring into that vista is like inhaling pure contentment.

The blueness winks and flickers through bamboo trees as I traverse a stone bridge to Karma Spa. (Mr Smith has elected to remain in the villa to keep an eye on the three bedrooms, outdoor shower, pool deck and kitchen with everything from a microwave to Häagen-Dazs ice-cream in the freezer.) For the next half-hour, I'm to relax in the spa's infrared detox sauna. It is tucked away in a glass-fronted cabin on a rocky outcrop, clinging to the brink as if it's about to abseil down. There's an oval pool, also cliffhanging, where you're simultaneously enveloped in warm Himalayan saltwater and suspended, god-like, high above the surf. This is life on the edge as it should be. Inside the cabinet, the heat has my circulation singing while I gaze at the horizon. Words for blue float through my mind: cobalt, sapphire, azure…

This ever-so-slightly tripped-out state is very Karma Kandara. The spa specialises in holistic hedonism. 'Pleasure is part of the cure' is the mantra on a menu offering a his 'n' hers Moët and Manicures treatment alongside more deeply soulful therapies from world-renowned healers. The Ultimate Oxygen Infusion facial even has plumping properties recommended by Madonna. The Karma group's owner John Spence, an ex music-biz Brit who was once Boy George's agent, encourages a 'five-star hippie' vibe. He loves a party and they happen frequently at Karma's Nammos Beach Club, at the bottom of the cliff, where you can be a lounge lizard by day, social butterfly by night. A Karma Chameleon, if you like. (Spence enjoys this gag, but swears he didn't name his resorts after the song.)

With the white, blue and focus on fun, I reckon this place channels Mykonos. 'It's Hellenic!' I declare, re-entering the villa with glowing skin and clear eyes. 'I don't agree,' says Mr Smith. 'I think it's lovely.' Bless him, he's still tripping on blue. We'd better eat.

Di Mare, Karma's restaurant, is a sun-drenched – or moonlight-bathed – white semicircle on the cliff edge, with fabric ceiling and open front. The Mod Med/Asian menu takes full advantage of the catch from down below.

Between courses, I'm lured from our table by Veritas, di Mare's climate-controlled wine treasure trove. Pop a plastic card into a slot and you can access samples of eight different tipples by the glass, kept fresh by Bali's first Enomatic dispenser. A wine ATM? Now, that's very good Karma.

Mr Smith is missing the next morning when I wake in our floaty-curtained four-poster. I locate him in Karma's main infinity pool, outlined against water and sky like a stuntman on a blue screen. 'I've been riding on the inclinator,' he says. 'It's great! I'll show you.' In the little white box we drop slowly down the green-clad cliff. At this time of day, Nammos is a picture of snoozy decadence. A four-poster day-bed beckons, and then the tide turns making it the perfect time for a snorkel on the reef. Later, hours vanish as we watch the resident monkeys swinging through the trees.

On our last night, we stroll hand in hand to the spa, where two massage tables await in that cliffhanging courtyard. With waves for music and the moon for light, we're rubbed into heaven by two amazing Balinese therapists. Afterwards we bask, just the two of us, suspended in the night air with the world at our feet and the stars overhead – I can see why this is a major scene for proposals. We top off the evening with a movie down at the beach, snacking on popcorn in *padang* leaves and grilled seafood (the Odeon, this ain't).

Following a few final rides on his beloved inclinator, Mr Smith joins me in our pool. We are wallowing contentedly when we spot a kingfisher – a bright blue bird on an endless sky-blue canvas. By now we're not even sure if it's real, or yet another psychedelic side effect of Karma Kandara's blue-induced bliss. Feeling blue never felt so good...

Reviewed by Amy Cooper

NEED TO KNOW

Rooms 46 villas, each with two to four bedrooms, except the Grand Cliff-Front Residence, which has five bedrooms.
Rates From US$865–US$965 for a two-bedroom Luxury Pool Villa; US$5,000–US$6,000 for the Grand Cliff-Front
Residences (sleeps 8–10). Rates exclude breakfast (US$25), and a 21 per cent tax and service charge.
Check-out Noon, but flexible subject to availability, and a 50 per cent charge up to 6pm. Earliest check-in, 2pm.
Facilities Spa, gym, library, gardens, free WiFi throughout. In villas: flatscreen TV, CD/DVD player, iPod dock, SMEG-
equipped kitchen with stocked refrigerator, glasses, dishes and flatware, washer/dryer.
Poolside Two levels of free-form, salt and chlorine pools sit just below the di Mare restaurant. The lower-level, shallow
pool is ideal for little Smiths. All villas come with private pools; with the Cliff-Front Residence, you get an infinity pool.
Children Smiths of all ages welcome. Villas with a third bedroom include twin beds; cots are free, and additional beds
cost US$75. Karma Kids Club, great for two- to 12-year-olds, operates from 9am to 8pm daily.
Also An inclinator descends the cliff to Nammos Beach Club, where non-motorised watersports are free for hotel guests.

IN THE KNOW

Our favourite rooms All spacious, thatch-roofed, white-washed villas are decorated in an elegant palette from cream to
cocoa via ochre and russet. For particularly pleasing panoramas, request the four-bedroom Villa 36 or three-bedroom Villa
10. The five-bedroom, three-storey Grand Cliff-Front Residence has unrivalled views, a cinema room, gym and spa pavilion.
Hotel bar Fruity concoctions and ice-cold beers can be found at Nammos Beach Club, but serious oenophiles will
enjoy the sybaritic sipping at Veritas, the resort's glass-clad wine bar overlooking the coastline.
Hotel restaurant Main restaurant, di Mare, is a high-ceilinged white-washed airy space, where chef Simon Blaby
serves a Mediterranean menu. It's all Greek and pizzas at the laid-back, veranda restaurant at Nammos Beach Club.
Veritas has an addictive tapas menu, including dishes such as seared scallops with roast garlic purée.
Dress code Strictly flip-flops and beachwear at Nammos; take the glamour up a notch after dark at Veritas and
di Mare – although summer-casual prints suit the mood better than dressy labels.
Top table Book ahead at di Mare for a perimeter table with eagle-eye views of the peninsula. The communal central table
is a sociable option; we're also drawn to the back wall's elevated padded banquettes for their broader ocean views.
Room service Available around the clock. Wood-fired pizzas and the signature Wagyu burger are delicious at any hour.
Local knowledge Look out around the resort for the fruits of Karma Kandara's artist-in-residence programme, which
nurtures the talents of painters, sculptors and musicians then try the healing hands at clifftop Karma Spa.

LOCAL EATING & DRINKING

For cliffs and culinary heights, Cire (+62 (0)361 848 2166) is a contemporary, Western restaurant at Smith-approved
Alila Villas Uluwatu, on Jalan Belimbing Sari, in Desa Pecatu. Chef Brandon Huisman commands the open kitchen at
Faces at the Balé (+62 (0)361 775 111). This intimate Nusa Dua eatery, on Jalan Raya Nusa Dua Selatan, is acclaimed
for its modern Med meets Indonesian fare. At Jimbaran Bay, pick of the seafood warungs is Bagus Cafe (+62 (0)812
390 7681), second from the end furthest from the Four Seasons resort. Also in Jimbaran at 18 Jalan Wanagiri,
is Pepe Nero (+62 (0)361 704 677) – a little gem of an Italian restaurant in an unlikely location with ocean views.

GET A ROOM!

For more information, or to book this hotel, go to www.mrandmrssmith.com – our expert team can take care of all your
travel arrangements. Register your Smith membership card to enjoy exclusive offers and privileges.

 SMITH MEMBER OFFER A wine appreciation session for two.

Karma Kandara Jalan Villa Kandara, Banjar Wijaya Kusuma, Ungasan, Bali 80362, Indonesia (+62 (0)361 848 2202;
www.karmaresorts.com)

SEMINYAK & TABANAN, BALI

COASTLINE Beguiling bars, buzzing beaches
COAST LIFE 24-hour party people

A stay along this short stretch of Bali's sultry south-west coast is enough to be beguiled by the island's contrasting charms – from the brash backpackers' hang-out Kuta and serenely sophisticated shores of Legian and Seminyak to the ravishingly remote black-sand beaches and emerald rice fields of the Tabanan Regency. Name your pleasure – consuming world-class cuisine, shopping at chic boutiques, lying on the beach for hours or surfing Bali's legendary breaks – you'll find it here. Afterwards, return to your luxe pad and dandy up for a night out on the town. Sunset cocktails are almost a religion in this part of the world, where it is mandatory to waft off to fabulous restaurants and sexy lounge bars until dawn. You are on holiday, after all...

GETTING THERE

Planes Wing your way to Ngurah Rai International Airport (www.baliairport.com), just south of Bali's capital Denpasar. If you need one, you can buy a visa on arrival (US$25 for 30 days); paying by cash will speed up the process.
Automobiles Ngurah Rai is just a 20-minute hop, skip and a jump south of the famous Kuta, Legian and Seminyak beach strip, and within an hour's drive of the Tabanan coast, further north. Some hotels offer free airport transfers, but if not, book a pick-up with the concierge. Taxis operate from the airport on a fixed-price scale. You can rent a car at the airport but traffic can be terrifying.

LOCAL KNOWLEDGE

Taxis Make sure the taxi clock is turned on (or at least agree on a fare) before you set off. Bali's best legit metered-taxi company is Blue Bird (+62 (0)361 701 111). For longer trips, your hotel can organise a driver for about US$30–$50 a day.
Siesta and fiesta Generally, Bali's banks and post offices open 8am–2pm Monday to Thursday, and until 12pm Fridays (post offices until 2pm), with banks also open until 11am on Saturdays (ATMs are accessible out of hours). Shops ply their trade around 9am to 8pm, and food haunts from 8am to 10pm. While the rest of Bali snoozes soon after sunset, Seminyak throbs well past the witching hour. In quieter, more rural Tabanan, you may need to rely on your hotel's wining and dining spots, or drive an hour to Seminyak for nocturnal action.
Do go/don't go The weather is at its most appealing in the dry season between April and September; as a general rule, monsoon clouds start to gather in October, with the humid wet season lasting until March. The European summer holiday crowd arrives in August.
Packing tips Kaftans, swimmers and Havaianas are cool and light for daytime; come evening, dress to impress and show off your tan. Don't forget your favourite hangover remedies for morning-after healing.
Recommended reads Miguel Covarrubias' *Island of Bali*, originally published in 1937, is still considered the most authoritative account of Balinese life and culture. One of a series, Alan Brayne's novel *Kuta Bubbles* follows a long-time Bali expat growing weary of paradise, and is the perfect beach page-flipper.
Local specialities You can eat almost any style of global food in the Seminyak area, but it'd be a shame not to try some of Indonesia's traditional rice dishes, satays and *ayam goreng* (fried chicken). Roving *kaki lima* (food cart) vendors are another authentic local option.

Also Before you hit the streets with your credit card, ask the concierge if the hotel has a Seminyak shopping map – it's much easier than trying to work out where things are from their addresses.

WORTH GETTING OUT OF BED FOR

Viewpoint The vista everyone wants is sunset over the Indian Ocean. Arrive early at Kuvé, the exclusive rooftop lounge at the ultra-glam beachside bar and restaurant Ku De Ta (http://bali.kudeta.net) to snaffle one of the egg-shaped rocking chairs.

Arts and culture Head north past the rice paddies of Canggu to Pura Tanah Lot, a Hindu sea temple perched on a rocky ocean-fringed outcrop, which you can walk to at low tide. The spiritually inclined can undergo a *melukat*, or karma-cleansing ceremony, on the volcanic sand at the adjacent hot springs. Prince Ajoaes (+62 (0)81 139 6974), a descendant of the King of Tabanan, carries out this local rite of passage to re-balance the spirit.

Activities One particularly magical experience is riding horses along the black-sand beach at Yeh Gangga, just west of Tanah Lot. During a two-hour expedition, the guides at Bali Island Horse (www.baliislandhorse.com) take you past rice paddies, temples, villages and a bat cave, as well as hugging the shoreline. You can even go for a swim on your pony. Looking for romance? Book in for an hour-long sunset ride. Alternatively, saddle up at Kuda P stables in Canggu (www.kudapstables.com).

Best beach The hearty party people somehow always manage early-morning power walks along Seminyak Beach – minus the stilettos but often accompanied by a four-legged friend. At any time of the day, it's a great spot for a stroll – stop at some of the gorgeous beachfront hotels for lunch or a drink – and a float in the ocean (one of the world's best hangover cures if you've been indulging in Seminyak's late-night delights).

Daytripper Drive north along Tabanan's gushing rivers and lush ravines to the surprisingly cool-climate mountain town of Bedugul, just south of Lake Bratan. Locals honour the lake's goddess at temple Pura Ulun Danu Bratan, which juts out into the water. There's also plenty of lake larks, including boat rides, parasailing, canoeing, banana boating and water skiing. Afterwards, gorge on the area's famous fist-sized strawberries at Candi Kuning Market. Press on towards bustling Singaraja on the island's north coast, stopping for a tropical rainforest walk to see Gitgit Waterfall. On the way back to Seminyak, treat yourself to a Firefly Supper (+62 (0)81 2399 9019; www.bigtreebali.com), a six-course torch-lit jungle banquet organised by Ben and Blair, a couple of expat organic farmers based near Jatiluwih.

Children Kids grow up fast enough without exposing them to Kuta Beach, known for its tacky bars and raging beer-fuelled fêtes. The one age-appropriate exception is Waterbom (www.waterbom-bali.com), which sports aquatic entertainment from action rides with names like Smashdown and Boomerang to slides and water-balloon throwing. Parents can relax in the spa or at the pool bar.

Walks Lace up your trainers and put some water in a backpack to trek north along the beach from Seminyak. It will take you about two hours, with patches of rocky scrambling, to get to the iconic 16th-century oceanfront Pura Tanah Lot temple.

Perfect picnic Canggu's laid-back residents try hard to keep Echo Beach a secret – it's a quaint spit of sand and great for ogling the surfers at its respected break. If you'd rather someone else prepped the produce, this is also where you'll find the Beach House Restaurant (www.echobeachhouse.com), ideal for sundowners on simple wooden picnic tables, followed by a fiery barbecue of freshly caught prawns and lobsters, steaks and marinated ribs all served with organic salads to the acoustical accompaniment of the rolling ocean. Take the Sunset Road towards Tanah Lot, then scout out the Echo Beach House sign as you approach Canggu.

Shopping The main boutique shopping street has at least three charmingly inconsistent names as it snakes along the Seminyak coastline. Start across from the Legian Hotel, picking up sterling-silver chopsticks and Wonder Woman–style silver cuffs by CV Jewellery found in Maru at Jalan Laksmana 7a. The Corner Store at Jl Laksmana 10a stocks kooky kids' clothes, from delicious apple-stamped dresses to tie-dyed tour tees for the family's littlest head-bangers. Around the bend, Karl Lagerfeld alumnus Michel Harcourt, at Jl Raya Basangkasa 1200a, offers his catwalk creations. Finish the ensemble with sky-high stilettos from Niluh Djelantik at Jl Raya Kerobokan 144. Sari Shop at Jl Raya Seminyak 36 is the place to load up on vintage batik sarongs. Style-setters nip to nearby Allegra for ethically farmed animal-skin accessories by home-grown talent Leyla, whose oversized braided beach bag is the unofficial Bali Birkin.

Something for nothing Stake out a square of sand in front of the Anantara Seminyak – you'll not only get a primo view of the colour-streaked sky but also of the frenetic regular football games between the local men.

Don't go home without... getting horizontal for a deep-kneading Balinese massage. The ancient holistic practice incorporates reflexology, acupressure and aromatherapy oils to stimulate blood flow and qi. Let the island's 'dancing fingers' soothe your knotty limbs at Jari Menari (www.jarimenari.com).

SEDUCTIVELY SEMINYAK & TABANAN

Kuta, Legian and Seminyak have long been a Mecca for surfers, with learner-friendly breaks as well as more advanced waves a kilometre out at Kuta Reef, best accessed by boat. If you fancy trying your luck on a board, book in with Double D Surf School (www.surfschoolbali.com), owned by twin brothers Dedik and Deduk. They grew up in the area, so know the breaks, plus they're friendly guys and offer a personalised service.

DIARY

February Across the island, locals celebrate Saraswati Day, devoted to the goddess of knowledge. Blessing ceremonies are held to protect books and even computers. **June–July** The month-long Bali Arts Festival (www.baliartsfestival.com) in nearby capital Denpasar showcases modern and traditional dance, handicrafts and music in the cultural event of the year. **September–October** Kuta Karnival (www.kutakarnival.com) is a popular 10-day beachfront gathering for events such as turtle releases, a kite festival, sunset dances and street art.

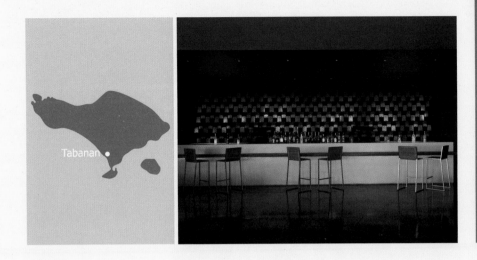

Alila Villas Soori

STYLE Sleek sea-kissed sanctuary
SETTING Jet-black sand, jade-green rice paddies

'Once we're alone in our Ocean Pool Villa, Mr Smith and I eye each other before whooping like children. This is, without question, the most glamorous place we have ever stayed'

The rice paddies and temples appear to have been engulfed by shopping malls lined with Givenchy and Bulgari boutiques in the 20 years since Mr Smith and I last visited Bali. Somehow, though, the island has retained its distinctive charm. Everything still appears to have that same human scale – the malls remain modest, the temples diminutive and the roads more like alleys.

Not that we notice any of this at first. The journey from Ngurah Rai Airport to Alila Villas Soori on the island's isolated west coast is an impressive indicator of the two days to come. After being met by a car organised by the hotel, the attention to detail en route is deliciously distracting: ginger-scented face flannels, exquisite snacks, cool bottled water and an aloe vera, ylang-ylang and lavender face spray. The driver even offers to phone ahead to ensure a meal is waiting in our villa when we arrive.

After another fragrant flannel (in case we managed to work up a sweat between opening the car door and

stepping out, perhaps), we are shown around the resort by the charming manager. Our first response is that this is one of the most beautiful hotels we have ever experienced. The combination of spectacular scenery – the villas overlook a turbulent ocean whose waves crash onto an iridescent black-sand beach – and the effortless elegance of the architecture make the Alila an aesthetic delight.

Once we're alone in our Ocean Pool Villa, Mr Smith and I eye each other before whooping like children. This is, without question, the most glamorous place we have ever stayed. Our bedroom opens into a living space that opens onto a private pagoda with day-beds overlooking the sea. Each villa has its own swimming pool, indoor and outdoor showers, and his-and-hers toiletries (they are discreetly changed over to his-and-his versions during the afternoon).

For the first half-hour Mr Smith and I are quite literally paralysed by luxury, unable to decide whether to use the day-beds in the lounge or the pagoda, or if, in fact, we should take a dip in the ocean, the 50-metre infinity pool or our own private one. Finally, we settle for soaking in the perfectly proportioned double bath, complete with ergonomic stone head rests. Considering these Mr Smiths are from drought-ravaged Melbourne and normally shower with buckets at their feet (to recycle the water to the garden) this is incredibly exciting.

For the next two days, we revel in the property. There's the complimentary afternoon tea to enjoy, accompanied by *gamelan* players, and we end up dining at all three of Soori's eateries. The first night is casual beachside Coast where I devour a gorgeous grilled snapper with Balinese spices, backdropped by waves glimmering under spotlights and a horizon illuminated by a lightning storm. The next day we visit the main dining area, Cotta, where I have *ayam taliwang* (barbecued chicken with red spice) and Mr Smith has rigatoni with

portobello mushrooms and truffled ricotta – a seamless curation of cuisines from East and West. Finally, we test informal Drift, where you can order café-style food among books and sofas by day, and enjoy fine-dining at night. In principle this is a great idea, but in practice eating a meal in the severe white room filled with hard-edged furniture was as cosy as chowing down at an Ikea showroom. The food is, as usual, terrific: lobster and mushroom quesadilla, smoked chicken pizza and chargrilled vegetables. All of this is then followed with a delicious green tea martini. Need I say more?

Perhaps it sounds like we are preoccupied with food, but between meals we do book in for massages in the tranquil, temple-like spa beneath the central reflection pool. Greeted with a cool lemon and honey drink, I relax with a reflexology massage, while Mr Smith has a more traditional Balinese massage. Both are heavenly and transport us into complete relaxation mode.

Lying in bed at night watching CNN (one of our few criticisms is the lack of bedside reading lights – although we've heard they've since been installed), we feel a million miles away from the world. In our designer retreat, surrounded by black volcanic rock walls and driftwood sculptures, we feel completely cocooned.

Rested beyond our wildest dreams, we venture out of the Alila grounds on our final morning. The resort's leisure concierges can organise all types of sightseeing opportunities (they call them 'journeys') and we opt, perhaps unsurprisingly, for the gourmet variety. Alila's sous chef, Made Suriana, acts as our guide to the real Bali. Made, a man of great dignity and knowledge, gives us a crash course in the island's culinary culture, taking us to markets and showing us deep-fried elvers (baby eels) caught in the local rice paddies. He explains that the small village eggs are the most expensive because they are the equivalent of what we know as free-range. Made also points out the many offerings – woven baskets filled with flowers and food – for sale. One of the cultural shifts in the past two decades is that women, traditionally responsible for creating these gifts to the gods, have now entered the workforce so don't have time to make their own.

Afterwards, guide becomes chef once again and Made prepares an extraordinary meal while demonstrating the basics of Balinese cooking. As we're eating, I think of the local people in the markets and how impoverished their lives are by our standards. Still, they devote so many of their scarce resources to their beliefs, making offerings of gratitude for what they do have. It occurs to me how little appreciation Westerners have for their blessings, and that there is much for us to learn in this small, beautiful island of smiling strangers.

Reviewed by Tony Ayres

NEED TO KNOW

Rooms 48 pool villas.

Rates US$510–US$1,090 for a one-bedroom villa; US$1,750–US$2,880 for a three-bedroom villa. Breakfast is extra at US$25 a person. Excludes 11 per cent tax and 10 per cent service charge.

Check-out Officially noon, but late departures can be accommodated. Check-in, 3pm.

Facilities WiFi throughout, library, spa, gym, bicycles, gift shop. In rooms: personal host service, flatscreen TV, preloaded Apple TV, iPod dock, Spa Alila toiletries, minibar, espresso machine.

Poolside At the resort's heart, lies a sleek 25m infinity pool with four submerged day-beds at the shallow end.

Children Younger guests are equally welcome in these divine natural surroundings. Baby cots are free and villa sofas can be adapted for children under 12 to kip on. Babysitting costs around US$11 an hour.

Also The luxurious Spa Alila is located beneath reception's glass-based reflective pond, allowing filtered light to bathe the space, creating the most soothing atmosphere for a coma-inducing Balinese massage.

IN THE KNOW

Our favourite rooms All the sublime minimalist pads enjoy ocean views, but book into a second-storey Ocean Pool Villa for a blue bonus: a sea-view bath tub. Villas 202 to 206 are best positioned to maximise the postcard-perfect panorama.

Hotel bar More lounge than bar, informal Drift resembles the living room in the beach house of one's most enviable friends. Sit back with an iced tea in hand (or opt for the Long Island version) while flicking through the latest style bibles. Drinks and tapas-sized savouries are up for grabs, with Drift switching seemlessly to fine-dining come evening.

Hotel restaurant Dine alfresco or undercover at Cotta, which serves innovative Western fare, as well as fine local favourites such as *bebek menyatnyat*, a creamy duck curry. Just steps off Kelating Beach is the resort's more casual offering, Coast, where fresh seafood is grilled simply over charcoal.

Top table Come well before sunset to snag one of the two beachfront tables at Coast.

Room service Room service – from the restaurant menus or specially requested comfort food – can be delivered 24/7.

Dress code Skip the stilettos in favour of Havaianas topped with cool kaftans – effortless chic is key.

Local knowledge After lazing by the beach or pool, active types can grab an Alila surfboard to tackle the nearby breaks, ride a horse along the black-sand beach or cycle through the rice paddies. The Leisure Concierge can also organise 'Journeys by Alila' exploring Tabanan's thrills, spills and culture, including visits to food markets, artisans and temples.

LOCAL EATING AND DRINKING

Apart from humble *warungs* on nearby beaches, there are few restaurants around here. Head towards Seminyak – about an hour's drive – to enjoy some of Bali's finest fare. Sarong (+62 (0)361 737 809), at Jalan Petitenget, has a pan-Asian menu encompassing grilled and tandoori dishes, curries and creative stir-frys. Newcomer Métis (+62 (0)361 737 888) has a tempting Gallic menu in a gorgeous rice-paddy setting. Watch the sun set with a cocktail, then indulge in tasty Italian fare at beachside La Lucciola (+62 (0)361 730 838), on Oberoi Road. Sit in the frangipani-fringed courtyard or under the thatched roof upstairs. Wrap up the night with drinks at legendary bar Ku De Ta (+62 (0)361 736 969)

GET A ROOM!

For more information, or to book this hotel, go to www.mrandmrssmith.com – our expert team can take care of all your travel arrangements. Register your Smith membership card to enjoy exclusive offers and privileges.

 SMITH MEMBER OFFER A 90-minute spa treatment for two; and, if you stay for two nights or more, dinner for two at Cotta restaurant.

Alila Villas Soori Banjar Dukuh, Desa Kelating, Kerambitan, Tabanan, Bali, 82161, Indonesia (+62 (0)361 894 6388; www.alilahotels.com)

Seminyak

The Amala

STYLE Holistic with a heart
SETTING Sybaritic Seminyak

'A full-blooming frangipani perfumes the air
of our Spa Villa, which has, as its centrepiece,
a courtyard plunge pool with Jacuzzi jets'

Busy, buzzy and boasting chichi shops, world-class restaurants and funky Euro-style bars – that's Seminyak, Bali's capital of cool. As much as Mr Smith and I love the decadence that comes wrapped in layers of tropical sultriness, we also thrive on peace and calm. Enter the Amala, tucked a few lanes back from the area's premier fashion strip. Surrounded by tranquil ponds and stands of bamboo, its ambience instantly stills the frenzied beating of my store-loving heart.

A full-blooming frangipani perfumes the air of our Spa Villa, which has, as its centrepiece, a courtyard plunge pool with Jacuzzi jets. The pool deck seamlessly flows into the living room on one side and an outdoor bathing area on another. Here, a shelf near the enormous tub is lined with luxurious handmade soaps, bath soaks and scrubs produced in the Amala's spa and scented with wild herbs, citrus and ginger. My favourite welcome gift, however, is a jar of freshly baked shortbreads, chocolate-chip cookies, sesame crisps and cinnamon swirls.

As my hand delves into the cookie jar for the fourth – OK, maybe the fifth – time, I remind Mr Smith that we need to keep our energy levels elevated for an afternoon of shopping. He accepts an offer of a cinnamon swirl as we head towards the door.

There's no doubt about it, Seminyak is a danger to most credit limits. Handcrafted jewellery, handbags, elegant footwear and high-end fashion labels are interspersed with street stalls selling everything from knock-off designer sunglasses and novelty lighters to Bintang singlets, the uniform of bogan Aussie tourists.

In no time we discover Mr Smith has natural bargaining skills and he's negotiating deals that would make a used-car salesman blush. I, on the other hand, have no such talent. If the first price ain't right, I quickly head for the door. Somewhat mercifully, the shopkeepers mistake my reluctance to haggle for that well-practised bargaining technique of feigning disinterest. Soon they're chasing me down the street and dramatically dropping their 'best price', by which point I'm too embarrassed not to buy. The 'turn and walk', as we dub my move, is quickly incorporated into a formidable double act on Seminyak's shopping strip.

Three fake Rolexes and a Gucci handbag later, we decide to head to the beach for retail respite. Big mistake. Our feet have barely touched sand when we're accosted by a string of barefooted hawkers all desperate to hock their wares London geezer-style. A briefcase full of sunglasses, offensive bumper stickers and a bizarre collection of hats are all coolly deflected with a shake of the head.

'Hey mister, you wanna buy some Raybans? Mrs, can I braid your hair? Massage? Mushrooms that will fly you to the moon?'

'What?' I stop dead in my tracks and turn to look at Mr Smith: 'Did you hear that?' His half smile of consideration tells me he did, and clearly. 'No, thanks,' I reply, giving Mr Smith a meaningful look.

The verbal assault continues but we walk on staunchly until finally we give in to a man who introduces himself as Ketut. As if by magic, Ketut pulls two icy Bintangs from a bucket and presents a couple of sun-bleached plastic chairs. It's the best offer we've had all afternoon and we obediently take our places in time to watch the sun set.

The Amala's overpowering sense of Zen has clearly taken effect when, the following morning, we wake early, bursting with energy. We head back to the beach, determined to beat the crowds. This time our strategy

pays off. The sand is virtually devoid of life and rows of vacant deckchairs stretch out before us. The clear blue water is like a bath – you could swim for hours and never get cold. After what seems like an age, I turn back to face the shore. The sun is bright and I squint in the glare, eyes straining to pinpoint what was, moments before, a lone umbrella on the shore. Now there's a throng of blue and white stripes lined up just beyond the water's edge. But what really makes me gasp is the sight of four enormous German shepherds catching waves in front of me. 'Did we really say no to those mushrooms?' asks a grinning Mr Smith who's paddled out to meet me. 'Those dogs can really surf!' Clearly, he's impressed.

After the plank-riding pooches, I'm in need of some respite and we return to the Amala to road-test one of the spa treatments. Faced with innumerable options, we take the easy way out and choose the signature 120-minute Amala Healing Ritual, a series of scrubs, foot rubs and massages with essential oils finished off with a soak in a flower-filled bath. Two hours later, Mr Smith and I are capable of nothing more than lying in the sun by our private pool.

Hours later, still delightfully discombobulated, it's time to eat. On closer inspection, the Amala's Bamboo Restaurant feels a little too public for a romantic rendezvous and we decide to eat in the privacy of our villa. In moments the sun-deck is bathed in candlelight and a dining table appears by the pool. Handmade gnocchi, organic chicken and freshly caught fish are followed by delicious desserts washed down with one of the best lattés in Bali.

In ancient Sanskrit, the word *amala* means pure and unspoiled. I'm sure we'll leave the Amala the next day feeling pure, but for the past 48 hours we've been thoroughly spoiled.

Reviewed by Mr & Mrs Smith

NEED TO KNOW

Rooms 12 villas, including a three-bedroom residence.

Rates Low season, US$235–US$580; high season, US$265–US$610. Prices include breakfast, in-room soft drinks, cookies and fresh fruit, but exclude 11 per cent tax and a 10 per cent service charge.

Check-out Noon, but flexible up to 6pm, subject to availability, and a 50 per cent charge. Earliest check-in, 2pm.

Facilities Spa, yoga studio, gift shop, gardens, free WiFi throughout, a small library of DVDs, books and magazines, a laptop for guest use. In rooms: flatscreen LCD TV, CD/DVD player, iPod docking station, minibar, free bottled still water.

Poolside All villas come with private pools. In addition there is a lap pool, shaded by palm fronds and surrounded by plenty of padded outdoor furniture.

Children The Amala keeps its peace with a strictly enforced policy of no children under 12.

Also Freebies at the Amala include butler service, available 24 hours, and a 15-minute welcome massage. You can book a car and driver for local drop-offs.

IN THE KNOW

Our favourite rooms Spa Villas have a Jacuzzi and herb-infused steam shower, but the plunge pool and kitchenette that you get with a Pool Villa just edges it for us. The decor is contemporary – white walls and lacquered black furniture with minimalist finesse and maximum gadgetry. The super-grand Amala Residence, with three bedrooms and large private pool, is ideal for groups or families with children over 12.

Hotel bar What the Amala lacks in a proper bar it more than makes up for with its drinks menu. A poolside bottle of Tattinger Reims Brut Reserve for decadent days; a fresh Booster juice for the morning after.

Hotel restaurant Chinese high-back wooden chairs and opium beds confer an imperial quality on Bamboo, the resort's otherwise minimalist and casual open-air dining room. The cuisine is Indonesian and seasonal, with a choice of vegetarian, salad and more indulgent options.

Top table Let the butler turn the villa's outdoor poolside table into a romantic affair with candles and wine for dinner *à deux*.

Room service It's fairly standard to have breakfast at your villa – or any other meal you choose: the restaurant menu is available to order in when the kitchen is open, with a reduced selection on offer between 11pm and 7am.

Dress code Korean honeymooners match their LVs and Polo ponies from head to toe, but others will feel entirely at ease draping a light shirt or gossamer beach frock over swimsuits.

Local knowledge A Masters-In-Residence programme offers the services of Bali's finest wellness gurus and healing hands. Consider booking an Aqua Wellness and Yoga Day with water woman Elisa Senese and yogini Beate McLatchie.

LOCAL EATING AND DRINKING

Chef owner Nicolas Tourneville is the genius behind classy **Métis** (+62 (0)361 737 888) in Kerobokan Kelod, for French Mediterranean cuisine and an entire menu of foie-gras dishes. Along the street, **Hu'u Bar** (+62 (0)361 736 443) is an ideal spot for lazing under the stars and sipping lychee martinis. Try **Ku De Ta** (+62 (0)361 736 969) on the sand at Seminyak, which combines a beach club, lounge bar and restaurant on the waterfront.

GET A ROOM!

For more information, or to book this hotel, go to www.mrandmrssmith.com – our expert team can take care of all your travel arrangements. Register your Smith membership card to enjoy exclusive offers and privileges.

 SMITH MEMBER OFFER Healthy canapés and a fruit platter on arrival; and a romantic candlelit bath experience set up in your room.

The Amala Jalan Kunti 108, Seminyak, Bali 80361, Indonesia (+62 (0)361 738 866; www.theamala.com; www.lifestyleretreats.com)

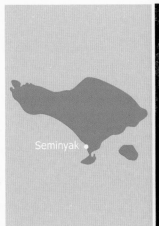

The Legian
& The Club

STYLE Oceanside opulence
SETTING Beach central

'Having a butler spoils you for life. You need to know this before you check in... you may never again be able to pour your own drink or fold your own clothes'

Having a butler spoils you for life. You need to know this before you check into the Club at the Legian; afterwards you may never again be able to pour your own drink or fold your clothes. You may even struggle to walk.

With my knowledge of butlers gleaned mainly from movies, I try to imagine the real thing as we travel to Seminyak. Will we be waited on by a penguin-suited Lurch intoning, 'You rang, sir?' Or perhaps a quaintly English Jeeves who will iron Mr Smith's newspaper while being implicated in various murder mysteries.

But first, we must find the Club, a super-private 11-villa hideaway close to its established mothership hotel, the Legian. Its entrance is so discreet our taxi driver misses it and instead delivers us to the much more visible lobby of the Legian itself, where the elegant bellboys summon a sleek black Lexus to relocate us across the narrow street. It's such a short distance, we protest. We could walk. The driver looks astonished and we realise that the Club, which describes itself as 'an oasis of sophisticated relief', intends to spare us even a whiff of exertion. There's a brief flash of Seminyak street bustle, a security-patrolled gate, then absolute peace. The villas stand around an ornamental pond, tropical gardens and the Club Lounge, with its bar, restaurant and nearby pool.

The Club delivers Legian luxury wrapped in an extra layer of personal attention. Each villa has a dedicated butler, and ours is Vina, who is not even slightly Lurchesque or Jeeves-like, but a smiling Balinese lady who combines serenity with the efficiency of an elite military unit.

She unlocks a wooden door and we step into our secret garden. There's a 10-metre swimming pool fringed by hibiscus and frangipani, an outdoor dining balé, manicured lawns, day-beds and, in the middle, a Balinese palace that, thanks to further ponds, appears from certain angles to be floating on water. Vina's introductory tour has more highlights than we can immediately absorb: a welcome bottle of Taittinger chilling in the fridge, bedroom with four-poster, bathroom with his 'n' hers wardrobes, a drinks cabinet proffering decanters of gin, vodka and whisky, jars crammed with cookies and nuts, and a minibar of further tipples. They're complimentary and refill magically whenever plundered.

The roll call of goodies continues: two sarongs, with tying instructions; tasteful straw sandals, a yoga mat, beach bags; board games, magazines and two iPods loaded with music for every taste. And my favourite: a huge bath outside among those ponds.

Left to our own devices, we explore our walled garden and conclude that it is, indeed, completely private. So we skinny-dip and Mr Smith takes a sarong-less stroll, communing with dragonflies. I'm concocting puns about bare-bottom botany when the doorbell rings, sending him scrambling for cover. No need, as Vina is clearly accustomed to guests exploring their inner naturist and allows time for modesty between ringing and entering through her special butler's door.

Want to know the truth about butler service? It's a little weird at first. Being resourceful travellers who, if necessary, will build a fire or catch dinner, we've unpacked our own suitcases and poured our own champagne. Then we remember that's Vina's gig. I fear we're under-achieving at being butlered, so we rustle up some dirty laundry and ask Vina to book a table at a much-recommended restaurant, La Lucciola. 'Think of more tasks,' I urge Mr Smith. You haven't known real luxury until you've suffered from butler angst.

Normally, we'd walk around the corner to La Lucciola, but this is the Club, where feet don't touch the ground. At sunset, Vina, black Lexus and driver arrive and deliver us to the door in moments. La Lucciola perches on a tranquil stretch of Seminyak Beach, and waves, candlelight and delicious Italian food paint a romantic idyll so dreamy that although we walk home we reckon Vina wouldn't mind — since it feels like floating.

The villa is so richly appointed you could nest indefinitely. But the next day we want to explore the Legian, as its facilities are available to Club guests. We recline on a sunlounger and watch the two-tier infinity pool and Indian Ocean vying to out-blue each other. Then, at risk of disappointing our butler, we walk along the beach towards Kuta and back along streets lined with shops running the gamut of tat to tasteful.

After the hubbub, we relish our private paradise. Apparently, some guests only emerge from their villa cocoon to visit the Club Lounge. Others punctuate their seclusion with trips to the Legian's spa, Pool Bar and the Restaurant, where we dine that night. Being VIPs (Vina's Important People), we're escorted to a prime table on the terrace. My river prawn *sambal* is spicy and fresh; Mr Smith's red snapper with chilli oil and water spinach is his favourite dish yet.

By now, we have endless errands for Vina. We've got her tracking down friends, finding shops, and asking the chef to make us a local dish called *martabak*. Just as we've finally surrendered every last shred of self-reliance, it's time to leave. Vina helps us pack and farewells us at the gate. 'Come with us and run our lives!' we want to cry, because after two days of splendid, cosseted indolence, we are convinced that survival skills are vastly overrated.

Reviewed by Amy Cooper

NEED TO KNOW

Rooms The Legian and the Club are sister properties that form one resort. At the Legian Hotel, there are 68 one- and two-bedroom suites; at the nearby Club, 10 one-bedroom villas and one three-bedroom villa.

Rates Low season, US$385–US$750; high season, US$650–US$1,300. Includes breakfast unless you've landed a discount on the rack rate (in which case, you pay an extra US$26). An 11 per cent tax and 10 per cent service charge applies.

Check-out Noon, but flexible subject to availability, and a charge of up to one day's rate. Earliest check-in, 2pm.

Facilities Spa, gym, library of board games and books, gardens, free WiFi throughout. In rooms: free internet (high-speed broadband/WiFi) in suites and villas; iPod dock (in suites), two Video iPods, Bose sound system, LCD flatscreen TV, Blu-Ray Disc Player, espresso machine.

Poolside At the Legian a seductive two-tiered 23m pool offers Indian Ocean views. The club Villas all have 10m private pools and there's a luxe 35m-long pool at the Club Lounge.

Children All ages welcome at this family-friendly resort. Baby cots are provided free and an extra bed for older children costs US$100. Book a Balinese nanny from around US$12 an hour with 24 hours' notice.

Also Villas at the Club come with a raft of extras: private airport transfers, in-room breakfast, afternoon tea, minibar treats, a local drop-off/pick-up car service and personal butler service. Free yoga lessons are on offer for all guests.

IN THE KNOW

Our favourite rooms Top-floor suites at the Legian command exceptional views over the hotel's garden. We like the generously proportioned third-floor one-bedroom Deluxe Suites. At the Club, to single out just one of the capacious dream homes would be foolish, unless it's the king-of-the-beach three-bedroom villa.

Hotel bar The Pool Bar and Ocean Bar at the Legian serve signature cocktails such as the Legian Mojito.

Hotel restaurant The Restaurant at the Legian offers themed dinners on certain nights, including hot favourite, the Friday night seafood barbecue. Club guests can enjoy a similar menu in the more intimate Club Lounge.

Top table Grab a seaside table at the Pool Bar for sundowners that lead into dinner. For Friday's seafood extravaganza, book ahead and request a waterfront table.

Room service Order from a globe-spanning menu throughout the day (and night).

Dress code By day, anything more demure than a bikini or board shorts goes. Add glamour after dark.

Local knowledge Consult the guest directory for listings of Bali's many temple ceremonies – the Legian concierge (or your Club butler) can arrange transport and advise on dress code.

LOCAL EATING AND DRINKING

Jalan Petitenget is a strip of wall-to-wall stylish bars and restaurants. At number 21, rice-paddy views, laid-back lounging and super-fresh seafood await at Sardine (+62 (0)361 738 202). Enjoy romantic cocktails and Western fare at glam La Lucciola (+62 (0)361 730 838), beachside by Temple Petitenget. The chef owner behind once acclaimed Kafe Warisan has moved his talents to number 6, aka Métis (+62 (0)361 737 888), where the superlative French fare proves that geography is no obstacle. Beach club, restaurant and lounge bar Ku De Ta (+62 (0)361 736 969) at 9 Jalan Kayu Aya in Seminyak, is a long-standing favourite. Compare and contrast its cocktail list, starting with its lychee martinis, at Hu'u Bar (+62 (0)361 736 443) on Jalan Oberoi, Petitenget.

GET A ROOM!

For more information, or to book this hotel, go to www.mrandmrssmith.com – our expert team can take care of all your travel arrangements. Register your Smith membership card to enjoy exclusive offers and privileges.

 SMITH MEMBER OFFER A 30-minute neck and shoulder massage each.

The Legian & The Club Jalan Kayu Aya, Seminyak Beach, Bali 80361, Indonesia (+62 (0)361 730 622; www.ghmhotels.com)

UBUD, BALI

COUNTRYSIDE Jungle valleys, rice paddies
COUNTRY LIFE Spiritual souls, artistic adventurers

Verdant rice terraces surround a thriving community of painters, mask-makers, musicians and monkeys in rustic inland Ubud. Spend your days wandering art galleries, markets and boutiques, before watching fire dancers and shadow-puppet performances after dark. Even before Elizabeth Gilbert drew global attention to Bali's cultural heartland in her bestselling autobiography *Eat, Pray, Love*, the one-time farming village swarmed with enlightenment-seekers, including A-listers Mick Jagger, Julia Roberts and Donna Karan. These days, this bustling town's charm is increasingly felt on its fringes – stroll through the jaw-dropping rural landscapes, explore the shaded jungle and witness the serene Balinese at work and play.

GETTING THERE

Planes Touch down at Ngurah Rai International Airport (www.baliairport.com), just south of capital Denpasar.
Automobiles The 30km drive north to Ubud will cost you about RP195,000 in an official airport taxi, but if you're feeling feisty you can haggle with one of the loitering cabbies beyond the airport perimeter. For a hassle-free transfer, however, organise a car ahead of time through your hotel.

LOCAL KNOWLEDGE

Taxis There are no metered taxis in Ubud (if you spot one, he'll have dropped someone off and be heading out again), but drivers are plentiful, especially along main drags Jalan Raya Ubud and Jalan Raya Campuan. Negotiate a price before you set off.
Siesta and fiesta Generally, Bali's banks and post offices open 8am–2pm Monday–Thursday, and until 12pm Fridays (post offices until 2pm). ATMs are accessible and easy to locate. Shops ply their trade from around 9am to 8pm, and food haunts from 8am to 10pm, or longer in tourist hubs. The prime night action in Ubud happens early evening with dance and cultural performances, but once they wrap you may find it tricky to eat out much after 9pm, although select backstreet watering holes will be open until midnight.

Do go/don't go Ubud's higher elevation may take the edge off the equatorial swelter, but the annual average rainfall is higher here, too. July to September is high season, when the climate is most appealing, but August is also the busiest time of year.
Packing tips This is no party town, so leave your best threads at home. Bring all things shiny and stretchy for basking, bathing and bicycling. Comfortable kaftans and loose linen will keep you cool and sun-burn free.
Recommended reads Love it or loathe it, Elizabeth Gilbert's *Eat Pray Love* raised Ubud's profile as a healing heartland and makes an easy, enjoyable read. Long-time Ubudian Janet de Neefe wrote a considerably deeper analysis of the place and people in *Fragrant Rice: My Continuing Love Affair with Bali*. Those curious about the daily lives of the peaceful locals should pick up *A Little Bit One O'clock: Living With a Balinese Family* by William Ingram.
Local specialities Don't miss the iconic *babi guling* – spit-roasted pig stuffed with chilli, turmeric, garlic and ginger.
Also Cycling is a fantastic way of exploring some of the villages and countryside around Ubud. Many hotels have bicycles available; if not, the concierge will certainly be able to organise pedal power for you.

WORTH GETTING OUT OF BED FOR

Viewpoint The Balinese consider the Ayung River and its many tributaries holy: the scenery along its steep, jungle-clad banks is awe-inspiring. Many of Ubud's luxury resorts overhang the river, providing great views. There is a good walk that takes you past the Sayan Terrace Hotel and down a track to the riverside (one of the locals will show you the way for a few rupiah).

Arts and culture Watching 50 half-naked sweaty men dancing around a bonfire may not sound like your ideal night out, but the *kecak* dance, performed by local group Cak Rina, is the most dramatic of Bali's famous dances; catch shows every full and new moon at the Arma Museum (www.armamuseum.com). Witness a *wayang kulit* performance at Oka Kartini (Saturday and Wednesday at 8pm; +62 (0)361 975 193), where as many as a hundred shadow puppets are sashayed across a fire-lit stage to act out tales from great Hindu epics, such as the Ramayana. Serious buffs will find one of the finest selections of Balinese and Indonesian art at the Neka Art Museum (www.museumneka.com).

Activities Go with the flow: raft on the white waters of the Ayung River or cycle down the mountain to the Elephant Safari Park with Bali Adventure Tours (www.baliadventuretours.com). For a more gentle distraction, the cooking classes at Casa Luna (www.casalunabali.com) include an early-morning market visit, hands-on demos and a sumptuous shared meal. Try a soothing therapeutic Ayurvedic treatment at the health and yoga centre, Amrta Siddhi (www.amrtasiddhi.com).

Best beach You'll have to descend from Ubud's lush heights to find the serene palm-lined stretch of Pasir Putih Beach in Candidasa. It's not a tourist-magnet, so you're guaranteed a slice of serenity.

Daytripper Go east for a different perspective of Bali's natural and cultural heritage. Serious climbers will have no trouble hiking up the now dormant volcano Mount Agung, Bali's highest peak at just over 3,000m. Aim to get to the top by 8am to enjoy a cloud-free view. On its slopes, visit the multi-tiered Pura Besakih or 'mother temple', a complex of 23 temples perched on parallel ridges. For an easier climb, walk up to the indigenous Bali Aga mountain village of Tenganan, known for its unique double ikat weaving, called *kamben gringsing*, and sacred leaf books or *lontar*. From here, it's a short journey down to the beach at Candidasa.

Children 'Throw down to the ground' is the translation of Ubud attraction *mepantigan* (www.mepantiganbali.com), which integrates various self-defence techniques, Balinese folklore and mud wrestling. It's meant to teach audiences about harmony between man, god and nature. It's impossible not to become engrossed as the *gamelan* gets louder and dancers begin fire eating then dancing like shadow puppets. Watch the action or encourage the kids to get dirty themselves at the Green School (www.greenschool.org) on Monday and Wednesday at 3.30pm.

Walks Long before eco was chic, Ubud native Darti (+62 (0)361 975 487) was picking up trash on his well-known rice-paddy walks. After a guided walk across rivers and through bamboo groves, Darti will take you for a feel-good shopping spree at Threads of Life (www.threadsoflife.com), a fair-trade non-profit enterprise that promotes women's empowerment and sustainable development through traditional Balinese ikat weaving.

Perfect picnic Watch for the water bridge over the road on your way into Ubud, then follow the signs on foot through the rice paddies to Sari Organik (+62 (0)361 780 1839), where you can enjoy fresh tofu dishes and just-picked salads from this alfresco snack-shack.

Shopping Frenchman Jean-François Fichot's handmade jewellery and tableware (www.jf-f.com) is as spectacular as Ubud's verdant landscape; seek out his silver filigree and jade-festooned seashell rings, Brazilian tourmaline chokers and buffalo-horn salad servers. Silversmith to the stars John Hardy (www.johnhardy.com) also does a fine

line in Balinese bling. Pick up one of Bali's most charming souvenirs, the game of *kocokan* at Studio 22K (Jalan Raya, near the entrance of Oka Kartini Hotel). Local artist Made Subrata has created a beautiful version of the traditional game played at temple shrines since ancient times, with a hand-painted mat covered in fantastical turtles, fish and snakes.

Something for nothing If Ubud is Bali's cultural heart, then the *gangs* (alleys) are its veins and art its lifeblood. You can lose a day just wandering between art galleries and craft workshops. Bali's growing community of female painters exhibit at the Seniwati Gallery (www.seniwatigallery.com); alternatively check out cutting-edge contemporary art at Komaneka Gallery (http://gallery.komaneka.com) and Gaya Fusion (www.gayafusion.com), both free to enter. Those with a sweet tooth may, however, want to consider carrying a few rupiah since Gaya's gelato is the island's best.

Don't go home without... spending an hour or so just watching the goings-on in the Sacred Monkey Forest Sanctuary, at the end of Jalan Monkey Forest. Regardless of the signs imploring visitors not to carry food, some wag will think he can outsmart the monkeys – big, whiskery, evil-looking things – by 'hiding' a hand of bananas in his backpack or packet of peanuts in his pocket. What ensues – virtually a primate ambush – would be scary if it wasn't so hilarious.

UTTERLY UBUD

Achieving total relaxation has become a mission in its own right in these idyllic surroundings. Ubud's spas and healing retreats range from rather basic to incredibly luxurious. One of the most popular treatments is the Mandi Lulur, a royal bridal ritual from Java, consisting of a massage, body exfoliation, yoghurt mask and flower bath.

DIARY

March Get in touch with your inner yogi at Ubud's Bali Spirit Festival (www.balispiritfestival.com), a five-day celebration of yoga, dance and music towards the end of the month. June In nearby capital Denpasar, the month-long Bali Arts Festival (www.baliartsfestival.com) showcases modern and traditional dance, handicrafts and music in what is considered the cultural event of the year. October Immerse yourself in the Ubud Writers & Readers Festival (www.ubudwritersfestival.com), which has become one of the biggest events of its kind in south-east Asia.

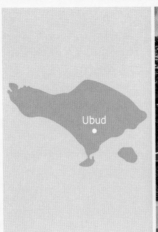

Como Shambhala Estate

STYLE Well-heeled wellbeing
SETTING Jungle wonderland

'If Bali is the Island of the Gods then it is highly likely Como Shambhala Estate, nestled in a misty, mossy valley, is where they reside'

If Bali is the Island of the Gods then it is highly likely Como Shambhala Estate, nestled in a misty, mossy valley, is where they reside. My suspicions were first aroused a few years back when Mr Smith and I travelled to this hidden wellness retreat, 15 minutes' drive from Bali's artistic and cultural centre, Ubud, for our honeymoon. At that time we were convinced that there were good spirits inhabiting the villas while we were hanging about borrowing their space.

This time around, having been shown to our Retreat Villa, called Vasudhara, with its own pool and couple's therapy room, we are tempted to stay put. It's just as I remember: the timeless, understated design, every detail created with care, from the proportions of the furniture and lamps to the incredibly pleasing doormats. We even measure up a chair I've instantly fallen in love with, taking photos and determining to have one made for our home. Everything just seems to work, including the established vegetation that appears to have been planted strategically to maximise shade and privacy.

On offer further afield is a full schedule of activities – cycling through the village, yoga classes, even talks on philosophy if that's your cup of Ayurvedic tea – but you could easily hole up in your room, ordering room service, dipping in the pool and getting the massage therapists to come to you. Mr Smith is keen on this option but eventually I convince him we need to explore – and eat. My restaurant of choice is Kudus House, one of the Estate's two dining options, and I call our PA to make a booking at the modern Indonesian restaurant housed in a 150-year-old former Javanese residence. He also offers to transport us to dinner in a buggy, but we choose instead to take a slow walk through the grounds, enjoying Ubud's cool evening breeze.

The sounds of the Ayung River below accompany the faultless meal and our plans to move to Bali, a plot that is systematically hatched each time we visit. I wish I'd written down what we ate – it was vegetarian and came with red rice – because I would do anything to be able to replicate it myself. We half-walk, half-float back to the villa, satisfied and feeling a million miles away from the pressures of home.

The following morning, while we're out cruising around Ubud, one of the locals comments that 'too much is never enough' when it comes to the Estate. Later, as I'm wrapped in a towel on our private outdoor massage suite, looking out over the valley, I realise just how true that statement is. When we last visited this holistic haven, the treatments were an absolute highlight. I guess they're still amazing, but as I fell asleep just minutes into my massage I'm not really in a position to speculate.

That evening a little magic comes our way (it must be those gods!). It has wings and a tiny pulsating light. A firefly frolics over our heads then lands on the lampshade. Mr Smith instantly reverts to childhood, amused and amazed at this twinkling miracle of science that has blessed us with its presence. We are completely fixated. The enchanting Ubud Valley had pulled us in and real life seems so distant – at least for one night.

The next day, we decide to make the most of the wellness options at the resort. I drag the yoga-fixated Mr Smith to a complimentary pilates class, although he has trouble understanding the small core movement exercises and wonders why there's not more 'go go go' involved. Later, we consult the friendly resident nutritionist, and have our pulses read by Como Shambhala Estate's Ayurvedic doctor. He holds my wrist and promptly tells me I think too much; that even when there is nothing to think about I think something up. I think he is pretty right in his thinking.

Many people come here for a week or more to take full advantage of all these fine-tuned spa and wellness programmes. The resort encourages a three-night minimum stay to ensure you leave feeling well and truly cleansed and detoxed on both a physical and emotional level – but we still wish we'd booked in for longer.

While we're packing our bags, I notice Mr Smith has collected a little stash of the Como Shambhala toiletries.

Now, I am usually a bit of a snob when it comes to hotel soaps, but even in this department the resort excels, with toiletries all scented with the Estate's signature Invigorate fragrance. Its amenities are made of natural botanical ingredients (so they're better for the environment), blending mood-elevating grapefruit, fennel, cypress and lime, while the body lotion in the bathroom is beyond silky smooth. It's the little things, as they say.

Como Shambhala Estate more than lives up to my memories of our first visit, having perfected the subtle art of being both luxurious yet understated. Of course, this time around we've spent quite a bit more time enjoying all the resort's amenities rather than spending all our time doing, well, honeymoon stuff. But there is one thing that is troubling me: the name of the resort. Really, it should be called the Como Shambhalaaaahhhh.

Reviewed by Nadya Hutagalung

NEED TO KNOW

Rooms 30 suites, housed in five shared residences, plus five Retreat Villas and four two- or three-bedroom Private Villas.
Rates US$720–US$3,570; US$1,400–US$15,900 for three- to seven-night packages, including breakfast, wellness consultation, daily activities, spa facilities and a personal assistant. You can book a whole residence (four or five suites) from US$2,300 a night. A 21 per cent tax and service charge applies.
Check-out Noon, but flexible subject to availability. Earliest check-in, 2pm.
Facilities Spa, gym, yoga studios, Jungle Gym, tennis courts, library, shop. In rooms: LCD TV, DVD player, free WiFi, minibar, tea/coffee, Como Shambhala spa products.
Poolside Each of the residences has its own pool and stand-alone villas have private pools. In most cases, they are infinity-edged, surrounded by decking and with beautiful jungle views. The spa, as well as a 25m lap pool, has hydrotherapy pools and jet beds.
Children The Private Villas are best suited to little Smiths. Under-12s stay free; for older children, an extra bed costs US$75 a night. Babysitting can be arranged for US$10 a child an hour.
Also A minimum three-night stay applies at this spa-focussed sanctuary, so guests can recharge, with compulsory half-board (daily breakfast and lunch or dinner). East meets West in the nine treatment rooms of the holistic Ojas spa, with a range of holistic therapies.

IN THE KNOW

Our favourite rooms They're all pretty spectacular. The one-bedroom Retreat Villas – each with a private treatment room – are ideal if you're planning on being a regular at the nearby spa. Of the Private Villas, Sukma Taru has valley views. The Principal Suites – one in each residence – are large and lavish. Go for the one in Tirta-Ening residence, which has a private entrance, terrace, waterfall pool, balé and Jacuzzi – oh, and a six-ton carved stone bath.
Hotel bar As if we'd let you poison your liver on a wellness retreat...
Hotel restaurant The tasty, locally sourced produce perfectly complements the wellness ethos. Kudus House serves Indonesian cuisine in a 19th-century Javanese villa; Glow is an all-day restaurant, with an open kitchen, offering local organic dishes with a healthy bent. At the Ojas spa and poolside, choose from a menu of snacks, sorbets and granitas.
Top table Glow's pavilion structure means every mouthful is accompanied by eyefuls of the Ayung valley. In Kudus House, request a table on the veranda.
Room service A wide-ranging menu of healthy snacks and meals is available 24 hours.
Dress code Cotton kurtas and Thai-style wrap trousers.
Local knowledge Relaxation isn't hard to come by... Choose from yoga, meditation, pranayama or pilates.

LOCAL EATING AND DRINKING

We doubt you'll want to derail your wellness programme by eating out, but if you're tempted make for the Three Monkeys (+62 (0)361 975 554) on Jalan Monkey Forest, where the magical rice-paddy panorama is well matched by simple Mediterranean fare and divine desserts. Head to hillside Murni's Warung (+62 (0)361 975 233), on Jalan Campuhan, for Indonesian and Western dishes served on four open-air levels decorated with Balinese art.

GET A ROOM!

For more information, or to book this hotel, go to www.mrandmrssmith.com – our expert team can take care of all your travel arrangements. Register your Smith membership card to enjoy exclusive offers and privileges.

 SMITH MEMBER OFFER A Como Shambhala aromatherapy gift; a 60-minute massage for two for five-night stays; or for seven-night stays, a two-hour bath body treatment for two.

Como Shambhala Estate Banjar Begawan, Desa Melinggih Kelod Payangan, Gianyar, 80571, Bali, Indonesia
(+62 (0)361 978 888; www.cse.como.bz)

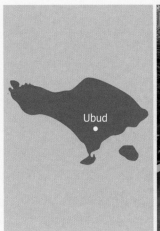

The Purist Villas & Spa

STYLE Remixed treasures, modern pleasures
SETTING Verdant village edge

'Every area has been designed to ensure maximum horizontal enjoyment, whether that's lazing on a sunlounger on the deck or slothing on the more secluded day-bed'

Trust Mr Smith and me to arrive in Bali at the same time as a megastar. Indeed Megawati Soekarnoputri, the former Indonesian president, has chosen today, of all days, to kick off her party's pre-election campaigning on the island, and she's brought along quite the entourage. As is often the case in Bali, the traffic has come to a grinding halt, and we're only a hundred metres from the airport. The happy-go-lucky nature of the Balinese means no one really seems to mind, but for this seasoned commuter, sitting in traffic is no way to start a holiday. Then I clock the giant posters of Mega's face beaming down on streets lined with banners and flags – girl power! – and can't help but smile back and surrender to the chaos. At least we have air-conditioning.

When we finally arrive in Ubud my cheery holiday vibe is restored: the Purist Villas define serenity. Set on lush tropical hills on the outskirts of town, there are just seven private villas, making this one of Bali's smallest boutique hotels.

As luck would have it, Mr Smith and I are staying in the smallest hotel's largest villa – an antique house transplanted from the island of Timor. Its carved timber panels have been extended upward to include a mezzanine level that is now the master bedroom, starring a king-size four-poster bed. As our butler Agus shows us around, it becomes apparent that the boudoir is not the only place suitable for a lie-down.

Every area of our Hill Villa has been designed to ensure maximum horizontal enjoyment, whether that's lazing on a sunlounger on the deck overlooking the main swimming pool, or slothing on the more secluded day-bed by our own pool. Inside, the living room's sofas offer the perfect vantage point for gazing up at the villa's *alang-alang* roof, and the second bedroom, with doors that open to the private pool, has two single beds that scream 'siesta'. Then, of course, there's the indoor/outdoor bathroom with a stone tub, perfect for soaking beneath the stars. 'We'll be making the most of that,' says Mr Smith.

With two days of intense relaxation ahead of us we set ourselves the arduous task of choosing a favourite resting place. In the heat of the day, that's our private pool. As we splash about, Mr Smith declares a cocktail the only thing missing from this idyllic scene. Two mojitos are promptly ordered – it is mid-afternoon after all. Not so promptly, the mojitos arrive. We don't really mind for we are now in total relaxation mode. While we sip contentedly, Agus asks us if we're dining in that night, as anything from the kitchen must be ordered well in advance to allow the staff time to prepare.

The ingredients for almost every dish are sourced from the local market, which means produce that's fantastically fresh, but it also requires anticipating your food mood and appetite up to three hours before you eat. With this in mind, I figure it wise to order another round of mojitos, too, correctly predicting an ongoing thirst.

Mandi Lulur might sound like the name of the latest teen sensation to storm the charts, but it's actually the flower bath treatment Mr Smith and I have booked at the spa. It's one of the hotel's signature pampering pleasures, originally devised in the 17th century for royal Javanese brides-to-be. A double treatment room means our bodies are pummelled and tweaked in unison before being rubbed down with a richly spiced, house-made body scrub to exfoliate the skin. We're then covered in detoxing yoghurt (mojitos, be gone!) before the session ends with a soak in a deep, warm bath topped with flower petals.

Muscles refreshed and skin silky-smooth, we return to our villa in a delightful daze just in time for dinner. We've decided to eat in the comfort of our new home (a wise move given our spa-sedated condition), but there's also the option of heading to the Living Room, the common dining area. The food is amazing and keeps us alert until dessert has been devoured. We crawl upstairs and crash before our plates are cleared, falling into the deep, otherworldly slumber usually reserved for children and the recently massaged.

While I pick over breakfast in the sun the next morning, Mr Smith jumps straight in the pool. Between his splashes, we decide today is all about adventure and braving Ubud's famed Monkey Forest. In fact, we are feeling so ready for action we resolve to travel there on motorcycles, exploring local rice paddies and villages along the way.

The thrill-seeking, however, is short lived. Channelling Casey Stoner, I give the throttle a few revs and drive straight into a nearby fence. Agus runs to my rescue, pulling off the bike and helping me from the ground. More amused than alarmed, Mr Smith tries to stifle his laughter, cursing the missed opportunity to capture the whole thing on film.

Cuts and bruises attended to, Agus arranges a driver to take us to the Monkey Forest. We spend the day communing with primates and exploring Ubud's art and craft markets before returning home to the villa. Wonderfully weary, we slide into the pool, bottles of Bintang in hand, to escape the heat and watch the sun set behind jungle-covered hills.

'We should come back to Bali next year,' says Mr Smith. I give him an approving nod: 'That should be enough time for me to get my motorcycle licence.'

Reviewed by Mr & Mrs Smith

NEED TO KNOW

Rooms Seven villas, of which two pairs can be adjoined to form larger residences.

Rates US$240–US$380, excluding 21 per cent tax and service charge. During peak times (mid-December to mid-January, and mid-July through August), there is a surcharge of US$30 a villa a day, and a minimum three-night stay.

Check-out Noon, but flexible subject to availability. Earliest check-in, 2pm.

Facilities Spa, yoga pavilion, library, bicycles, gardens, free WiFi throughout. In rooms: flatscreen TV, CD/DVD player, minibar, free tea, bottled water, fresh fruit.

Poolside The Garden, Hill and Bamboo Villas each have private pools. The remaining villas have direct access to the jungle-fringed main infinity pool.

Children Little Smiths are welcome at the Purist and free baby cots are provided.

Also The ethos here is home away from home – so you can dine or enjoy spa treatments at your villa.

IN THE KNOW

Our favourite rooms The decor in all villas teams Balinese trinkets and soft furnishings with sleek, contemporary furniture and design. We like Timor Villa for its hand-carved rough wood exterior and thick, antique floorboards. Garden Villa comes with the largest private pool. Hill Villa stands out as a quirkily decorated duplex with two bedrooms. For larger groups, the River Villas combine into one large residence, as do the Timor and Garden Villas.

Hotel bar Staff can be called upon at any time to mix drinks in this covered open-air nook.

Hotel restaurant An open-air Javanese *joglo* house has been recycled here as the hotel's dining area, although most guests enjoy dinner at their villa or by the pool. Breakfast brings fresh fruits, pancakes or native *nasi goreng* (a rice and chicken dish). By night, go Balinese with a salad, grilled fish or curry under the stars.

Top table For in-villa dining, the jungle-facing outdoor living area of the River Residence is hard to beat. For other guests, the Purist's bijou bar doubles as an excellent spot to dine, accompanied by the river and countless crickets.

Room service A selection of food is available around the clock, with breakfast served between 7am and 11am.

Dress code The high degree of privacy means no one needs to dress up. Jungle nights can be cold, so pack accordingly.

Local knowledge Plan to spend serious time in the intimate, minimalist spa here.

LOCAL EATING AND DRINKING

Bali Buddha (+62 (0)361 976 324), on Jalan Jembawan, is a café above a shop, serving home-made, mostly vegetarian, fare. A Full English breakfast and Balinese tapas exemplify the diversity you'll find at Ubud institution Nomad (+62 (0)361 977 169). Expect French fine dining and an impressive wine list at Mozaic (+62 (0)361 975 768), where you can eat on the terrace or in the tropical garden. The food is as beautifully presented as the open-air, conservatory-style dining room is elegant at modern Japanese restaurant Minami (+62 (0)361 970 013). Across the Tjampuhan River Indus (+62 (0)361 977 684) serves Indonesian and Western dishes – sometimes with Latin dance evenings or, at Full Moon, accompanied by jazz.

GET A ROOM!

For more information, or to book this hotel, go to www.mrandmrssmith.com – our expert team can take care of all your travel arrangements. Register your Smith membership card to enjoy exclusive offers and privileges.

 SMITH MEMBER OFFER An Anti-Jetlag package for two, including a 30-minute neck and shoulder massage on arrival, healthy mocktail and Balinese offering box.

The Purist Villas & Spa Jalan Tirta Tawar, Banjar Kutuh Kaja, Ubud, Bali, Indonesia (+62 (0)361 974 454; www.thepuristvillas.com)

SURF'S

Time zone GMT +7 hours.

Dialling codes Country code for Laos +856: Luang Prabang (0)71 — drop the zero if calling from overseas.

Language Lao (including the Vientiane dialect and the northern dialect favoured in Luang Prabang). English, French and Thai are widely understood.

Currency Lao kip (LAK), Thai baht (THB) and US dollars (US$) are all accepted. ATMs are a rare find, but there are a couple dishing out dollops of kip.

Tipping culture Most Laotians don't tip, but Johnny (or Joanna) Foreigner is expected to leave about five to 10 per cent.

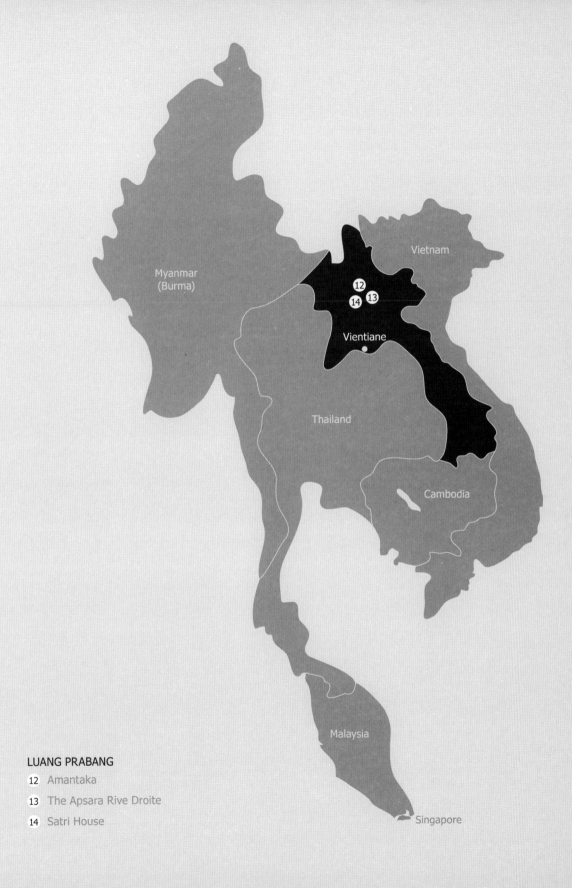

Myanmar
(Burma)

Vietnam

12 13
14

Vientiane

Thailand

Cambodia

Malaysia

Singapore

LUANG PRABANG

12 Amantaka

13 The Apsara Rive Droite

14 Satri House

LUANG PRABANG

CITYSCAPE French history, Mekong mystery
CITY LIFE Living on a prayer

Lying between mist-shrouded mountains on the palm-lined banks of the Mekong, languid Luang Prabang is every bit the land of the lotus eaters. Years of war and some cranky communist ideas may have taken this historic town off the travel map for nearly two decades, but for those beating a path back to its Unesco-protected temples and colonial villas, the northern Laotian outpost is still one of the most charming destinations in south-east Asia. Serene to the point of somnolent, the old quarter is bursting with grand French mansions and traditional wooden houses. The pleasures to be enjoyed here are simple and lingering: Lao coffee sipped in a street café; the hypnotic drum beat of the monks' call to prayer; or a walk beneath boughs of fragrant frangipani trees.

GETTING THERE

Planes Wing your way into Luang Prabang International Airport (www.luangprabangairport.com) from Bangkok, Chiang Mai, Siem Reap or Hanoi, among other regional airports. Bangkok Airways (www.bangkokair.com) and Vietnam Airlines (www.vietnamairlines.com) offer the smoothest flight connections. An airport taxi into town costs about US$6.

Boats Several cruise boats connect Huay Xai (the bustling Mekong River port on the Thai border) with Luang Prabang – handy if you're coming from Chiang Mai or Chiang Rai in Thailand. Luang Say Cruises (www.luangsay.com) offers a two-day river experience, with an overnight stay in the rustic town of Pak Beng. Don't even consider the speedboats unless you enjoy tinnitus, cramp and death-defying velocity.

Automobiles Luang Prabang is compact and easy to explore on foot. For trips further afield to the Kuang Si Falls or Pak Ou Caves (nicer by boat), you could hire a car and driver: prices start at US$30 a day.

LOCAL KNOWLEDGE

Taxis There are no metered taxis, but plenty of *jumbos* (eight-seater motorised three-wheelers) or tuk tuks. You'll hear the more diminutive vehicles before you lay eyes on them: the two-stroke engine whines like a hornet.

Your ride will cost about US$2; a little more if your jumbo is, ahem, jumbo-sized. Hotels can arrange cars if asked.

Siesta and fiesta Banks open weekdays 9.30am–4pm. Shop times vary widely, but the core hours are 9am until about 9pm. Lao people usually dine early, so local places close before international eateries. Night spots warm up around 9pm, but the universal closing time of 11.30pm means they cool down pretty soon afterwards.

Do go/don't go Pleasantly cool and dry weather arrives from November to February, but corresponds with a peak in tourist numbers. The wet season (peaking in August) is not a complete washout, though, as showers are usually brief and paint the countryside in a vivid palette of greens.

Packing tips A hod: the value of Lao's coinless kip currency is so low that you'll have to carry around brickloads of cash to pay for even small items (we suggest you take low-denomination US dollars or Thai baht instead).

Recommended reads Unravel the mysteries of the Laotian nation with *A Short History of Laos: The Land in Between* by Grant Evans. Dervla Murphy's *One Foot in Laos* may inspire you to travel into the hinterland.

Local specialities Lao cuisine has long lived in the shadow of its neighbour Thailand's fare, but undeservedly so:

common dishes such as *laap* (minced meat or fish with herbs, greens and dried chilli flakes) may have a shared ancestry, but, among other ingredients, it is finger-friendly sticky rice that sets Laotian menus apart. A culinary sponge, it soaks up sauces, eradicating the need for fiddlesome cutlery. Luang Prabang's French heritage means you'll not only feast on traditional Lao fare: there's also fine French dining – not to mention fantastic Asian fusion. Savour a signature Luang Prabang salad (made with coriander, mint and crisp watercress) and you'll realise fusion was invented way before it popped up in Wolfgang Puck's recipe files. Other unmissable snacks include nori-style *kai phen* (Mekong River weed with sesame seeds and chilli) and *jaew bong* (a gingery dip with water-buffalo skin and dried chillies).

Also Amaze your friends back home with an authentic Lao banquet: a gourmet cooking masterclass with Tamarind (+856 (0)20 777 0484; www.tamarindlaos.com) provides an informed guide to the Lao hearth – you'll learn to cook six dishes in a serene lakeside setting.

WORTH GETTING OUT OF BED FOR

Viewpoint If you're up early to offer alms to the monks, then you might as well stay awake and roll with the karma. Ascend the steps to the summit of Mount Phousi and take in the verdant views over low-rise Luang Prabang – it's blissfully quiet around sunrise.

Arts and culture Wat Xieng Thong is the postcard-perfect temple, with its roof arcing effortlessly to the floor. It's an original survivor from the 16th century, before the Black Flag (not Henry Rollins' seminal punk outfit, but a band of marauding Chinese) used it as a base during their 1887 assault on the town. For more cultural capers, the Royal Palace Museum (+856 (0)71 212 470; US$2), housed in the former royal residence, boasts treasures including the portrait of King Sisavang Vatthana, whose royal shoes appear to follow you across the room in the most alarming manner, changing direction in the process.

Activities Luang Prabang is about adventure as well as culture, with fitness-boosting forays into the countryside, hikes to hilltop villages, cycle rides through lush forests, or kayaking along pretty rivers. Several reliable operators offer one-day cycling and kayaking trips or opt for a longer combination including trekking and elephant encounters: try Tiger Trail Outdoor Adventures (+856 (0)71 252 655; www.laos-adventures.com) or Green Discovery (+856 (0)71 212 093; www.greendiscoverylaos.com).

Daytripper Venture to the Kuang Si Falls (Tat Kuang Si), a series of tumbling cascades that wend their way through the Lao jungle. The limestone formations give the place an otherworldly atmosphere and have turned the waters a vivid turquoise. There are swimming holes beneath the main falls, including one with an impressive rope swing for Tarzan-channelling Mr Smiths to try.

Children Introduce the kids to some gentle giants at an elephant camp in the surrounding countryside. Elephant Village (www.elephantvillage-laos.com), a centre for rehabilitating former working animals, offers half-day treks to the wondrous waterfall of Tat Sae; big kids (Smith seniors included) will love it too.

Walks Traffic remains mercifully light in old Luang Prabang, and tour buses are banned downtown, making it pedestrian-friendly. Start at one end of Sisavangvong Road near the post office and head to the other end near Wat Xieng Thong, wending your way through small alleys and secluded wats to spy half-timbered colombage houses, saffron robes and smiling residents.

Perfect picnic Every visitor makes a pilgrimage to the Pak Ou caves to pay homage to the thousands of Buddha images hidden there over the centuries. Though busy, the caves' dramatic location in towering limestone cliffs above the Mekong is still worth the detour. Make it more memorable with a private picnic on a deserted Mekong island en route. There are several seasonal spots where this is possible (ask your hotel for details), plus some abandoned wats for a romantic if eerie backdrop.

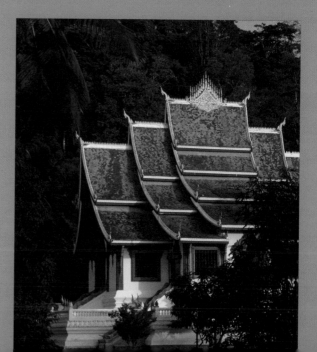

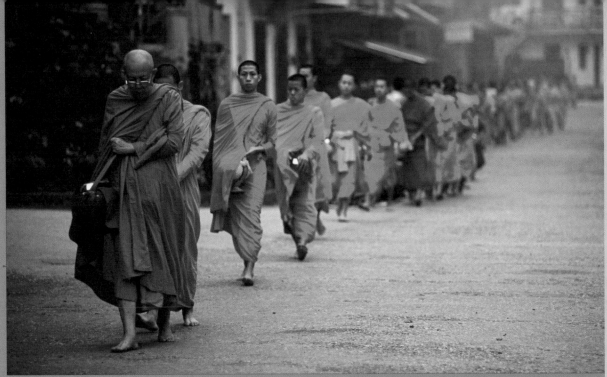

Shopping Luang Prabang has a host of tempting shopping opportunities, but given that this is laid-back Laos, there is not much of a sales pitch – enter a boutique and you may need to wake up the sales assistant. The one exception is the Night Market, strung out along Sisavangvong Road each evening. Touting silk scarves, Hmong-style slippers and throws, it's a buzzy place to browse and check the pulse of prices. Many sellers are minority women from nearby villages, so purchases made here will benefit the local economy. On Sakkarine Road, Ock Pop Tok (+855 (0)71 254 406; www.ockpoptok.com) is a fair-trade textile gallery showcasing crafts with flair (the shop name means 'East meets West').

Something for nothing Most temples are free to enter and very striking, but if you're all templed out, soak up soothing aquatic views instead. The Mekong and Nam Khan rivers embrace the old town peninsula before merging at its tip. Cross the dry-season bamboo bridge over the Nam Khan for lush vistas over the local side of town, where farmers grow vegetables and peanuts on the river's banks.

Don't go home without... a Laotian scarf from Caruso Lao (www.carusolao.com) – they also offer original homewares including wooden tableware, ebony vases and shimmering silks.

POWERFULLY LUANG PRABANG

Many of the Mekong region's historic and sacred sites are a throwback to bygone empires, but Luang Prabang's allure lies in the fact it's a living, breathing entity. Nowhere is this more tangible than in the city's 36 ornately roofed and elaborately decorated Buddhist wats (temples). Every morning, a bright blaze of tangerine fabric snakes its way through town, as hundreds of monks spill onto the streets in search of spiritual succour. Cynics might contend that the daily dose is just for tourists now, but if you venture into the back alleys, you'll find the tradition alive and well.

DIARY

Mid-April Lao New Year (or Bun Pi Mai) is the highlight of the country's calendar. As well as water fights and a liberal smattering of talcum powder, Luang Prabang plays host to a colourful elephant procession. **May** Bun Bang Fai is the Rocket Festival, an ancient ritual to summon the rains, which see locals making merry before firing bamboo rockets wildly into the sky. **October–November** During the Bun Nam water festival, Luang Prabang stages long-boat races on the Mekong River – a sort of Henley Regatta for the masses, only with Lao-Lao rice wine instead of Pimm's.

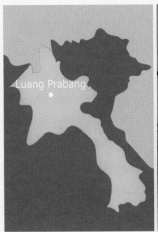 

Amantaka

STYLE Contemporary colonial
SETTING Under Mount Phousi

'Luang Prabang is the hottest destination in Asia... considered to be the best preserved and most authentic small town in former Indochina'

Celebrity spotting has never really been my strong suit. Once, at Nell's in New York, I spent a whole evening sitting next to Al Pacino thinking he was an over-tanned, gold-bechained banker rather than one of the most successful actors of his generation. 'What does Al do?' I asked my friend, who was obscurely related to him, later in the taxi. 'What do you mean, what does Al do?' he replied.

But in the sharply air-conditioned oasis of the Amantaka library in Luang Prabang, it is Mr Smith who fails to clock the boyish Hollywood megastar being discreetly ushered to his room by the GM. Distinctly un-Dunhillish in dressed-down trackie pants, and with what I can't help thinking is a rather bogan bottle-blond job, he does look more backpacker than Cool Britannia pin-up. But that's Jude Law alright. I'd recognise Sienna Miller anywhere.

Our frisson with fame is fleeting. Luang Prabang is too much of a star attraction herself to allow for lengthy distraction. It's day two of our stay and our retreat back to the hotel – OK, and the scrumptious afternoon tea, complete with pandan leaf–covered delicacies – is short and sweet. It's time to climb the mountain and see this charming Laotian backwater from above.

Mount Phousi is a modest, fin-like hill at one end of the little isthmus running between the great Mekong River and its tributary, the Nam, that essentially defines the heart of Luang Prabang, and, by default, the spiritual ground zero of Laotian Buddhism. At night, spot-lit in the smoky agricultural haze that pervades the town in spring, its graceful golden stupa seems to float above the town like a benign religious UFO. After a sweaty ascent – we're too hot to count the steps – we also realise it attracts 99 per cent of the local insect and gecko population; the white walls of the temple look like an Agnès B shop display in the pulsating late afternoon sunlight. Below us, the town stretches out lazily towards the river, and glints of gold cross the hilly countryside. It's all so transfixing we stay too long and have to take the long way down at dusk, mosquito swarms following us like thought bubbles. The back path releases us at one of the town's countless temples. The courtyard is deserted save for a mangy dog or two, while the boy monks say their evening prayers inside.

These days, Luang Prabang is (understandably) the hottest destination in Asia. It's enjoyed a privileged Unesco World Heritage status since 1995, and is now considered to be the best preserved and most authentic small town in the whole of former Indochina. Development in Luang Prabang is small-scale and low-rise and, out of respect for its living Buddhist culture, none of the central hotels have a swimming pool. Traffic is light and slow, and you are as likely to be overtaking one of the rickety local vintage cars, as they are you. This place is a genuine boutique bolthole.

We're guiltily glad, though, that Amantaka sits just outside the rectangular central grid. Not only does it have a grand swimming pool – we do desultory laps each morning – but our suite also has its own terrace and smaller pool. It's a perfect example of heritage restoration. Once the Catholic hospital, its clay-tiled and generously veranda'd dormitories stand sentry around an elongated, grassy central compound and it's hard to spot the one modern addition to the pack. An air of genteel and restorative calm is established within its walls; you can almost sense the wimpled nuns gliding about with tiffins while poor consumptive locals lie wanly on the beds inside.

The suite itself is a model of understated elegance. Mr Smith thinks it verges on the antiseptic, but I love it. High ceilings accommodate the mosquito-netted four-poster bed with ease; pistachio-coloured shutters throw shadows on the white walls; the bathroom sports a jaunty art deco look with its black and white tiles and retro fan. All that's missing are our linen suits, sun hats and a scratchy gramophone record for sundown. The common areas are very Foreign Correspondents Club too – convivial, ceiling-fanned rooms neither cavernous nor cramped. We take dinner in the dining room on our first night – a fiery four-course Laotian feast complete with the region's ubiquitous speciality sausage – and think ourselves very *The Year of Living Dangerously*.

Luang Prabang has that kind of effect. Chronology recedes, timelessness exudes, and the power of place levels locals, monks, travellers and even celebrities. On our last cycle through town – an old-fashioned upright bike with basket is the de rigueur vehicle – we overtake our friends from the library and share a languid hello. Mr Smith recognises them this time, but nobody bats an eyelid all the same.

Reviewed by Mr & Mr Smith

NEED TO KNOW

Rooms 24 suites, including 16 with private pools.
Rates US$700–US$1,400, including airport transfers. Excludes breakfast at US$25 a person, 10 per cent tax and 10 per cent service charge.
Check-out Noon, but flexible; until 6pm you'll be charged 50 per cent of the nightly rate. Check-in, 2pm.
Facilities Free WiFi throughout, library with laptops, spa, gym, yoga studio, boutique and art gallery, gardens. In rooms: Bose stereo, iPod dock, preloaded iPod in Mekong and Amantaka Suites, minibar, Lemongrass House toiletries.
Poolside Lucky couples in a pool suite can live the celebrity lifestyle sprawled by their private pond. The main pool is spacious enough for serious swimmers and is nicely cushioned between the gym and spa, depending on your mood.
Children Welcome: free cots and beds for under-12s. Baskets for infant guests come with baby wash and talcum powder.
Also A four-night minimum stay applies over Christmas, New Year and Easter holidays. Smoking in outdoor areas only.

IN THE KNOW

Our favourite rooms Ouch, tough choice with all those private pools on offer. Pool Suites 14 and 15 both offer views towards temple-topped, mist-swathed Mount Phousi. Khan Pool Suite 7 has an extensive garden hidden beneath tropical trees. The two Amantaka Suites are simply enormous, but you might lose each other from time to time.
Hotel bar Combining black-and-white photos of Buddhist monks with elegant teak sofas, rattan armchairs and trad newspaper racks, the Lounge Bar is open on demand for all guests. Enjoy a Laojito: we won't spoil the surprise.
Hotel restaurant The Restaurant at Amantaka offers grand dining under soaring ceilings. Sample some sensual Lao flavours with *mok pa* (steamed fish in banana leaf) or play closer to home with a duck ragout.
Top table Gravitate to the poolside terrace on a balmy evening. Stars above, oil lamps below, this is why we love to travel. For a table that tops all others, request a romantic dinner in the courtyard of your suite, complete with a private butler, traditional Lao music and candles to light the way to bed.
Room service Available 24 hours, room service spans a selection of Lao and Gallic-influenced dishes.
Dress code Mod-colonial to suit the surrounds (it is set in a former French hospital building resonating with old-world charm). By mod we mean modern: make sure Mr Smith doesn't crack out his parka and start singing Jam anthems.
Local knowledge Amantaka offers tempting Guest Experiences for immersion into the Luang Prabang scene. Explore the old city on foot, make a temple offering, cruise the Mekong River, learn the art of the elephant mahout or splash under a waterfall, all with a local guide. Culture vultures should visit the Buddhist Archive, which showcases restored photos of monastic life dating back to the 19th century. For another kind of spiritual high, the Aman Spa boasts steam and sauna rooms and a double Jacuzzi. Oh yeah.

LOCAL EATING AND DRINKING

Don't be put off by cheesy images of Eighties castaways – **Blue Lagoon** (+856 (0)71 253 698; www.blue-lagoon-cafe.com), on Ban Choumkhong, is an elegant eatery serving up Lao spice and French fare. For authentic Lao cuisine, try casual, café-style **Tamarind** (+856 (0)20 777 0484; www.tamarindlaos.com, on Ban Wat Nong. Its cooking classes also come highly recommended. For colonial grandeur head to **Villa Santi** (+856 (0)71 252 157), on Royal Sakkarine Road, a former royal residence with a fab terrace for people-watching.

GET A ROOM!

For more information, or to book this hotel, go to www.mrandmrssmith.com – our expert team can take care of all your travel arrangements. Register your Smith membership card to enjoy exclusive offers and privileges.

 SMITH MEMBER OFFER An Asian Blend Massage for two.

Amantaka 55/3 Kingkitsarath Road, Ban Thongchaleun, Luang Prabang, Laos (+856 (0)71 860 333; www.amanresorts.com)

Luang Prabang

The Apsara
Rive Droite

STYLE Chic gîte retreat
SETTING The *right* bank

'We congratulate ourselves on staying in a hotel with a view of the town but with the ambience of a village guesthouse... with a large pool, manicured gardens and an excellent restaurant'

The tiny launch is bobbing furiously in the fast current of the Nam Khan River. Our destination, the Apsara Rive Droite, is up the hill on the other bank, but first we have to negotiate steps, a bamboo dock and the rocking boat. The river is low and the boatman has certainly done this a thousand times, but it all adds to the sense of adventure. This is, however, not the place for high heels.

There are four paths to the hotel, sister to the well-established and chic Apsara, which is on the busy Luang Prabang side of the river. You can catch the hotel's own ferry – a journey that takes two minutes, walk across a narrow bamboo bridge a few metres upstream, cycle over an old railway bridge with a path two planks wide, or take a taxi that loops round to the new concrete and steel bridge and takes 15 minutes. During our stay, we try them all – cycling is the most fun – and each time we congratulate ourselves on staying in a hotel with a view of the town but with the ambience of a village guesthouse. A rather luxurious guesthouse, it has to be said, with a large pool, manicured gardens and an excellent restaurant.

The Apsara Rive Droite lobby references Indochina in a modern way, with huge swaying lampshades, a row of glass Buddhas in bubblegum hues and a cartoonish mural of an Apsara girl from Angkor. Apsaras are celestial dancing water nymphs and Mr Smith notes a number lying in a row by the pool as we check in, before I distract him with the promise of a gin and It in our ground-floor quarters. The huge, shady room is richly furnished in dark wood in a style best described as masculine glamour. The Lao silk bedspread and giant wall hanging are in muted tones of sand, black and garnet, large green wooden doors lead onto the veranda and a fan stirs the tropical air. The walls are decorated with black-and-white photos of indeterminate vintage and, alongside the grand desk under the shuttered window, trigger vague ambitions of a literary nature. These are soon squashed by the sybaritic enticement of the wicker day-bed on our terrace with its view of the pool, gardens and the *rive gauche* beyond.

After a swim we test the crisp white and grey bathroom – the shower is big enough for two with a showerhead the size of a dinner plate. A sliding mirrored wall above the basin turns out to be a window into the room,

allowing you to chat with your best friend in the bed next door. It's a quirky touch that proves to be surprisingly congenial. Another friendly feature is the minibar's moderate pricing, which means we use it as we would the fridge at home.

The Rive Droite is laid-back, very spacious – there are only nine rooms across two floors – and, although it's only been open a few months, it's the sort of place you feel you've been coming to for years. Ivan, a laconically witty Englishman who owns both establishments, seems to be in the two places at once, a useful feat as he's on hand to explain matters to tuk tuk and taxi drivers who invariably take us to the old Apsara. Memo to hotel: print the directions on your address cards in Lao as well as English. The manager is groovy, friendly, unflappable and totally efficient too, and the Lao staff members are fantastic, although the barman has an idiosyncratic touch with the gin and tonic, serving it in three separate glasses – one for spirits, one for ice and an empty third in which to introduce them both to the mixer.

When it comes to dinner we are on much firmer ground. The hotel's big sister is famed for its fare and the smaller menu at the Rive Droite is equally stunning – definitely the best meal of our stay. Like the interiors, the food

dabbles in a range of influences but isn't a slave to any. A lip-smacking Lao version of *baba ganoush* is served alongside a papaya and beef salad, spicy noodles with pork and delicious crumbly sausages. I don't know if there is a Lao word for piquant, but this would be the time to use it.

The hotel, in common with several other lodgings in Luang Prabang, offers guests the free use of bicycles – the glorious old-fashioned sort with baskets, dynamo lights and kickstands. The rutted village lanes around the Rive Droite give our buttocks a good work-out, but this is the best way to explore the vicinity, as well as get into town to experience the temples and architecture. Being on the undeveloped right bank of the Nam Khan also means we can discreetly watch the dawn alms-giving, a daily exchange between monks and village women that, across the river, has become something of a tourist jamboree.

If you want to see locals being tourists and having a good time, head to Tat Kuang Si, a magnificent series of waterfalls and limestone swimming holes. It can be a hair-raising climb to the top if it's been raining but it's worth it for the views and the highest pool, which can only be reached by scrambling through the falls. On the way down we dally by the sun bear and tiger enclosures, housing animals that have been rescued from poachers. The Rive Droite organised the trip at short notice and for the same price you'd pay a town tour operator. If we wanted one, offers Ivan, our new best friend, he could rustle up a picnic in 20 minutes. When we get back, tranquil, fresh and clear-eyed, Mr Smith and I both agree that we've lucked upon a sanctuary built for the discerning and seasoned traveller.

Reviewed by Fiona Gruber

NEED TO KNOW

Rooms Nine rooms.

Rates Low season, US$140; high season, US$195, including breakfast and airport transfers.

Check-out Officially midday, but flexible depending on availability. Check-in, 2pm.

Facilities Free WiFi in public areas, bicycles, gardens. In rooms: minibar.

Poolside Because of the small number of rooms, there's a real sense of privacy by the pool. Although located on the banks of the Nam Khan, bamboo and tropical foliage hide it away from river traffic.

Children To maintain the aura of escape, Rive Droite does not cater for children under 12. Extra beds for older kids can be added to rooms for US$20 a night.

Also While everyone else is tuk-tuking around, Rive Droite guests can rock up in the centre of town by boat. Just hold those heels until you are on dry land though, Mrs Smith, as there are lots of stairs at either end of the crossing. A minimum two-night stay applies. Smoking is allowed on balconies and outdoors only.

IN THE KNOW

Our favourite rooms Numbers 8 and 9 are poolside if all the little geckos are making you feel like a lounge lizard. Room 1 has expansive (but no more expensive) views over the river to town.

Hotel bar The Rive Droite Bar is open from 8am to 10pm and provides the pull of poolside cocktails as the day wears on. Shake off (or turn up) the tropical lethargy with a lychee daiquiri.

Hotel restaurant Offering a small but effortlessly sophisticated menu, the kitchen at the Apsara Rive Droite takes its lead from mother hotel the Apsara across the river. Sample tasty treats with a twist, including dried beef and lemongrass salad or spicy buffalo sausage.

Top table During the dry season, position yourself outside and under the stars. If the rains are putting a dampener on things, then choose a cosy corner in the small bar/restaurant area.

Room service You'll have to dress and hit the restaurant as there's no in-room menu.

Dress code Stylish silks from Jim Thompson, Thailand's famous fabric house. Don't own any? Do some emergency shopping while passing through Suvarnabhumi Airport in Bangkok.

Local knowledge Try a romantic picnic, Apsara-style. Cruise by boat up the Mekong River to an abandoned wat swathed in history and atmosphere. Your private butler will serve up an elegant lunch of East meets West delights, best enjoyed with bubbles. Alternatively, ride around the local area on one of the hotel's bicycles to see how the real Lao live, away from the gentrified heart of Luang Prabang.

LOCAL EATING AND DRINKING

Directly across the river on Kingkitsarath Road, the Apsara (+856 (0)71 254 670; www.theapsara.com) is a delightful stop for dinner. Try the lemongrass and coriander fishcakes. Want a decent glass of red in an alluring spot? Pack Luck Wine Bar (+856 (0)71 254 839; www.packluck.com), on Sisavangvong Road, has a sassy selection of drops from around the world and is a favourite watering-hole for expats. When you're yearning for French patisseries and fab coffee, head to Le Café Ban Vat Sene (+856 (0)71 252 482), on Sakkarine Road, one of the city's first Western-style establishments. Take a table on the footpath and watch the Luang Prabang locals go by.

GET A ROOM!

For more information, or to book this hotel, go to www.mrandmrssmith.com – our expert team can take care of all your travel arrangements. Register your Smith membership card to enjoy exclusive offers and privileges.

 SMITH MEMBER OFFER Dinner for two at the hotel's restaurant, excluding drinks.

The Apsara Rive Droite Ban Phanluang, Luang Prabang, Laos (+856 (0)71 254 670; www.theapsara.com)

Luang Prabang

Satri House

STYLE Right royal residence
SETTING An amble from the old town

'It's a smart daffodil-yellow colonial house that looks more civil service bridge club than mini royal palace once built for a minor Laotian prince'

In the fading heat of the afternoon, we arrive at Satri House. A languid boules game is in progress opposite, and the rack of antique black bikes outside suggests the day's exertions are largely over for the rest of the guests. From the street, the property is modest and unshowy. It's a smart, daffodil-yellow colonial house that looks more civil service bridge club than mini royal palace, although we learn later that it was built somewhere at the beginning of the 20th century (no one really seems able to pinpoint a date) for a minor Laotian prince.

Once inside, a generous and more traditional complex opens up, with different buildings creating a series of courtyards and gardens, beautifully manicured and scattered unobtrusively with tables and chairs or sunloungers – several of which we trial over the course of our stay, books and lop-sidedly mixed G&Ts in tow. Our room, though – all creaky polished wood floors, 'ethnic' sepia photographs, billowing mozzie nets and signature silk soft furnishings – is at the front of the original house on the street. It's not the biggest room in the hotel, but it has an intimate, deeply sexy charm. From the broad balcony I watch the boules game below. Is that money I see changing hands? There's clearly a book running; it's a distinctly Asian version of French post-colonialism, after all.

Dinner is equally Indochine. Old friends also in town join us at our candlelit table by the pool to share a wonderfully eclectic mix of bean-sprouty spring rolls, spicy fish curry and soft, I'd-swear-they're-from-the-Rue-de-Buci baguettes. Something happens in the balmy hill station air; we get to reminiscing and before we know it we've retired into the genteel deco drawing room and are swilling cognac in big glasses and taking up smoking again. Mr Smith looks so handsome with a cigarette. We are almost inspired to wire in a story on communist insurgents and return to our rooms to finish our novels to the smell of burning mosquito coils.

A leisurely two-wheeled excursion around town the next morning does little to shake our Graham Greene-ish torpor. There's something about a wicker basket that makes you pedal slower, too. Desultory temple-touring ensues – they are strangely exquisite, low-eaved, jauntily painted things – with frequent stops on either side of the long, finger-like promontory that constitutes downtown Luang Prabang to gaze out over the two rivers that frame it. Both are dry and low, with the Mekong narrowed at points by sandbanks. But its grandeur is unmistakable – in full flood it must be both monumentally awe-inspiring and completely terrifying. Later, we catch a boat and follow a series of bamboo walkways to the other side and explore more temples, almost alone. At one temple, three children point to a fissure in the rocky hillside and lead us in pitch darkness down a hundred steps to a forlorn cave full of broken Buddhas. At another, a barefoot monk with an Elvis Presley hairdo strums an out-of-tune guitar. Everyone, including us, is on the verge of sleep, even the boy collecting a toll at one of the bridges. We tiptoe past guiltily.

Heartily pleased with ourselves after our day of high culture, we return to the *petit palais* for a nap of our own, first by the pool, then, after a cooling shower, in the four-poster privacy of our room. At this point, Mr Smith gets it into his head to check his email. Now, the internet has certainly made it to the Lao People's Democratic Republic, but only on its own terms. That extends to intermittent wireless broadcast to the front rooms of Satri House. A person in Armani-like silk trousers is summoned to no avail. The manager is called and there appears a short, athletic Frenchwoman with a severe haircut and more evidence of the faint echoes of Gallic imperialism. She is at a loss to explain the lack of a signal.

'Well, it works for me,' she offers, with that shrug that French children must be taught in Grade One. Mr Smith is mildly outraged – he is prone to mounting the high horse of moral dudgeon – but I find it rather endearing. Don't we require the French to be nonchalant? And who on earth needs broadband in heaven anyway?

So heaven is what we give ourselves over to – up at the crack of dawn the next morning to witness the famous alms-giving ceremony, into the jungle during the day to swim in cascading waterfalls, and back at night eating Luang Prabang sausage on the banks of the Mekong. This town weaves a special spell – laid-back backwater and place of pilgrimage, exotically foreign and strangely familiar, simple, sophisticated, rustic, refined – and there's no better vantage point to enjoy it than from that balcony outside Room No. 1 at Satri House.

The boules game is still happening when it's finally time to leave. I know I'll be back and, if they're still at it, I'll wander over and put down my own stake on the little card table on the gravel – and then I'll never go home again.

Reviewed by Mr & Mr Smith

NEED TO KNOW

Rooms 25, including seven Junior Suites and three Satri House Suites.

Rates Low season, US$180–US$380; high season, US$240–US$480, including breakfast.

Check-out Noon, but flexible subject to availability. Check-in, 2pm.

Facilities Free WiFi in the lobby, bar and by the pool, spa, library, gardens. In rooms: flatscreen TV on request, minibar, local-brand toiletries.

Poolside In a stroke of inspired indulgence, there are two pools to recline beside. The main pool sits in the shade of the original royal house. The new pool is below, near the spa complex (which boasts high-ceilinged treatment rooms).

Children Cots are free for infants and extra beds cost US$30 a night for under-12s.

Also Peruse the elegant lobby while awaiting your welcome drink: built for a branch of the Lao royal family, this is a place of refined taste, replete with antiques and regional handicrafts. Smoking on balconies only.

IN THE KNOW

Our favourite rooms Room 222 has an inviting terrace with views over the garden and pool. An equally panoramic vista over the pool and spa is on offer in 523, but it also has his 'n' hers sinks. Feeling flush? Satri House Suite 422 promises seclusion and its own lounge bedecked with antiquities. Every room boasts four-poster beds, retro phones and wooden furnishings from an era when quality meant more than quantity.

Hotel bar Satri Bar is open 11am to 11pm, but the bartenders will keep the drinks flowing if you have the legs.

Hotel restaurant Satri House Restaurant is the place to sample a symphony of Lao and Thai spices. Try *sa pa*, a do-it-yourself fish wrap with banana flower.

Top table Hold court on the balcony facing the spa pool – at night, when the low lights illuminate the grand buildings, it's the epitome of atmospheric. Alternatively, romance it up in the private pavilion overlooking the lotus pond.

Room service Available 24 hours, but with a more limited menu of Lao classics and Western snacks.

Dress code Regal, as Satri House was once fit for a prince. Or revolutionary (Marx and Spencer will do at a pinch, but Soviet is hipper) if that's easier – Souphanouvong was the Red Prince after all.

Local knowledge Inspired by the subtle silks of Satri House? Release your inner weaver. Ock Pop Tok (+856 (0)71 212 597; www.ockpoptok.com) runs weaving classes at its Living Crafts Centre. Learn about natural dyes, craft a scarf or try making silk. Come on, Mr Smith, get with the programme – you can always fashion a tie.

LOCAL EATING AND DRINKING

Glide effortlessly from your dandy surrounds to aristo Lao cuisine at L'Elephant (+856 (0)71 252 482), on Ban Wat Nong, considered one of the best tables in town by those in the know. The restaurant at the Apsara (+856 (0)71 254 670), on Kingkitsarath Road, comes highly recommended for its upmarket take on Lao cuisine.

GET A ROOM!

For more information, or to book this hotel, go to www.mrandmrssmith.com – our expert team can take care of all your travel arrangements. Register your Smith membership card to enjoy exclusive offers and privileges.

 SMITH MEMBER OFFER A Jet Lag massage for two in Satri House Spa.

Satri House 057 Photisarath Road, Ban That Luang, Luang Prabang, Laos (+856 (0)71 253 491; www.satrihouse.com)

Time zone GMT +8 hours.
Dialling codes Country code for Malaysia +60:
Langkawi (0)4 – drop the zero if calling from overseas.
Language Bahasa Malaysia (or Malay), although
English is also widely spoken.
Currency Malaysian ringgit (RM).
Tipping culture Not necessary – most establishments
will add a 10 per cent service charge to the bill.

Myanmar
(Burma)

Vietnam

Laos

Thailand

Cambodia

15

Kuala Lumpur

Singapore

Brunei

LANGKAWI

15 Bon Ton Restaurant & Resort

LANGKAWI

COASTLINE Andaman archipelago
COAST LIFE Surf-and-turf adventures

Langkawi may be Malaysia's best-known holiday hang-out, but this peaceful patch of paradise is so laid-back, it's horizontal. While hordes graze the beaches of southern Thailand's nearby islands, the 99 jewels of this artful archipelago go relatively unspoilt. Tourism is centred on main hub Pulau Langkawi, leaving the many smaller islets to wilder whims. Play Robinson Crusoe castaway on palm-fringed sands or head underwater to frolic with the fish; if beach boredom bites, swap open-toed sandals for sturdy walking shoes and set off inland for an afternoon trek. With home-grown fusion food and some of the best spas in Malaysia thrown in for good measure, you won't want to leave.

GETTING THERE

Planes Fly into Langkawi International Airport, near Kuala Muda on the west coast, served year-round by Malaysia Airlines (www.malaysiaairlines.com) direct flights from capital Kuala Lumpur and Singapore. In high season, several major international carriers run direct long-haul flights to the island.

Boats Ferries run between Kuala Perlis or Kuala Kedah on the Malaysian mainland and Kuah town on Langkawi, taking an hour and an hour and a half respectively (www.langkawi-ferry.com). You can also catch a ferry to Langkawi from Georgetown on Penang (two and a half hours) or Satun on the southern Thai coast (one hour).

Automobiles Langkawi is a relatively easy island to navigate, and rental cars offer the best way to explore. Make savings by asking your concierge to recommend a car from an outside agency, or pick one up yourself at Kuah ferry jetty. Drive carefully at night, however; Malay villagers, motorbikes and livestock have a cavalier approach to road safety.

LOCAL KNOWLEDGE

Taxis Taxis are cheap and readily available at the airport or at Kuah town jetty. In the more developed areas, such as beach strips Pantai Cenang or Pantai Tengah, you can easily flag one down outside your hotel.

Siesta and fiesta Most shops open at 10.30am or 11am and close between 6pm and 7pm. Restaurants and cafés ply their trade in the evenings from about 6pm onwards; many also serve lunch or mid-afternoon snacks.

Do go/don't go Langkawi enjoys consistently good weather all year round. Showers during the August and September rainy season are usually short and sharp, providing just enough downtime for a quick nap.

Packing tips Light cotton and linen clothes that scream, 'I'm in a ridiculously relaxed, sunny frame of mind'. Mosquito repellent to avoid becoming an insect buffet; jungle attire for trekkers.

Recommended reads IB: A Life – The Autobiography of Ibrahim Hussein, celebrating the respected Malay artist whose work is exhibited on Langkawi. Take stock with A Short History of Malaysia: Linking East and West by Virginia Matheson Hooker.

Local specialities Blending rice, spice, noodles and seafood, traditional Malay food is a must-try. For the most popular dining areas, hightail it to Kuah town, Telaga Harbour, Pantai Cenang and Pantai Tengah. The latter two brim with every kind of restaurant imaginable – from upmarket, trendy eateries to backpacker cafés. Chow down on char kway teow or nosh on nasi campur for some local street cred.

Also To catch sight of the majestic hornbill, grab a pair of binoculars and take a slow sunset drive along the trails of central Gunung Raya's protected reserve. Three species call Langkawi home, and the island's tallest mountain should soon reward you with a glimpse of this amazing rainbow-billed bird.

WORTH GETTING OUT OF BED FOR

Viewpoint For an inspiring bird's-eye view ride the Langkawi Cable Car (www.langkawicablecar.com.my), which rises to the summit of one of the island's highest peaks, Gunung Machinchang, in the north-west. The vistas are simply breathtaking: on clear days, you can even see Thai islands on the horizon.

Arts and culture Pop into the Ibrahim Hussein Museum and Cultural Foundation (www.ihmcf.org), on the island's north-west coast near Teluk Datai. One of Malaysia's top artists, Hussein died in 2009 but his avant-garde spirit can still be felt within his sensuous and intricate artworks.

Activities Unsurprisingly, given Langkawi's lush landscapes, kayaking and trekking are popular pastimes. Explore the mangroves and jungle with a guide (your hotel can arrange one for you). Wannabe Tarzans should book a rainforest canopy zipline adventure with Juergen Zimmerer (www.langkawi.travel/lca.htm). For more controlled swinging, golfers can tee off at three fantastic courses: the Golf Club Datai Bay (www.dataigolf.com), Gunung Raya Golf Resort (www.golfgr.com.my) or Langkawi Golf Club (+60 (0)4966 6187). Spas are equally evolved here; one of the best is at Smith hotel the Datai (www.ghmhotels.com). If you're yearning for a yoga fix, Langkawi Yoga holds classes (www.langkawi-yoga.com). For a special gourmet hit, food fanatics can whip up their own Malay marvels at Cook with Shuk (www.thelighthouse-langkawi.com/cook.htm).

Best beach Pantai Cenang and Tanjung Rhu are our top tips for beach bums. The former is a 2km stretch of sand on the south-west coast, a five-minute walk from Smith hotel Bon Ton Restaurant & Resort. Keep going until you reach quieter Pantai Tengah further south, dotted with exquisite dining options. Pantai Tanjung Rhu boasts white sands and swaying palms, ideal for doing, well, nothing (blissfully).

Daytripper Spend a day exploring some of Langkawi's 99 islands. There are several boat operators that will whisk you away for fishing, snorkelling or island-hopping. Crystal Yacht Holidays (www.crystalyacht.com) offers a three-hour sunset barbecue cruise around deserted coves as well as a longer, six-hour Geopark Adventure Day Cruise, including secluded swimming, private beach picnics, and a jungle walk.

Children Take your animal-loving kids along to Langkawi's sole animal shelter LASSie, which has become an essential link between the islanders and their ever-growing stray cat and dog population (www.langkawilassie.org.my). Let mini-Smiths eyeball sharks and turtles from a 15m glass tunnel in the walk-through tank at Underwater World Langkawi (www.underwaterworldlangkawi.com.my). One of the largest aquariums in south-east Asia, the centre also hosts sea dragons, puffer fish, a colony of rockhopper penguins and even a menagerie of marmosets.

Walks Stretch your pins and discover some of the island's tallest trees and strangest animals on a four-hour jungle trek with Langkawi Canopy Adventures (http://www.langkawi.travel/lca.htm). Quirky creatures you might encounter include flying lemurs, giant squirrels or a bewilderingly tiny slow loris.

Perfect picnic After stocking up on supplies from any of Pantai Cenang's grocery stores, hop on a speedboat at Porto Mali jetty and head for picturesque Pulau Dayang Bunting ('Island of the Pregnant Maiden'), just 15 minutes south of Langkawi's main island. Surrounded by densely forested limestone outcrops, its tranquil freshwater lake was surely designed with idyllic dips in mind.

Shopping Although it's touted as a duty-free zone, Langkawi is not known for rewarding shopping; however if you really need some retail therapy, mosey down to Langkawi Fair, the island's largest shopping centre, near the jetty at Kuah. This huge mall has more than 150 different retailers flogging swimwear, local handicrafts, books and cameras.

Something for nothing Langkawi is blessed with several jaw-dropping waterfalls. The most beautiful and accessible is Seven Wells, known to locals as Telaga Tujuh, a short walk or drive from pretty beach Pantai Kok in the island's north-west. It's quite a sight: water cascades into seven pools. If you're lucky (and/or hallucinating), you might encounter a few fairies – local legend says that this is where they come for their supernatural ablutions. Temurun Waterfall, near Teluk Datai, is also worth a look.

Don't go home without... descending below the waves of the Pulau Payar Marine Park, about an hour's boat ride south of Langkawi, where you can snorkel or dive off a cluster of small islands above the reef. East Marine (www.eastmarine.com.my) offers daytrips and longer expeditions, setting off from the Royal Langkawi Yacht Club in Kuah.

LIP-SMACKINGLY LANGKAWI

South-east Asia's fruits are among the world's most delicious, colourful, and, to Western eyes, odd. Visit eco-tourism hub Mardi Langkawi Agrotechnology Park in Lubuk Semilang Recreational Park (+60 (0)49 532 550), in Jalan Padang Gaung, to find out more about quirky local produce – and, more importantly, to sample a selection.

DIARY

January A high point of island social life, the annual Royal Langkawi International Regatta draws in sailors from all over the world (www.langkawiregatta.com). February Traditional Hindu holiday Thaipusam sees devotees piercing their bodies with skewers and hooks. March Le Tour de Langkawi is one of the best bicycle races in Asia and a hoot to watch (www.tdl.com.my). April Sea-sport-centric Langkawi International Water Festival sees kayak races, underwater treasure hunts, beach netball, fishing competitions and cook-offs take over the island. October The Hindu festival of lights, Deepavali, is a glittering visual treat. When the island's Muslims celebrate Hari Raya Puasa at the end of the fasting month, markets sprout up across Malaysia, selling festive clothes, foodstuffs and knick-knackery.

Bon Ton
Restaurant & Resort

STYLE Rustic Malay restoration
SETTING Lagoon-side Pantai Cenang

'Our favourite touch of all is an on-site reasonably priced internationally stocked wine shop – with free 24/7 ice-bucket service no less'

Langkawi

Fresh and exotic: our frozen cocktails from Chin Chin are the best Mrs Smith and I have tasted so far during our three-week Asian adventure. This bodes well for our time at Bon Ton Restaurant & Resort. Framed by rainforest-clad hills and the sparkling Andaman Sea, the setting proves as delicious as our drinks, as we savour white-sand-flanked surroundings and watch the sun set over bird-flocked lily ponds.

Some people build hotels; others convert interesting buildings into hotels. We, however, don't know anyone else who would think to gather eight individual timber houses from Kedah state in Malaysia, bring them all to Langkawi and lovingly rebuild them, creating a boutique hotel-village in a gorgeous island setting. Employing an eye for design and taste for luxury, Narelle, the owner, has restored these antique villas beautifully. From White Frangipani to Black Coral, the themed pavilions provide elegant, historic lodging that's as far removed from a chain-hotel room as is possible.

We love Bon Ton for its schizophrenia. Rarely does having to change rooms each night prove to be such a treat. Due to our late booking, this is a necessity that gives us the opportunity to experience more of the resort's unique stilted Malaysian boudoirs.

White Frangipani is the rendezvous for our first night, and the raised antique house positively radiates romance and rustic charm. The enormous bed is fanned by an old-fashioned propeller ticking away overhead and overlooked by an exquisite intricately carved Malay wooden screen. A snoop beyond to the hanging wardrobe reveals an unexpected added amenity: a fluffy cat asleep in the laundry basket. Sneaking past the furry snoozer, we find a spot to elicit our own purrs: a private balcony with an under-the-stars bath.

The following evening, another high-ceilinged, timber-framed number is our exciting new sybaritic residence. We take advantage of the dreamy double bed, clad in crisp linen and festooned with a seductive mosquito net. It is lovey-dovey in its draping, not that there are loads of bugs lying around in smoking jackets and kimonos whispering sweet nothings. (Although so soul-stirring is our come-hither bed, I wouldn't be surprised if that was the effect on the mood even for its insect residents.)

Mysteriously, although the hotel is full for our stay, we still feel as if we have it to ourselves. Well, almost. Observing cosy corners and comfy cushions more closely, we spot many contented-looking cats. Narelle's pet project – if you'll excuse the pun – is the island's animal sanctuary next door, providing an excellent afternoon's diversion for cat-cuddlers like Mrs Smith.

Bon Ton Restaurant & Resort offers the discerning globetrotter more than feline entertainment and comfortable tropical quarters, though: the island-famed restaurant Nam lures diners from other hotels with its innovative fusion cuisine. Narelle is, in fact, a well-known foodie in Malaysia. Originally from Australia, she has spent 20 years in the region and gives guests the chance to sample authentic, unpretentious Malay food, all complemented by an impressive wine list.

If the way to your heart is through your stomach, you'll be smitten with Bon Ton after one bite in the restaurant. Yet what really fast-tracks Bon Ton's way to a permanent place in our affections are the considerate touches that abound. An in-room Mosquito Kit (containing every possible weapon required in the war against the mozzie), having our laundry pressed to perfection without an

inflated hotel mark-up (simply the price charged by the local launderette), discreetly hidden fridges in each room (with a little note attached to say tomorrow's breakfast of pastries and fresh fruit will wing its way over soon) and bathrooms stocked with locally produced toiletries are all winning features.

And move over rip-off minibars. Our favourite touch of all is an on-site, reasonably priced, internationally stocked wine shop – with a free 24/7 ice-bucket service, no less. It's attention to details like this that distinguish Narelle as someone who is committed to looking after each and every guest. Keep your eyes peeled and you'll spot her doing her daily rounds, ensuring everybody's experience delivers above and beyond expectations.

Little wonder Mrs Smith and I spend much of our final morning discussing how we might wangle a few more nights at Bon Ton. Seeing how sad we are at the prospect of being prised from our Malaysian paradise, Narelle prescribes some Bon Ton medication: a couple of our favourite mango daiquiris. She then hugs us before sending us tearily on our way to the airport. 'We'll be back as soon as we can,' we tell her. An hour later we are as good as our word, having managed to change our flights.

Sipping cocktails, stroking cats and checking in to a fabulous new room, we reflect on how very lucky we are to have 24 more hours of this intoxicating, beautiful and wondrous place. Chances are, as you read this, we'll have changed our flights yet again.

Reviewed by Mr & Mrs Smith

NEED TO KNOW

Rooms Eight traditional Malay villas.

Rates RM490–RM1,190, depending on size of villa; rates include breakfast.

Check-out Noon, but flexible subject to availability. Earliest check-in, 2pm.

Facilities Art and textiles gallery, cigar room, private dining room, books, magazines, DVDs and music, free WiFi throughout, computer/printer for guest use. In rooms: TV, DVD/CD player, tea/coffee-making facilities, toaster, fridge.

Poolside Flanked by palms, the pool and Jacuzzi area is a sliver of blue and white cut into the grass – its sunloungers providing views of the surrounding mountains and coconut groves.

Children Cots and baths for babies can be provided for free and babysitting can be arranged for RM10 an hour, if booked one day in advance. Baby monitoring equipment is available and there's a stash of pool toys for young ones to play with.

Also Supplied to your fridge the night before, the Continental breakfast of breads, jam, honey, fruits, yoghurt, juice and home-made cake is a largely DIY affair to enjoy from the privacy of your villa.

IN THE KNOW

Our favourite rooms Each of the eight antique, timber houses is unique; five have open-air bathrooms with freestanding wooden bath tubs. Palm Villa tops our list with its ornate, carved windows and sumptuous decor in turquoise and lime green. All houses are beautifully furnished with traditional Malay fabrics, antiques and carefully picked decorative details, and have pool and lagoon views.

Hotel bar Chin Chin lounge bar is based beside the Nam restaurant in a 60-year-old wooden Chinese shophouse, filled with antiques and atmosphere. Liqueur coffees and cocktails are specialities – grab a Short Island Iced Tea to enjoy on the sunset deck.

Hotel restaurant The renowned restaurant, Nam – perhaps the most popular, and best, on the island – blends Eastern and Western cuisine with a dose of spice to create an imaginative and inventive gourmet menu. Plump for *Nyongya*, the signature platter, which features nine Malay and Chinese dishes served on a banana leaf.

Top table To secure a front-row seat as the sun goes down, nab tables 1, 2 or L6, then watch water buffaloes cooling off in the lagoon while you eat.

Room service A selection of dishes from the Nam menu is available in-room until 11pm.

Dress code Laid-back loungewear to suit your rustic retreat – you're far from the fashion houses here.

Local knowledge Pack your binoculars for lying back on the loungers and star-gazing. Set in a former coconut plantation fronting onto a lotus-strewn lagoon, Bon Ton is five minutes' drive from Pantai Cenang beach if you fancy a dip.

LOCAL EATING AND DRINKING

A simple yet satisfying restaurant for Thai-influenced Malay dishes, **Wan Thai** (+60 (0)49 661 214), at 80-82 Langkawi Mall in Kuah town is extremely casual and popular with foreign visitors. **Mare Blu** (+60 (0)49 593 830), on Perdana Quay in Telaga Harbour Park, is a delightful Italian restaurant with harbourside views and an excellent wine list; dine at one of the outdoor, waterfront tables. Owned by Malaysia's former prime minister, **the Loaf** (+60 (0)49 594 866), along Perdana Quay at Lot C9, is a bakery and bistro, which serves 60 varieties of bread, moreish snacks and light meals; call ahead – the opening hours can be erratic.

GET A ROOM!

For more information, or to book this hotel, go to www.mrandmrssmith.com – our expert team can take care of all your travel arrangements. Register your Smith membership card to enjoy exclusive offers and privileges.

 SMITH MEMBER OFFER A welcome drink and a lime margarita each.

Bon Ton Restaurant & Resort Pantai Cenang, Langkawi 07000, Malaysia (+60 (0)49 551 688; www.bontonresort.com.my)

Time zone GMT +8 hours.

Dialling codes Country code for Philippines +63: Cebu Province (0)32 – drop the zero if calling from overseas.

Language There are 171 languages here, but the official language is Filipino. In major tourism areas, many locals speak English or a version of Filipino and English called 'Taglish'. Spanish is also spoken.

Currency The Philippines peso (PHP); US dollars (US$) are also widely accepted.

Tipping culture Some restaurants automatically add a service charge of 12 per cent. Elsewhere, tipping for good service, although not expected, is appreciated.

Manila

16

CEBU & MACTAN ISLAND

16 Abacá Boutique Resort

CEBU & MACTAN ISLAND

COASTLINE Marine Eden
COAST LIFE Mangoes, music and manta rays

Ferdinand Magellan may have had more interest in converting islanders to Catholicism than admiring the scenery, but the Portuguese explorer can't have missed Cebu's tropical shorelines when he first landed in 1521. Floating in a 166-islet archipelago, the island is the throbbing heart of the Visayas region: Cebu City is now the second-largest metropolis after Philippine capital Manila, offering all the urban pleasure with less of the chaos. Away from the mega-malls, a stay on neighbouring Mactan Island offers circumnavigations far less arduous than Magellan's, with laid-back *banca* cruises that only drop anchor for onshore lazing. Like the mixed-up Pinoy pudding *halo-halo*, the best-spent holidays are all about getting the balance right.

GETTING THERE

Planes Wing your way into Mactan-Cebu International Airport on Mactan Island (www.mactan-cebuairport.com.ph), the region's secondary gateway. Plenty of international airlines fly in directly, but you're most likely to touch down in Manila and connect to Cebu with a domestic carrier: Cebu Pacific Air (www.cebupacificair.com), Philippine Airlines (www.philippineairlines.com) or Zest Air (www.zestair.com.ph).

Boats Alternatively, make the transfer from Manila by boat: the journey takes almost 24 hours, but you can book suites or family rooms aboard a SuperFerry (www.superferry.com.ph). Cebu's port sees inter-island ferries and catamarans depart daily: check schedules with SuperCat (www.supercat.com.ph) and OceanJet (www.oceanjet.net).

Automobiles With two short bridges connecting Mactan and Cebu, it's easy to nip between the two islands. Self-drive cars are available, but you're better off hiring wheels with a driver; Cebu City's one-way systems can be tricky.

LOCAL KNOWLEDGE

Taxis Aim for a metered taxi and make sure the click is ticking. Otherwise, agree on a fare before getting in, or ask your hotel to arrange a car for you. Most people get around by *jeepney*; these ornately decorated mini-buses are cheap and full of character(s) – handy if they're going your way.

Siesta and fiesta Traditionally, life starts and finishes early here; locals tend to eat around 6pm, with tourists filling bars and restaurants from 7.30pm, and clubs warming up from 10pm. Shopping malls open 10am–8pm, and are often also the centre of nightlife. If you need to go to the bank (usually open 9am–3pm), you'll be asked to leave your firearms at the door.

Do go/don't go The heat can be searing from March onwards; visit between September and February for balmier temperatures. Avoid Holy Week in March/April, when this Catholic country all but shuts down.

Packing tips Bring your snorkel and mask for ocean explorations, and diving certification if you're planning to go deep. A preloaded iPod will slot nicely into the docks aboard smarter *banca* charters. The Philippines is hot, hot, hot: light layers are the way to go.

Recommended reads National hero José Riza's iconic 19th-century love story *Noli Me Tangere* gave Filipinos a national identity and sparked a revolution. Peter Bacho's award-winning novel *Cebu* offers a grittily realistic look at life through the eyes of an American-born Filipino priest.

Local specialities Cebuano fare is a mixed bag, fusing Malay and Polynesian staples with borrowings from Chinese, Spanish and American cuisine. If you're the sort of person who likes buffets, sharing platters and finger foods, you'll be right at home here: most Filipinos eat five meals a day, enjoy unusual flavour combinations and even have a special word (*pulutan*) for the snacking sessions between main chow-downs. Tapas-style *longganisa* sausages are tasty, and Cebu's famous *lechon baboy* (spit-roasted pig) is said to be the world's finest, but confectionery is what really gets sweet-toothed Pinoy going: look out for sticks of *masareal*, made with peanuts, sugar and flour; *otap*, a coconut cookie; *ampao* puffed-rice cakes; and *hopia*, pastries with mung-bean.

Also The Philippines' favourite beer, San Miguel, has a factory on Cebu. Locals are also partial to their rum and home-made *tuba* (coconut wine), available at most basic street shops in varying degrees of toxicity.

WORTH GETTING OUT OF BED FOR

Viewpoint Tops Lookout, a viewing deck on Mount Busay on Cebu Island, offers a gasp-inducing panorama of Cebu City, Mactan Island and the bridges connecting the two. Visitors pay a small fee to go inside the 'park' area at the top, where there are picnic tables and stalls selling barbecued snacks.

Arts and culture Take in Cebu's cultural highlights on a half-day historical tour. Your hit-list should include Colon Street (the oldest thoroughfare in the Philippines), Magellan's Cross, ruined Portuguese stronghold Fort San Pedro, Basilica Minore del Santo Niño, and the Casa Gorordo Museum, former residence of Mactan's first bishop.

Activities It's from the sea, not the land, that Cebu and the surrounding islands are best viewed, so hop into a kayak, grab a windsurfer, or board a *banca* – it takes around two hours to circumnavigate Mactan. Alternatively, try island-hopping, dolphin-spotting or sunset cruises, stopping for a romantic dinner on a deserted beach. Even Jacques Cousteau would be impressed with the dive sites here, a regular parade of manta rays, moray eels, pygmy seahorses and a rainbow of reef fish. Check out the crystalline waters of Moalboal on the south-west side of Cebu; or take a two-hour drive north to hop over to the tiny island of Malapascua for an underwater encounter with thresher sharks.

Best beach The shores of sleepy Bantayan Island off the north-west coast of Cebu have the kind of powdery white sand and turquoise waves the country is famous for, especially around the palmy village of Sante Fe. There's no good snorkelling here, but it's the perfect spot for reading and catching rays.

Daytripper The island of Bohol, two hours from Cebu by ferry, has overtaken Boracay to become the Philippines' top tourist destination. Its famous Chocolate Hills are a visually arresting display of 1,776 conical mounds spread across 30 square kms. Bohol is also home to the tarsier – one of the world's tiniest (and possibly cutest) primates. It's a protected species; if you want to see them, go to the government-funded Tarsier Visitor Centre at Corella.

Children Nippers will enjoy meeting Nemo's reef-dwelling friends on a fish-feeding adventure in the shallow waters of Gilutongan and other local marine sanctuaries off the coasts of Mactan or Olango (www.islandsbanca.com).

Walks It's only a short walk, but for followers of Taoism it's an important and symbolic one. The 81 steps up to the Taoist Temple in the hills to the north of Cebu City represent the 81 chapters of Taoist scriptures. A pleasant climb rewards you with dragon statues, views across Cebu and tranquillity (silence is observed around the temple).

Perfect picnic Take a boat across diamond-clear waters to a white-sand strand for a romantic beach barbecue. Islands Banca Cruises will arrange everything from a sleek boat to the candlelit desert island – complete with masseuse and violinist (+63 (0)917 630 0736; www.islandsbanca.com).

Shopping Side-step commercial mega-malls SM City or Ayala and take a *jeepney* or tricycle downtown to Carbon Market (MC Briones Street): hot and chaotic, Cebu's oldest and biggest market is where locals go to buy fish, meat, fruit and veg, shoes and clothing. This is the place to get authentic handicrafts made from home-grown abaca, rattan and bamboo. Cebu is also famous for its guitars: pick up a custom-made instrument from one of the guitar workshops in Abuno, near the airport, where acoustic six-strings, mandolins and ukeleles have been made for generations. Try family-owned Alegre Guitars factory, where you can also watch master craftsmen hand-building guitars.

Something for nothing The undeveloped white-sand beaches of Malapuasca are the perfect place to chill out; bring a picnic and relax under peaceful palms.

Don't go home without... experiencing the Marmite of Mactan desserts: *halo-halo* or 'mix mix'. It usually features crushed ice, coconut milk, *ube* (purple yam), fruit and berries, but it could also include sweet potato or kidney beans, all stirred together in a tall glass like some crazy kind of knickerbocker glory; every vendor will have their own jealously guarded recipe.

MOUTHWATERINGLY MACTAN ISLAND

Mactan Island could feasibly lay claim to the current gastro obsession with cooking 'three ways': SuTuKil (STK), in which your chosen ingredient is triply served – grilled (*sugba*), in broth (*tula*) and as a sort of ceviche (*kilaw*) – is best sampled at one of the basic fishermen's stalls in the Mactan Shrine area of Lapu-Lapu City. Pick your seafood feast from the freshly landed haul on display, and have it cooked to order – it's served up in its three guises at no-nonsense plastic picnic tables overlooking the mangroves.

DIARY

January Colourfully costumed Cebuanos parade the streets with deafening drums and dancing for Sinulog, or Fiesta Señor, Cebu's biggest, loudest and most popular festival (www.sinulog.ph). Held on the third Sunday of the month, it honours the Holy Image of Señor Santo Niño de Cebu. Get to President Osmeña Boulevard early to secure yourself a square foot among in-the-know locals. **March/April** Everything but the churches closes for Holy Week, covering Palm Sunday, Good Friday and Easter Sunday. **June 12** Philippine Independence Day. **December 30** The death of Dr José Rizal, respected scribe and revolutionary hero, is commemorated with a national holiday.

Mactan Island

Abacá Boutique Resort

STYLE Tasteful tropical base
SETTING On the waterfront

'Wrapped in thick, chocolate-brown towels, we sip calamansi sodas – the citrusy local fizz – sprawling on curvy contemporary furniture in a poolside cabana'

Local children slowly relocate their ball game from the road, before nondescript black gates open to reveal a tropical garden. 'Now this looks like my kind of place,' Mr Smith finally concedes. He has been silent and underwhelmed by the landscape – a herky-jerky mix of empty roadside plots and overly cheery Waikiki-pink hotel complexes – during the ride from the airport.

Ever enthusiastic and efficient, I've made better use of the journey. By the time we reach Abacá's discreet doors, our personal butler Raffie – who met us off our flight and is soon to become my new best friend – and I have identified suitable dinner venues while he pointed out historical sites and markets along the way. Raffie also informs us that jobs are now plentiful in the area thanks to Mactan Island's tourism boom. The information partly salves our guilty consciences about this indulgent holiday, and partly explains the welcoming, friendly nature of the locals we'll meet over the coming days. The only interruption to our chatter is the surprising

sound of UB40's 'Red Red Wine' resonating from the passenger seat. It is Raffie's mobile phone – the hotel is calling to establish our ETA. We like their style.

With only six suites, three villas and enough nooks and crannies to find some solitude, Abacá resembles a private residence. We feel even more at home when we're shown to our room, the expansive Seaview Pool Villa. Two keys are required to get in: one to enter the bougainvillea-canopied walled plunge-pool area (our minds race with the romantic possibilities), and another for the villa proper. Floor-to-ceiling windows allow for views from the pool deck to the big blue sea. We rush through Raffie's in-room check-in, throw on our swimsuits and slip into the resort's sultry infinity pool.

Wrapped in Abacá's thick, chocolate-brown towels, we sip calamansi sodas – the citrusy local fizz – sprawling on curvy contemporary furniture in a poolside cabana, a buffet of sunscreens thoughtfully provided nearby for vitamin D–deprived urbanites like ourselves. At first glance, the resort's modern design, dark woods and cream fabrics tempt us to reference Bali and cookie cutters. We never actually do, though, because subtle elements – sinuous rattan chairs by Cebuano designer Kenneth Cobonpue (who made Brad Pitt's bed), local antiquities and traditional handicrafts, the juiciest mangoes you've ever tasted, big-hearted hospitality – remind you that you are experiencing the best of the Philippines.

Mr Smith soon retires to the spa for a eucalyptus and rosemary scalp and shoulder massage, while I stroll out to the waterfront to chat with a young local girl who is knee-deep in the sea, collecting shellfish for her dinner. A valiant effort in the teeny health club follows. Of the resort's many laudable green policies, my least favourite keeps the air-conditioning off until a guest expresses interest. The complimentary Gatorade and water and shiny

new equipment, however (not to mention the decadent breakfasts), inspire me to return in the days that follow.

Instead of sampling Maya, a Mexican restaurant about 40 minutes away (also owned by the Abacá group) that night, we opt for local fare. An Abacá driver takes us five minutes down the road to the pick of the waterfront seafood restaurants, where you literally point out your preferred catch of the day. Afterwards, he walks us around the historic Magellan Marker and other monuments in a pretty community garden. On our return to Abacá, someone has adorned our pool deck with glittering candles. Behind door two, in the villa, are bedtime brownies. It is all too delicious to resist.

The luxed-up version of a traditional *banca* boat Raffie has booked for us arrives soon after a sinful breakfast the next morning, bobbing by the resort's waterfront about 30 minutes ahead of schedule.

By the time we step aboard the all-white deck, Raffie has already stocked it with fresh towels, fruit, drinks, lunch and chocolate-chip cookies. Sprawled on beanbags we decide that even the most jaded traveller would find it difficult not to feel giddy with excitement. We giggle with glee much to the amusement of our crew, who take us snorkelling at the Gilutongan Marine Sanctuary, then on to the postcard-worthy Pandanon Island, where we picnic on the white-sand beach.

Mr Smith rewards himself on our return for the day's active start with another massage. Easily seduced by a gigantic bathroom and standalone tub, I retreat to our villa. On the way, I stop by the restaurant to confirm our booking and, I confess, to scout out the best table. I find it is reserved – Raffie had already chosen it for us.

When we booked Abacá, we didn't know that the resort was built around a well-known restaurant of the same name. Chef Wade Watson's diverse menu includes phenomenal grilled seafood and imported beef, perfectly thin pizzas from the wood-burning oven, a decent selection of wines by the glass, and diet-busting desserts to follow. The home-made breads alone feel criminal in a place where you have to don a swimsuit the following day.

By the time we are heading back to the airport, any doubts we'd had about holidaying in the Philippines, which tends to get a bad rap from snooty travellers, have been dispelled. Abacá is beautiful, the service is thoughtful and efficient, and the food we sampled was wonderful. This is truly a world-class resort in a country full of spectacular spots begging to be discovered. From the beds to the *banca* and the butler, we were well and truly converted.

Reviewed by Sofia Suarez

NEED TO KNOW

Rooms Nine, comprising six suites and three villas.

Rates US$320–US$580, including return airport transfers, welcome drink, breakfast, evening cocktail and butler service. Excludes 12 per cent tax and 10 per cent service charge.

Check-out Noon, but flexible subject to availability, and a small fee. Earliest check-in, 2pm.

Facilities Library with books and DVDs, spa, gym, kayaks, gardens, free WiFi throughout. In rooms: flatscreen TV, DVD player, iPod docks with preloaded iPods and iPads on request, fridge, minibar.

Poolside The 30m black-tiled infinity pool has a submerged seat so Smiths can cool off while gazing out across the Hilutungan Channel towards nearby Olango Island. Grass-thatched cabanas with day-beds provide welcome shade.

Children Little Smiths are welcome. If eight years old or younger, children stay for free and the hotel supplies baby cots and extra day-beds for older children, also gratis. Babysitting can also be arranged.

Also Personalised 24-hour butler service starts when you're picked up from the airport and includes everything from newspaper delivery to ironing. Your butler can also arrange excursions, activities, drivers or restaurant reservations.

IN THE KNOW

Our favourite rooms The other two villas have their own plunge pools, but the Oceanfront Spa Villa (Villa 7, or Tawhay) boasts a large balcony for private sunbathing and dining overlooking the spa and seafront.

Hotel bar The bar has a fine selection of single malts and plenty of the new 'It' drink – and owner Jason Hyatt's personal passion – tequila (try the margaritas). There's also an extensive list of global wines.

Hotel restaurant Oceanfront Abacá restaurant offers Californian-meets-Mediterranean fine dining with a laid-back jazzy ambience and candlelit, open-air simplicity. Try Australian chef Wade Watson's grilled and roasted dishes, straight from the wood-burning oven. The home-made bread is hard to resist, as are the cooling shakes and juices.

Top table Table 4 is a romantic spot for two; or ask staff to convert Cabana Number 1 into a dining area, for a wave-serenaded feast. To see how the magic happens, take the Chef's Table, next to the kitchen.

Room service A selection from the restaurant menu is available until 12am – or later by request, but order in advance.

Dress code Anything goes – beachwear, shorts and sandals are fine, though you might want to spruce up for evenings.

Local knowledge At the pretty spa, the Filipino Hilot Massage is our top tip to bliss you out. Leave room in your suitcase for Abacá's natural spa products, which feature ingredients spanning mother-of-pearl, bamboo, walnut and even caviar.

LOCAL EATING AND DRINKING

On Mactan Island, Krua Thai (+63 (0)32 495 4818), near Marina Mall on Airport Road, has a reputation for authentic Thai flavours, including spicy soups, noodle dishes and curries. It's also good for vegetarians – something of a rarity in the carnivorous Philippines. Just down the road from Abacá, Rice Café (+63 (0)32 236 8888), at Be Resorts Mactan, is the go-to spot for pan-Asian dishes, from local fare to Indonesian, Indian and Thai treats. A short drive away in Cebu City, on neighbouring island Cebu, Maya (+63 (0)32 238 9552), at Crossroads Mall, offers tasty, genuine Mexican dishes, plus hundreds of tempting tequilas. For fine home-style cuisine, make for Laguna Garden Café (+63 (0)32 233 8600), at the Ayala Center shopping mall, an elegant eatery with set menus for all occasions.

GET A ROOM!

For more information, or to book this hotel, go to www.mrandmrssmith.com – our expert team can take care of all your travel arrangements. Register your Smith membership card to enjoy exclusive offers and privileges.

 SMITH MEMBER OFFER
A bottle of sparkling wine and 10 per cent off spa treatments.

Abacá Boutique Resort Buot, Punta Engano Road, Lapu-Lapu City, 6015, Mactan Island, Philippines
(+63 (0)32 495 3461/8456; www.abacaresort.com)

SKINNY

Time zone GMT +8 hours.
Dialling codes Country code for Singapore +65.
Language The national language is Malay, but English and
Mandarin are the most widely spoken and understood.
Currency Singapore dollar (SG$).
Tipping culture Bars and restaurants usually add a
10 per cent service charge to the bill, so additional
tipping is not the norm.

Malaysia

18

17

SINGAPORE

SINGAPORE

CITYSCAPE Skyscrapers and shophouses
CITY LIFE Clean and cosmopolitan

Singapore has come a long way, baby. Scratch the squeaky-clean surface of this former colonial trading post and you'll find an aromatically spiced blend of Malay, Chinese, Eurasian and Indian culture, neatly displayed against a landscape of glossy skyscrapers, lush parkland and tropical shoreline. Spend your mornings eyeballing designer glad rags in super-chilled labyrinthine shopping malls, then stop for lunch in a curry house before exploring historic temples and poking around Little India and Chinatown, all within minutes of each other. Later, soak up the sun on Sentosa Island, try your luck at Sands Casino, and feast on amazing Asian-fusion culinary feats in one of the city's smart restaurants.

GETTING THERE

Planes Singapore's superb Changi Airport (www. changiairport.com) is served by more than 80 international carriers, including Singapore Airlines (www.singaporeair.com), British Airways (www.ba.com), Qantas (www.qantas.com), Virgin Atlantic (www. virgin-atlantic.com), Emirates (www.emirates.com), KLM (www.klm.com) and Malaysia Airlines (www. malaysiaairlines.com).

Trains You can reach Singapore by rail from Malaysia and Thailand: travel in style on the Eastern & Oriental Express (www.orient-express.com). From the airport there's a fast 30-minute train transfer to the city on the MRT, Singapore's tube system, but the catch is you can only take one small piece of luggage on board. Within the city itself, you can't beat the MRT: it's cheap, clean and super-efficient. Buy a Tourist Day Ticket for unlimited journeys – you can use it on buses, too (www.smrt.com.sg).

Automobiles Don't bother hiring a car; the public transport is excellent and metered taxis plentiful.

LOCAL KNOWLEDGE

Taxis Easy to hail on the street (except during rush hours and just before midnight), cabs are the most convenient and economical way to get around the city centre. Expect surcharges for journeys in rush hour, at night, on public holidays or to certain destinations.

Siesta and fiesta Shops are usually open daily from about 10am to 9pm, although die-hard shopaholics will be delighted to learn that the Mustafa Centre in Little India is open 24 hours (www.mustafa.com.sg). Banks open their doors from 9.30am to 3pm Monday to Friday, and until 11.30am on Saturdays.

Do go/don't go Singapore is in the tropics and prone to sudden downpours all year round, but the rainiest months are October–January. In a country where shopping is the national pastime, it makes sense for the sales to be exceptional: May–July brings the Great Singapore Sale, an eight-week retail extravaganza (www. greatsingaporesale.com.sg). Pick up a Tourist Privilege Card from any visitor centre and you'll get extra benefits.

Packing tips Aside from all the 'S-ssentials' (sunglasses, swimwear and sunscreen), bring your best sandals, mules and flip-flops: shoes will feel way too clammy. Mosquito repellent will fend them off, but if you do get bitten, Singapore's famous Tiger Balm will soothe any itchy bits.

Recommended reads Paul Theroux's entertaining *Saint Jack* follows a hapless expatriate in 1970s Singapore; *Makansutra*, the street-food guide, will direct you to the best hawker stalls in Singapore.

Local specialities Singapore is renowned for its dining scene. Chinese, Malay, Eurasian and Indian culinary traditions can be sampled everywhere from the hawker street-stall centres selling *mee goreng* and oyster omelettes to formal restaurants offering elegant, modern fusion creations. For something truly unique, head to the Katong quarter for the cuisine of the Peranakans (Nyonyas or Straits Chinese), a sophisticated blend of Chinese and Malay flavours.

Also One of the best ways to see Singapore is by boat. For a fabulously kitsch experience, hop on a replica Ming Dynasty junk and cruise around Sentosa and neighbouring islands Kusu, Lazarus, Sisters and St John's (www.watertours.com.sg).

WORTH GETTING OUT OF BED FOR

Viewpoint Zip up to the vertigo-inducing New Asia Bar or the City Space lounge bar in the Equinox Complex (www.equinoxcomplex.com), on floors 70–72 of Swissôtel the Stamford, for stunning views of downtown Singapore. On a clear day, you can even see distant Malaysia.

Arts and culture Boasting an iconic building, the National Museum of Singapore on Stamford Road (+65 6332 3659; www.nationalmuseum.sg) is well worth a visit. We also love Mint Museum of Toys (+65 6339 0660; www.emint.com) at 26 Seah Street, next to Raffles Hotel. This cleverly displayed private collection offers a privileged peek at the playthings of the past. For a fascinating reminder of how the well-heeled 19th-century locals used to live, drop into Baba House at 157 Neil Road, a meticulously restored early colonial Straits Chinese home (www.nus.edu.sg/museum/baba).

Activities Singapore's coast is lined with sports clubs – charter a boat or go windsurfing or sailing with SAF Yacht Club (+65 6758 3032; www.safyc.org.sg). Tag along with a guide from Singapore's foremost culinary school, at-sunrice, on a Spice Garden Walk introducing Asia's aromatic herbs; afterwards, demonstrations at the school show you how to spice up your Thai, Malay and Singaporean dishes (www.at-sunrice.com).

Best beach Sorry to break it to you, but there are no beaches to speak of in Singapore – just narrow patches of sand. That said, for quality tan-time sashay to Sentosa Island, connected by a short bridge and cable car.

Daytripper Book into Spa Botanica (+65 6371 1318; www.spabotanica.com) on Sentosa Island, a brisk 20-minute drive from the city, and indulge in a lazy day of wallowing in natural volcanic mud baths, soothing massages and cleansing facials. After your pampering, have an Italian lunch at Il Lido (+65 6866 1977) which boasts serene views of greenery and sea.

Children Wow them with sharks, dugongs and stingrays while you glide along beneath them in an 83m glass tunnel at Underwater World Singapore Sentosa Island (www.underwaterworld.com.sg), or try a rollercoaster ride at Resorts World Sentosa (www.rwsentosa.com). Then venture off to spot nocturnal animals at the Night Safari on Mandai Lake Road (www.nightsafari.com.sg).

Walks Singapore looks its best either at dawn or dusk, so slip on some joggers and head out to Alexandra Road. Cut through Forest Walk and along the curvaceous Henderson Waves Bridge for a 'Me, Tarzan' treetop view of the surrounding jungle.

Perfect picnic Have your hotel pack you a picnic basket and then head to East Coast Park, a popular spot for runners, cyclists and rollerbladers all doing their thing against a backdrop of sea, sand and sky.

Shopping Singapore is renowned for its bargain watches, with up to 35 per cent off big-name brands. Try the Hour Glass (www.thehourglass.com), which has a handful of boutiques around town. Electronics are also cheap here – Sim Lim Square mall is the place to go for anything blinking, digital or with a screen (www.simlimsquare.com.sg). Charmingly narrow Haji Lane is lined with former 19th-century shophouses transformed into trendy little boutiques. Ogle the pretty lifestyle must-haves at

Egg3 at 33 Erskine Road (www.eggthree.com). And – this being the natural home of the retail addict – you shouldn't miss the giant, marbled mall experience for your vital Gucci and Prada fix. The pick of the crop are Ngee Ann City (www.ngeeanncity.com.sg), Paragon (www.paragon.sg), ION Orchard (www.ionorchard.com) and Mandarin Gallery (www.mandaringallery.com.sg). Bring a spare credit card.

Something for nothing For a welcome respite from the city's urban sprawl, wander through the Singapore Botanic Gardens (www.sbg.org.sg) at dawn; its spectacular showcase of the region's flora is worth the wake-up call. (The gardens open at 5am.) If you're more nightjar than early bird, stroll along the Changi Point Boardwalk on Singapore's easternmost tip at sunset.

Don't go home without... a Singaporean accent. Just add an emphatic 'Lah!' to the end of your every utterance.

SEDUCTIVELY SINGAPORE

Select a couple of woven cane chairs between potted palms and beneath a ceiling fan and order yourself a Singapore Sling in its birthplace, the Raffles Hotel's legendary Long Bar (+65 (0)64 121 816). Controversy surrounds the pre-mixed Sling recipe used today, and it's a bit touristy, but it's still an old-world pleasure to sip the sweetly sour combination
of gin, Cointreau, cherry brandy, Bénédictine, Grenadine, Angostura bitters, pineapple and lime.

DIARY

April Michelin-starred chefs roll into town for the World Gourmet Summit (www.worldgourmetsummit.com). May–June The Singapore Arts Festival showcases cutting-edge world premieres and performances (www. singaporeartsfest.com). September The Formula 1 teams thunder around Marina Bay (www.formula1.com). October ARTSingapore is south-east Asia's answer to Art Basel (www.artsingapore.net). November–December Orchard Road is transformed into a twinkling fairy tale of Christmas decorations; it's gauchely kitschy, but hard not to love just the same.

Sentosa Island

Capella Singapore

STYLE Clash of the centuries
SETTING Southern Sentosa Island

'Mrs Smith and I feel like we've left Singapore behind and stumbled onto the set of some dark, devious but deliciously decadent spy thriller. I half expect to be handed a dirty martini upon stepping out of the car'

This is the kind of entrance that deserves to be accompanied by the strains of the legendary James Bond theme. Driving up to the neo-colonial-meets-futuristic digs that are the Capella Hotel on Sentosa Island, Mrs Smith and I feel like we've left Singapore behind and stumbled onto the set of some dark, devious but deliciously decadent spy thriller. I half expect to be handed a dirty martini upon stepping out of the car. Of course, if we were in a Bond film, this fabulous place would undoubtedly be the lavishly decked-out hideaway of the movie's villain, most likely some Eurasian drug lord or terrorist with a penchant for contemporary art. Which would mean that, instead of a weekend of pampering, Mrs Smith and I would be bound into some ridiculous Rube Goldberg–designed death trap while said baddie lectures us about his plans for world domination. Thank heavens for real life then. Because the missus and I are very much looking forward to relaxing in what is Singapore's only true luxury resort.

Designed by Sir Norman Foster, Capella Singapore is nothing if not dramatic. The reception area – housing the lobby, library and Chinese restaurant and leading to the ballroom – is in a lovingly restored colonial mansion dating back to the 1880s. Behind this iconic building is an ultra-modern, steel-clad structure that resembles something out of *Gattaca* – you know, the 'Jude Law when he still had hair and was a hottie' movie, as Mrs Smith describes it. It hangs over a gorgeous array of swimming pools and, just past the beach, the South China Sea. This sleek sci-fi-style space contains the hotel's guest rooms (the swanky villas are spread throughout the estate), all offering a sensational view of the ocean.

Mrs Smith and I check into our large, comfortable and very well equipped Premier Sea View room. Decked out by modern-tropical interiors whiz Jaya Ibrahim, it is tasteful and minimal, with a neutral colour palette and a nice use of natural materials, namely wood and marble. After plugging in our iPod, unpacking and playing with the remote-control panel that adjusts the room's lighting to one of four different moods, we get down to some serious decisions: where to eat and what spa treatments to book.

Chinese food or a more diverse, casual menu? Capella has two restaurants: Cassia offers modern Chinese cuisine, while the Knolls is your typical hotel coffee shop, albeit more nicely decorated than others we've seen. The Knolls menu offers a range of Western, Asian and classic Singaporean dishes. Prices are a little high. I know you expect to pay a premium in any fancy resort, but it's hard to justify shelling out more than 10 times what the same dish would cost in any one of a hundred hawker centres or coffee shops around town. With that in mind, Mrs Smith and I decide to breakfast at the Knolls the following day and dine instead at Cassia.

Cassia (pronounced 'kay-sha') is a beautiful space. Andre Fu, one of Asia's hottest young designers, has created a truly glam, sexy restaurant. Mrs Smith and I love the half-moon banquettes and opt to sit side by side. The menu takes a bit of getting used to. This is Chinese food presented through a very Western filter, with dishes organised by starters, mains, starches and desserts. Every item is priced per person as well, which leads to a debate about whether sharing – the norm during a Chinese meal – is even allowed. Once we figure it out though, we are thrilled by the food, which is inventive and flavourful. I especially enjoy my final starch, a young coconut stuffed with seafood fried rice and topped with melted mozzarella cheese. Yum! Dinner was followed by a well-made Hendrick's Gin martini at Bob's Bar, sipped outside to enjoy the evening breeze.

Who would have thought that tea could get someone so excited? While breakfast at the Knolls is simple, Mrs Smith spends quite a bit of time chatting with the staff about the fabulous range of teas available. Capella has worked with a Singaporean brand, Gryphon Tea Company, to offer a nicely curated list of more than 30 premium Chinese, English, Indian and Japanese blends. Mrs Smith particularly likes the smart, well-written guide to the teas – I have to stop her from pinching it – and, over the weekend, samples several of the beautiful and quite rare Chinese offerings.

It's tempting to never, ever leave Auriga Spa. Both of us agree it is definitely the most well designed and beautiful part of the resort – Zen-like, mystical, embracing, calming. And that's before we even start our treatments. Mrs Smith disappears into the women's wing, only to emerge some four hours later raving about her massage, the vibrating beds in the lounging room and the scented showers. That's right. The showers in the women's wing each have a distinct aroma. She also loves the steam room which, when combined with the ice fountain and vitality pool, explains why I don't see her for half the day.

In the meantime, I have retired to our room, popped in a DVD from the hotel library and wolfed down a club sandwich. So when Mrs Smith finally reappears, fully rested, energised and eager to frolic, this sad sack of a husband burps and holds her off until his lunch has fully digested. Because there are things other than swimming that one shouldn't do on a full stomach.

Reviewed by Aun Koh

Rooms 112, including 11 suites, 38 villas and two colonial manors.

Rates SG$647–SG$1,500; two-bedroom villas and three-bedroom colonial manors, SG$2,000–SG$12,000, excluding breakfast (SG$38), a 10 per cent service charge and seven per cent tax.

Check-out Noon, but flexible subject to availability. Earliest check-in, 3pm.

Facilities Spa, gym, library of books and DVDs, business centre, tennis court, free WiFi throughout. In rooms: flatscreen TV, DVD player, Bose sound system, iPod dock, Nespresso coffee machine, minibar with free soft drinks.

Poolside Three tree-shaded, lounger-lined swimming pools come with South China Sea views. All villas have private plunge pools; manors have their own lap pools.

Children This resort is better suited to adults – leave the little Smiths at home in safe hands.

Also Smoking rooms and designated smoking zones are available. Dogs under 6kg can be accommodated.

IN THE KNOW

Our favourite rooms All rooms have an urban vibe: smart and fuss-free, in soothing earth tones, devised by Indonesian designer Jaya Ibrahim. Constellation rooms have capacious patios and outdoor Jacuzzis (Rooms 517 and 510 offer sea views). For a superlative home away from home, opt for a stately, three-bedroom colonial manor.

Hotel bar Smart and air-conditioned inside, dotted with day-beds alfresco, Bob's Bar serves the usual suspects, along with regionally inspired cocktails such as the Kaffir Lime Mule and Kumquat Sidecar. They also make their own ginger beer.

Hotel restaurant Cassia is a chic fine-dining Chinese restaurant in shades of black, beige and ivory. It serves Cantonese and fusion dishes, such as barbecued boneless duckling with sliced mango and lemon sauce. All-day diner the Knolls offers an East meets West menu. The tea bar, stocked with more than 30 varieties, is a great spot to linger after meals. A wine-matched gourmet dinner can be arranged by the pool, on the beach or in your room.

Top table In all cases, the best tables are about the view: at Bob's, if weather permits, go alfresco; at the Knolls, request a table on the terrace or by the window; at Cassia, you want the veranda.

Room service Available 24 hours, with a reduced menu after 11pm.

Dress code Something silk or Asian-inspired for Cassia; linen casuals everywhere else.

Local knowledge Capella guests enjoy free access to Sentosa Golf Club, or book a signature treatment at the Auriga Spa – we love energising New Moon, a foot rub, body scrub and massage using soothing seaweed and eucalyptus.

LOCAL EATING AND DRINKING

The owner of Il Lido (+65 (0)68 661 977) at Sentosa Golf Club is a fan of Philippe Starck and Flos, so he fills his sea-facing, sunlit dining room with iconic European design. The extensive Italian menu features dishes such as Wagyu beef cheek and veal ravioli. No, you're not in Ibiza, but you may feel you are at Cafe del Mar (+65 (0)62 351 296) on Siloso Beach – a hip, daytime hang-out, where the beautiful laze on sunloungers and a DJ plays from noon till dusk on weekends. Tanjong Beach Club (www.tanjongbeachclub.com) takes its name from its Sentosa strip of sand, and has a great daytime menu and cocktail list. It's difficult to find a one-stop night spot as all-inclusive as St James Power Station (+65 (0)62 707 676) – a red-brick complex of 10 bars offering musical allsorts.

GET A ROOM!

For more information, or to book this hotel, go to www.mrandmrssmith.com – our expert team can take care of all your travel arrangements. Register your Smith membership card to enjoy exclusive offers and privileges.

 SMITH MEMBER OFFER English High Tea for two at the Knolls.

Capella Singapore 1 The Knolls, Sentosa Island, 098297 Singapore (+65 (0)63 778 888; www.capellasingapore.com)

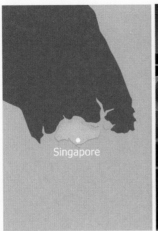

Naumi

STYLE Vine-entwined urban luxury
SETTING Plush, polished CBD

'The rooftop infinity pool has the reputation of being one of the most glamorous spots to catch some rays in the whole city, so I am keen on a romantic afternoon dip'

Singapore

Hello. My name is Mrs Smith and I am an addict. For me it's all about the lines. No, no, not those sort of lines – the sleek, delicious undulating contours of designer furniture. At the Naumi my fixation is fed the moment we enter our Deluxe Room. Don't get me wrong: there's none of that stark minimalism that looks amazing but is about as comfortable as a bed of nails. This is all about stylish functionality.

A bright orange Zanotta armchair is the focal point in an otherwise muted living room, where a frosted-glass lamp hangs over a khaki three-seater sofa – it has a vaguely mod Chesterfield style – that doubles as a cosy love nest. A sleek flatscreen TV separates the living and sleeping areas, and Mr Smith makes a beeline straight for it, swivelling it around to make sure we can watch it from both lounge and bed. We can. The king-size bed, flanked by Artemide table lamps, provides greater spin to the designer tale. To one side sits an iPod dock, and I find myself visualising a situation in which I walk alone, revelling in the sights of Singapore, while Mr Smith spends entire days horizontal, downing free drinks from the minibar while listening to the Beatles on his MP3 player. A quick call to our Naumi aide, assigned on arrival (how West Wing is that?), means that Wii and XBox consoles, together with the latest games, could also be brought to our room within minutes. I can see I'm going to have to keep an eye on the outgoing calls.

Hidden surprises are what really whet my interest though. There are plenty here, discovered as I throw open cupboard doors and explore the suite. Inside the pantry there's a Nespresso coffee machine; beside that, a wooden box is filled with Naumi organic tea bags. A mirrored cupboard opens to reveal shelves of gleaming cutlery, a toaster, microwave and hotplate. There's more than enough kitchen regalia to whip up something for one's self should the mood take you, though you'll perhaps not be surprised to learn we chose to pass on this option.

In the marble-clad bathroom, I find myself burbling like an idiot. 'Honey, they've got amazing toiletries!' I manage to say, while simultaneously inhaling soothing aromas and slathering body balm infused with orange peel, pink grapefruit and lemon rind onto my hands and legs. The doorbell rings and Mr Smith drags himself from a prone position to answer it. He returns with three extra facial products. There's only one word to describe my reaction when he presents them: ecstatic. Talk about a wonderful touch.

It hasn't always been like this. Before September 2007, the Naumi was known as the Metropole Hotel, a fairly conservative, budget-conscious spot popular with business travellers. Its location, in the centre of town right near Raffles City, means that it's still popular with that crowd but is also attracting more jet-setting types, like Mr Smith and myself.

Having completed a full room dissection, I harangue Mr Smith into pulling on his bathers. The rooftop infinity pool has the reputation of being one of the most glamorous spots to catch some rays in the whole city, so I am keen on a romantic afternoon dip. Sunsets, swimsuits, you can imagine the rest. Coming out of the lift, I'm floored by the dangerously sexy pool surrounded by designer chaises and shaded, round seats (with their pull-over-for-privacy sun shields, Mr Smith and I dub them the love pods) and a breathtakingly gorgeous view of Singapore's skyscrapers in the nearby financial district. Maintaining our cool while bubbling with excitement on the inside, we take our places on Dedon sunloungers,

order margaritas and assess the scene. At one point, I'm struck by the thought that perhaps a couple of laps might do me some good, but, much like the urge to check out the three fitness rooms (cardio, weights and yoga), it passes rather quickly.

With both our stomachs growling like mildly threatening rottweilers behind a gate, we gather ourselves for dinner. The Naumi has a bar in its lobby – entwined floral motifs feature prominently from intricate white prints on the see-through, neon-illuminated screens to the subtle embossed patterns on its sumptuous chairs – and while it does serve casual meals, we decide to head out to find food. We toy with the idea of burgers from Seah Street Deli at Raffles Hotel or stir-fries from the Arch, and even think about dressing up in our most stylish togs for a candlelit meal of modern French fare at Gunther's on Purvis Street. In the end, we wander down to the Chijmes dining, shopping and entertainment complex for dinner at the delightful Japanese Dining Sun restaurant. Dimly lit with a lofty ceiling and open kitchen, it is, it turns out, the perfect place for super-fresh *teppanyaki*, *sushi* and *sashimi*.

Afterwards, Mr Smith takes me to Tea Bone Zen Mind, a tea café located just a few doors away from Naumi, where we spend some time relaxing and sipping infusions from Japan, China and Taiwan. After much rumination – and even more tea – Mr Smith and I agree that the Naumi is ideally sited for sampling the gourmet goodies on offer in Singapore's restaurant-packed business district. Particularly for the design obsessed among us.

Reviewed by Evelyn Chen

NEED TO KNOW

Rooms 40, including 15 suites.
Rates SG$420–SG$2,000, excluding 10 per cent service charge and taxes. Breakfast, SG$25.
Check-out Noon. Late check-out up to 6pm subject to availability and a half-day charge. Earliest check-in, 2pm.
Facilities Gym, yoga room, DVD/CD library, free WiFi throughout. In rooms: huge plasma TV, DVD/video player, sound system with iPod dock, XBox 360 and Nintendo Wii on request, yoga mat, Nespresso machine, minibar and free local calls. All suites include well-fitted kitchenettes.
Poolside On the 10th floor, the skinny infinity pool and surrounding deck offer expansive views of the Singapore skyline.
Children Mini Smiths are welcome, but this hotel is firmly aimed towards couples.
Also For female guests, there is a Ladies Floor, secluded from the rest of the hotel by a security glass door. Feminine, extra touches include a selection of magazines to borrow.

IN THE KNOW

Our favourite rooms The leviathan Luxury Suite is the most alluring prospect, with indulgent perks such as the wine chiller, mother-of-pearl coffee table and its own steam room to tempt you. Lovebirds should flock to the Executive Patio Suite; the private high-walled patios, shrouded by leafy foliage, give you your own little bower to canoodle in.
Hotel bar Wallpapered with signature floral trails, Naumi Bar & Lounge is a cream-and-black-hued coffee lounge by day and a whisky bar by night, with more than 17 labels to choose from.
Hotel restaurant Doubling as a casual dining area, the Lounge Bar offers healthy Asian and Western à la carte dishes and a set lunch and dinner menu, including delicious salads and desserts.
Top table Take nibbles and cocktails to the rooftop pool deck and savour the skyline view.
Room service Noodle dishes and Western options such as pizzas and pasta can be served in-room 24 hours a day.
Dress code City sleek, indoors or swimwear and your hotel-supplied sarong up on the roof.
Local knowledge You don't need any… On arrival you'll be assigned a personal Naumi Aide to make sure you have everything you need – or want – during your stay, 24 hours a day.

LOCAL EATING AND DRINKING

Championing fresh ingredients and simple but sensational Gallic cooking, **Gunther's Modern French Cuisine** (+65 (0)63 388 955), at 36 Purvis Street, has become a hot ticket under chef Gunther Hubrechsen. On the second floor of the fashionable Chijmes restaurant complex, an atmospheric former monastery at 30 Victoria Street, **Japanese Dining Sun** (+65 (0)63 363 166) serves up seasonal Tokyo-inspired treats in a casual contemporary space. Raffles Hotel is a Singapore institution, and its casual New York-style **Seah Street Deli** (+65 (0)64 121 816) makes a tasty port of call for burgers, sandwiches and salads. Just across the road, **the Arch** restaurant (+65 (0)68 373 132), at 32 Seah Street, offers local Peranakan (Straits Chinese-influenced) fare in intimate surrounds. Down the street at 38a, **Tea Bone Zen Mind** (+65 (0)63 335 400) serves up a sensuous selection of pan-Asian teas, as well as tempting snacks, ideal for relaxing and regrouping.

GET A ROOM!

For more information, or to book this hotel, go to www.mrandmrssmith.com – our expert team can take care of all your travel arrangements. Register your Smith membership card to enjoy exclusive offers and privileges.

 SMITH MEMBER OFFER Breakfast for two served in your room.

Naumi 41 Seah Street, Singapore, 188396, Singapore (+65 (0)64 036 000; www.naumihotel.com)

Time zone GMT +7 hours.
Dialling codes Country code for Thailand +66:
Bangkok (0)2; Chiang Mai (0)53; Hua Hin (0)32; Khao
Yai (0)44; Koh Samui (0)77; Phang Nga (0)76; Phuket
(0)76 – drop the zero if calling from overseas.
Language Thai is the main language; English is
widely understood in Bangkok and tourist areas,
such as Phuket, Koh Samui and Chiang Mai.
Currency Thai baht (THB).
Tipping culture Tips aren't expected, but are
gratefully received, and you might want to round
up taxi fares and food bills. Established restaurants
usually add a 10 per cent service charge.

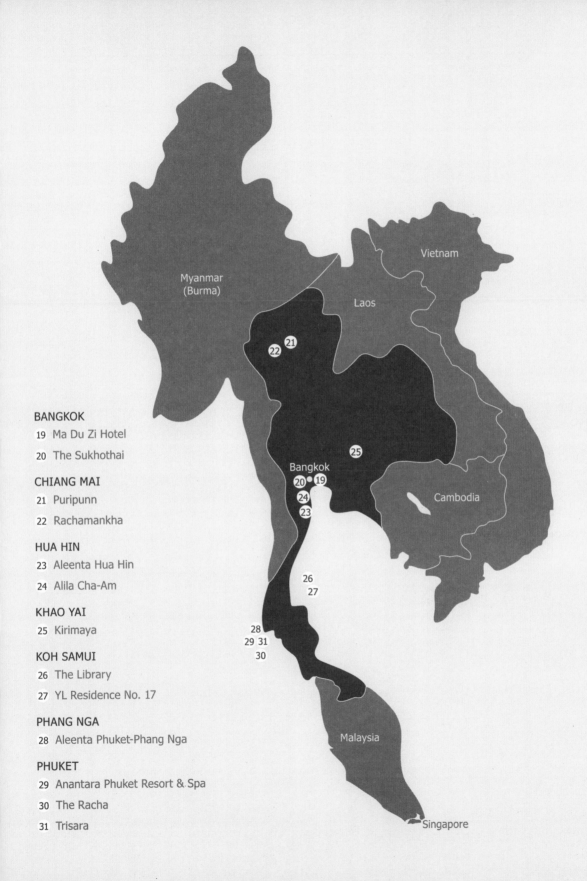

BANGKOK

19 Ma Du Zi Hotel

20 The Sukhothai

CHIANG MAI

21 Puripunn

22 Rachamankha

HUA HIN

23 Aleenta Hua Hin

24 Alila Cha-Am

KHAO YAI

25 Kirimaya

KOH SAMUI

26 The Library

27 YL Residence No. 17

PHANG NGA

28 Aleenta Phuket-Phang Nga

PHUKET

29 Anantara Phuket Resort & Spa

30 The Racha

31 Trisara

BANGKOK

Sultry and engaging, Thailand's capital is a warm whirlwind of sights, sounds, smells and tastes. This Venice of the East is criss-crossed with canals, thronging with traffic, and packed with temples, palaces, markets and malls. Whatever you do, don't be put off by Bangkok's travails: no other city on earth offers such a staggering array of affordable pleasures (and we don't mean in the notorious red-light district). From sumptuous day spas and exquisite dining to on-the-hoof street snacks or boutique browsing, gratification is never more than a moment away. Bangkok may have become a byword for exoticism, but the only word that matters in the City of Angels is *sanook* – a Thai term that translates to 'easygoing fun'.

GETTING THERE

Planes The international and domestic hub is Suvarnabhumi Airport (www.bangkokairportonline.com), 25km east of the city centre. Metered taxis will take you into town for about THB250–300, plus the THB50 airport surcharge and road tolls. The official AOT (Airports of Thailand) limo service costs THB1,000 – watch out for touts.

Trains Bangkok's main station runs efficient services to all areas of the country (www.railway.co.th), as well as to Singapore and Malaysia. Two urban rail systems operate within Bangkok: the sleek Skytrain (BTS) serves 25 stations on two lines; the Metro (MRT) visits 18 stations. Tickets are dirt-cheap, but not transferable.

Boats Bangkok's express boat taxi service is a cheap, efficient and excellent way of avoiding traffic (www.chaophrayaboat.co.th). Our tip: skip the dedicated tourist boats and hop on the public express boat to see more of the city and its people.

Automobiles Unless you plan on spending your time here frustrated and/or bored, do not rent a car. Bangkok is renowned for its marathon traffic jams.

LOCAL KNOWLEDGE

Taxis The open-sided, three-wheel auto rickshaws known as tuk tuks look fun but are best avoided. Take a metered taxi instead: there's a flat hire rate of THB35 with fares usually rounded up to the nearest THB5. Most taxi drivers won't speak English, so have directions in Thai to hand.

Siesta and fiesta Business hours are 8am–5.30pm on weekdays. Banks usually open between 8.30am and 3pm during the week. Malls often stay open until 9pm or 10pm. Many bars and low-key restaurants keep entertaining into the small hours.

Do go/don't go Temperatures are on the cooler side of roasting from November to February, but between April and July, the mercury can shoot up to 40ºC. The rainy season runs May to October.

Packing tips Bangkok sells plenty of threads at rock-bottom prices, so pack light and reinvent your wardrobe during your stay. During the rainy season, a Pakamac™ will be your BFF.

Recommended reads To grasp the nuances of Thai popular culture, pick up a copy of Philip Cornwel-Smith's entertaining *Very Thai*. John Burdett's detective thrillers *Bangkok 8* and *Bangkok Tattoo* are pulpy but engaging.

Local specialities Bangkok is a gastronome's paradise, feeding visitors everything from the victuals of Chinatown and the planet's finest street food to upscale international cuisine at the city's gamut of gourmet restaurants. The most authentic (and usually the freshest) food is to be found at the ubiquitous roadside stalls strewn across the city. Head to the cosmopolitan spots of Convent Road, Silom or Sukhumvit soi 38 where there are numerous vendors selling a variety of tasty delights, such as *kuaytiao* (noodles) served with or without soup; chicken rice; *som tam* (papaya salad) and grilled chicken and *moo daeng* (roast red pork). Ask for *pet nit noi* – just a little spice or *pet mak mak* when you're feeling bolder.

Also Bangkok's astonishing number of transvestites and transsexuals (*katoeys*) are almost universally accepted by Thailand's tolerant population. Many work normal jobs, but some of the more flamboyant members of the ladyboy community take to the stages of transgender cabaret. The best of the bunch is the professional Calypso Cabaret (www.calypsocabaret.com); it's well worth catching one of their twice-nightly dinner shows.

WORTH GETTING OUT OF BED FOR

Viewpoint Admire a sunrise riverside spectacular from atop Thailand's tallest temple: the aptly named Temple of the Dawn, Wat Arun. The cruise itself is half the pleasure, providing a chance to watch the city wake up. Head to the river and take a private boat or board the Chao Phraya river bus to the temple, then ascend 76m up the mythical-Khmer-being-emblazoned *prang* (spire) to enjoy the uplifting views of the city.

Arts and culture Bangkok is dotted with impressive edifices testifying to its importance as a royal and spiritual centre. The Grand Palace is a bewitching visual feast, home to Wat Phra Kaeo, the sacred temple of the Emerald Buddha. The Thailand Creative & Design Centre (www.tcdc.or.th) in the Emporium shopping centre hosts regular contemporary design exhibitions. Jim Thompson House hosts a stunning collection of furniture, art and antiques at 6/1 Soi Kasemsan 2, off Rama 1 Road (www. jimthompsonhouse.com).

Activities Charter a longtail boat from Oriental or Chan Pier to explore the city from the river – head up Khlong Bangkok Yai for a close-up view of Wat Arun and a peek at Bangkok's riverside. Allow two hours and expect to pay about THB1,000. Gain an introduction to Thai cuisine in the refined surrounds of the Blue Elephant Cooking School at 233 South Sathorn Road (+66 (0)26 739 353). If you're feeling fit, join ABC Amazing Cyclists for a ride out to the lush Bang Ka Jao and Grasshopper Adventures (www.grasshopperadventures.com) for nighttime tours around the old city.

Daytripper Siam's former royal capital, Ayutthaya, is a smorgasbord of crumbling antiquities and tucked-away temples, 80km north of Bangkok. These spiritual sanctuaries are not lifeless relics but living, breathing spaces, still populated and tended by saffron-robed monks. The Chao Phraya winds its way up from Bangkok, and several companies offer cruise tours (boat one way, air-con coach the other). One of the better efforts is the *Ayutthaya Princess*, which leaves the Shangri-La Hotel pier at 8am every morning – your hotel can book for you.

Children Despite first impressions, Bangkok is brilliant for kids (though not for pushchairs). Renew a belief in giants with an up-close view of the reclining Buddha's 3m long feet at Wat Pho. Siam Ocean World (+66 (0)26 872 000; www.siamoceanworld.co.th) is one of the largest aquariums in south-east Asia with 30,000 marine animals and a specialist shark tank. Let your under-14s loose in Funarium to burn off energy indoors (www.funarium.co.th).

Walks Resident photographer, writer and passionate foodie Korakot Punloprusksa (Nym) can take you on a magical mystery tour through the city's riverside communities and the bustling Night Flower Market, finishing up at Wat Suthat in time to hear the monks chanting. Contact Nym at info@thailandinstyle.com.

Perfect picnic Forget sitting outside when the weather is sweltering hot: don your white linens, polish your Queen's English and take afternoon tea in the Authors' Lounge at the historic Mandarin Oriental hotel. Just make sure you book ahead: it is justifiably popular (+66 (0)2 659 9000).

Shopping The biggest shopping centre is the leviathan Siam Paragon (www.siamparagon.co.th). For edgier offerings, hop across the road to Siam Square district, an atmospheric warren of mini-boutiques and food stalls that's Bangkok's answer to Soho. Drop in on girly treasure trove It's Happened to be a Closet (sic) on Soi 3 for retro-style clothes, shoes, a mani/pedi and slice of cake. If you're magnetised by markets, don't miss Chatuchak Weekend Market, next to Kampaeng Phet Metro station, where Thais and foreigners alike flock to empty their purses and fill their bellies.

Something for nothing To gain an insight into Bangkok life, watch people as they play in Lumpini Park, the city's largest central green space. Be amazed at the activity: runners looping the circumference; people practising t'ai chi and yoga; elderly Thai-Chinese women ballroom dancing; mass aerobics sessions and even open-air karaoke.

Don't go home without... indulging in a pampering treatment at one of Bangkok's many salons. Pretty up tired talons and trotters with a mani/pedi at a Take Care beauty salon at Siam Paragon (+66 (0)26 107 771) or Sukhumvit soi 33 (+66 (0)26 620 805); Healthland (www.healthlandspa.com) is the locals' choice for massage.

BEATIFICALLY BANGKOK

In spite of prolific commercialism, Bangkok retains a profound spiritual side rarely found in modern cities, and it's not surprising to stumble upon a shrine as you trundle between shopping centres and high-rise office blocks. The best example is the famous Erawan Shrine at the Ratchaprasong intersection, wedged between some of the city's largest malls and five-star hotels. This highly revered deity attracts Thais who come to 'make merit'; watch while they conduct prayer rituals (often with Louis Vuitton bag in hand) and marvel at the traditional Thai dancers.

DIARY

January–February Chinese New Year is extravagantly celebrated by Bangkok's Thai-Chinese population and Chinatown is awash with festive colour. March Dozens of Thai designers send their creations up the catwalk for Bangkok International Fashion Week. May Visakha Bucha Day celebrates the life of Buddha; a major highlight is the candlelit evening procession around Wat Benjamabophit. October Silver screenings around town for the World Film Festival (www.worldfilmbkk.com). November Every river and khlong glitters with a romantic flotilla of tiny candlelit craft for the Loy Krathong celebrations. December Tap toes and snap fingers at the Bangkok Jazz Festival – one of Asia's biggest (www.bangkokjazzfestival.com).

Ma Du Zi Hotel

STYLE Exclusive city sanctuary
SETTING Shops and saloons of Sukhumvit

'Inspired by the decor – caramel meringue lamp, shaggy cow-print stool, wastepaper basket strapped into corset criss-crossed with red stitching – we headed shopping'

As Mr Smith flicks through a manga-style comic that explains how to use the amenities in the room, I absentmindedly wonder out loud: 'Nuttaporn or Pimp?' Mr Smith looks perplexed, but that could be because he still hasn't worked out why the whirlpool bath, big enough to hold all of the passengers on Noah's ark, is filled up not by a tap but by a gushing rain shower above it. 'My Thai name,' I persist. 'Should it be Nuttaporn or Pimp?' Admittedly we'd tittered when encountering a few Porns and Pimps on an earlier shopping trip, but they were all lovely lasses who didn't seem to find their names amusing in the slightest. It transpires that the suffix 'porn' is a popular one in the Land of Smiles – there's Amporn, Pasaporn and Jatuporn, but none has as good a ring to it as Nuttaporn. With guidebooks advising you to learn the language and embrace the culture, I feel almost obligated to adopt a local name.

Since we arrived at Ma Du Zi, I've been trying to immerse myself in all things Bangkok. In fact, I'm still feeling the irascible effects of some lip-smacking *som tam* (spicy papaya salad) and use this as an excuse to glug down an icy Singha beer from the minibar. Earlier we'd scaled 25 floors (with the help of an elevator) to Long Table at Column, just around the corner from the hotel. There we'd taken in the crimson sun slinking down and the stunning skyline firing up, while taking advantage of the happy hour. I'd also used this as an opportunity to order the friskily fresh *som tam*, which I can never get enough of when I'm in town. Cockily, I'd insisted on having it *pet mak mak* (very spicy). I got my comeuppance when I nearly went into anaphylactic shock and had to exit with a spluttering walk of shame, tears streaming.

By now Mr Smith is up to his eyebrows in fragrant bubbles, courtesy of the infinity soak bath and organic Panpuri bath oils and salts with jasmine flower extract. Any hotel in the region worth its grain of salt (and intent on keeping some local flavour) accessorises its bathrooms with Panpuri. It's a brand so virtuous I'd be surprised if Gwyneth Paltrow – she of the macrobiotic diet and holistic lifestyle – didn't have the supplier's number on speed dial. The only animal-based ingredients you'll find on the labels are honey and beeswax. Several shops stock it, but the main branch, complete with its own Panpuri Spa, is located in the Gaysorn shopping centre, only a few minutes away by Skytrain.

Allowing him to wallow in peace, I finish off the Singha and hang my shopping in the teak walk-in wardrobe. There's no having to elbow each other out of the way with ample room for both of you and all of your acquisitions. Trust? Commitment? Communication? No, the secret to a long and happy marriage is a walk-in wardrobe. Preferably, one each. As Mr Smith's luscious bath turns him into a shiny pink prawn cocktail, I also feel a glow, albeit a post-purchase one, as I survey my impulse buys with no regrets. I'm not even going to let Mr Smith put me off my playsuit from Mob.F, which he maintains looks like a super-sized babygro.

Aimed at forward-thinking fashion followers (oxymoron intended), the recently launched Mob.F in the Siam Center brings together 42 fashion labels, sporting both established and up-and-coming Thai talents. Thanks to the store's White Café, Mr Smith was able to sip on a zesty cocktail and decorate his own cupcake while I browsed.

Inspired by some of Ma Du Zi's decor – the spun caramel-coloured meringue-meets-nest lamp, the shaggy cow-print bathroom stool and a wastepaper basket that appears to be strapped into a corset with criss-crossed red stitching – we then head to the Shop @ TCDC (Thailand Creative & Design Centre) in the Emporium mall. Originating as a space to showcase international designers, the focus has shifted to promoting young Thai creators, with tongue-in-cheek crockery, digital-print cushions, wire chairs and horse-shaped lamps all up for grabs.

Because he's not flushed enough, Mr Smith leaves the misted-up wet room to make himself a pick-me-up, following the comic's instructions diligently to ensure his Illy espresso is fashioned to barista standards. Earlier Mr Smith had been a bit prickly when I'd

reminded him that I had some work to cram in, but as he settles into a leather swivel chair, flicks on the widescreen TV and puts his feet up on the perfectly placed stool, he's as happy as a clam at high water – especially since the picture is complemented by Bose surround sound. Luckily for me, our Studio 53 suite, number two on floor Z, has a separate lounge-cum-study overlooking a pretty garden. The austerity of the fax and printer are counter-balanced by a soothing green sofa, just in case work gets on top of you. My head conjures lusty daydreams about replicating a similar working environment at home, but this is not conducive to meeting deadlines. Neither is flicking through the books crammed full of vivid photographs from across the region – another nod towards creating an indigenous ambience in the rooms.

With the sun setting, the bar is beckoning. When Mr Smith and I first arrived, we knew instantly this was the place for us. Ma Du Zi doesn't have a lobby, as such; it's been replaced by a convivial round bar with scarlet stools. Harnessing the hotel's family-run feel, here you can enjoy a drink with fellow guests, before moving into the impressive Ma Du Zi Restaurant by Yuya, where stiff white tablecloths and sleek seats are enlivened by leather bookcases and marble filigreed windows. Yuya, the new chef at this French eatery, is actually Japanese, but his tortes and confits are strictly continental.

'Leekpie!' Mr Smith suddenly exclaims. It's my turn to look bewildered. His plate, boasting a blushing pink Wagyu steak and an ornate asparagus parcel (I'd opted for the delicate red snapper from the set menu), shows no evidence of either a leek or a pie. 'Your Thai name,' he concludes. I'm so engrossed in my food that I rashly agree. Leekpie it is then.

Reviewed by Lyndsey Steven

NEED TO KNOW

Rooms 40, including 11 suites.

Rates THB4,650–THB25,000, including breakfast.

Check-out 2pm, or later subject to availability (after 6pm, you pay an extra half a night's tariff). Check-in, 12pm.

Facilities Free WiFi throughout, book/DVD library, gym, lounge. In rooms: flatscreen TV, DVD/CD players, Bose sound system with MP3/ipod port, fax/printer, minibar, espresso machine with Illy coffee, locally made Panpuri toiletries.

Children Welcome, but this is more of an adults' playground. Free cots and extra beds for kids can be supplied.

Also Part exclusive private home, part gentlemen's club, this hotel is stylish, seductive and sophisticated. Ma Du Zi means 'come and see', but unless you're a guest, it's impossible to enter without prior arrangement.

IN THE KNOW

Our favourite rooms The fifth-floor 79 Suites have their own cosy reception area and a collection of Chinese art worthy of any gallery. If you're seeking daylight, each of the six Corner 63 Suites has a wall of floor-to-ceiling windows that let the sunshine flood in.

Hotel bar You can't miss the glorious white round bar; you'll come across it as soon as you enter the hotel. Perch on a high red leather stool nursing a whisky sour, or retreat to the lobby's Tea Room, where dark slate walls, tactile rugs and gorgeous butter-soft suede sofas envelop you in relaxed sophistication. There's a well-honed list of wine and cocktails, including the signature Ma Du Zi Martini for Bond-style assignations.

Hotel restaurant The elegant Ma Du Zi Restaurant by Yuya, helmed by Japanese chef Yuya Okuda, has been wowing local diners with its original mix of French cuisine and oriental ingenuity. With dishes such as bouillabaisse with fresh seafood and miso and cinnamon-infused roasted stuffed quail, the idea is to entertain and enchant, not just fill you up. But it's not so posh you can't enjoy a simple burger (made with Wagyu beef, naturally) or salad. The window screens, with filigree patterns inspired by Granada's ornate Alhambra palace, cast slinky shadows throughout.

Top table Hide away at one of the corner tables to maximise your mystique.

Room service A 24-hour menu of tasty Thai and European food.

Dress code You may be in the tropics, but Ma Du Zi cuts an upscale dash, so keep it city chic.

Local knowledge Fitcorp Asia run 'boot camps' at Benjakiti Park, across from the hotel – check out the timetable online (www.fitcorpasia.com). If retail therapy is more your bag, Emporium (www.emporiumthailand.com) is a one-stop shopping destination for international labels, top Thai designers such as Greyhound and Soda, and the third outlet of It's Happened to be a Closet (sic). This fabulous, den-like boutique is stuffed with girly fashion, jewellery, shoes and bags, and even has its own nail spa and café. The centre's chic food court and supermarket are also worth a visit.

LOCAL EATING AND DRINKING

For authentic spicy Thai food in a pretty garden setting, try Balee Laos (+66 (0)26 631 051). Bo.Lan (+66 (0)26 029 623) is an elegant mod-Thai restaurant owned by a Thai-Australian couple who trained with chef David Thompson at his Michelin-starred London restaurant, Nahm. If you're after stunning city views and killer cocktails, as well as the longest dining table you'll find in Bangkok, head to The Long Table (+66 (0)2 3022 5579).

GET A ROOM!

For more information, or to book this hotel, go to www.mrandmrssmith.com – our expert team can take care of all your travel arrangements. Register your Smith membership card to enjoy exclusive offers and privileges.

 SMITH MEMBER OFFER A bottle of red, white or sparkling wine on arrival.

Ma Du Zi Hotel 9/1 Ratchadaphisek Road, Klongtoey, Bangkok 10110, Thailand (+66 (0)26 156 400; www.maduzihotel.com)

Bangkok

The Sukhothai

STYLE Stately sanctum
SETTING Bustling embassy enclave

'Riviera chic meets Thai charm in the shape
of a platoon of khaki-clad boys who scurry
after your every need'

There's a delicious aroma wafting through the lobby. Even harried and edgy, our spirits start to lift. We glance about and notice sinful tables of treats arranged in the Salon. We've arrived in time to feast on the weekend Chocolate Buffet. The temptation is definitely there, but for the past hour all we've wanted to do is head towards the sanctuary of our room. It took us some time to inch the mile and a half up Sathorn Road. Then, at a point tantalisingly close to the Sukhothai, a Mercedes-Benz blocked half the road. The driver, slipping off to buy noodles, simply left his car unattended.

That the Thai drivers around us took this in their stride, waiting with fatalistic patience for the noodle-buyer, was both charming and infuriating. My less-than-Buddhist response was pointless and, in its own good time, the traffic moved on and we turned into the hotel's tree-lined drive. Security guards ushered us through with a sharp salute and an oddly out-of-place Prussian heel-click. At once, where there was chaos, now there is calm. And chocolate.

The Sukhothai is named after the ancient northern kingdom ruled over by Ramkhamhaeng, Thailand's answer to King Arthur, a monarch who united the region's warring factions after the fall of Angkor and ushered in a golden age of order. It is an apt comparison. Where Bangkok's best hotels often fall victim to over-the-top gilt and ostentation, the Sukhothai's designers have shown admirable restraint.

Externally this pared-down style has been taken to extremes – the façade is perhaps a little too austere – but it comes into its own with the interiors, which are all muted tones and clean lines. It's where traditional Thai meets art deco head on in a pleasing, soothing mix. The atmosphere is hushed and unhurried, and our traffic-frayed tempers begin to cool under the gentle smile of the woman who greets us in elegant Thai silks.

We check in and are led to our room, all olive-toned silk walls, teak furniture, floors and trim. Though it's a very Western rendition of the Asian ideal, it does draw deeply

on the best of Thai decor to deliver deceptively simple luxury. We walk out onto the generous balcony, overlooking the pool, and take in a lush tropical view punctuated by the Bangkok skyline.

Our bathroom is more of a mini-spa, packing the full range of fab fittings into a relatively small space. Two vanities ensure there will be no squabbles over basin space, the bath is deep and wide enough for two, and the separate shower cubicle comes with massage showerhead – one that actually works for a change – combined with a wall-jet system. The leaf-toned shower tiles scream tropical-rainforest grotto.

The Sukhothai's rooms have three defences against the outside world: a sliding glass door to keep out the noise; a roll-back insect screen to hold bugs at bay; and silk-lined teak shutters that tell the whole damn lot to keep a distance. After a well-earned wallow in the tub, Mrs Smith and I choose the final option and settle into the fluffy pillows of our stylish self-contained retreat.

When morning comes, heralded by a superbly laden breakfast tray, our thoughts turn to how to make the most of cool-season Bangkok. A trip to Chatuchak Market, perhaps, to winkle out some Burmese antiques? A jostle in Chinatown to find the best *yum cha* this side of Hong Kong? Or a ride in the lift down to the pool for a morning of bone idleness?

Lounging by the pool is a very special experience. The Pool Terrace Café & Bar, with its awning of canvas and box-hedge borders, may be more resonant of Cap d'Antibes than Thailand, but that's not a complaint. Riviera chic meets Thai charm in the shape of a platoon of khaki-clad boys, who scurry to meet your every need. Throughout the hotel service is cheerful, discreet and efficient, but it noticeably shifts up a gear when you're beside the pool. As this is the haunt of a large, glamorous and gregarious gay contingent, Mrs Smith and I can't help but wonder whether the two occurrences are related.

After a punishing morning lying in the sun, devouring club sandwiches and drinking rosé prosecco, we retire to our room to consider our options for the

afternoon. I suggest a game of tennis, but Mrs Smith is far more interested in a spot of Thai massage in the spa. We decide to compromise, and pull up the drawbridge – well, close the shutters – for a siesta. We doze deliciously to the sound of gentle splashing from the pool below.

Refreshed, we head to dinner. There's a choice of three restaurants at Sukhothai: La Scala, classic northern Italian with Asian twists; the Celadon, a Thai restaurant surrounded by lotus ponds; or the Colonnade, a serene space in the main building. As we're planning to indulge in the Colonnade's sumptuous brunch the next day, and the most authentic Thai food is to be found on Bangkok's streets, we opt for La Scala. Visually delightful with a laid-back ambience, the eatery proves an excellent choice. The food is a pleasure and the wine, in a town where prices are generally eye-watering, is very good value. In fact, it's such good value that we order a second bottle. It turns out we can't finish it, but the waiter arranges for it to be sent to the room as we're settling the bill. It arrives before we do. These people are good.

The Sukhothai is a wonderful pit-stop in the rat race of Bangkok. And apart from the bathrobes (though the hospital-issue designs hanging in the bathroom during our stay have since been replaced by stylish waffle-cotton numbers, I hear) it's pretty well faultless. But even those robes can be happily overlooked. Perhaps the hotel was just toughening us up to face the real world, and the nightmare of the Sathorn Road beyond the chocolate-coated cavern of the Sukhothai.

Reviewed by Bill Condie

NEED TO KNOW

Rooms 210, including 47 suites.

Rates THB6,900–THB82,000, including buffet breakfast. Excludes 17.7 per cent tax and service charge.

Check-out Noon. Late check-out is available for half a day's room-charge before 6pm. Earliest check-in, 2pm.

Facilities Spa, gym (with Jacuzzi, sauna and steam bath), squash court, tennis court, aerobics studio, ballroom, shopping arcade, limousine hire, laptop rental, doctor. Health drinks and snacks are served on the terrace throughout the day. In rooms: large flatscreen LCD TV, iPod dock, CD player, free WiFi, complimentary minibar with soft drinks and beer.

Poolside Fringed with palms, the outdoor infinity pool is surrounded by wooden sunloungers. Healthy snacks and drinks are served on the terrace all day.

Children Under-12s stay free, with rollaway beds provided in all rooms except the Superiors. Cots are available.

Also The alfresco massages are recommended: book a poolside treatment in one of the hotel's open-air pavilions.

IN THE KNOW

Our favourite rooms The Sukhothai's 12 Garden Suites have romantic balconies overlooking the fairy tale courtyard gardens and lotus ponds. They are sexily splashed with livelier colours than the other rooms, although all rooms are draped in rich Thai fabrics, with plenty of polished teak. The enormous Sukhothai Suite, pied-à-terre to many a passing head-of-state, boasts a fitted kitchen and, most impressively, a grand piano.

Hotel bar The slinky Zuk Bar has garden views, low-slung sofas and floor-level lighting. There's an open-air lounge, too, which opens onto a terrace. Enjoy cocktails, wines and whiskies late into the night.

Hotel restaurant The award-winning Celadon serves authentic Thai cuisine in elegant air-conditioned salas, and on open-air terraces overlooking a lotus pond. La Scala offers fine Italian dining in a sleek, romantically lit, dark-wood restaurant. Colonnade, open all day, features a selection of Western and Asian favourites, and whips up a mean Sunday brunch.

Top table By the massive windows in the Colonnade, so you can gaze down at the water gardens.

Room service Why dine at the Colonnade, when the Colonnade menu can come to you? The menu is a mere phone call away 24/7, although from 11pm–6am, there's a reduced late-night selection available.

Dress code Unassailably A-list – add a layer to counteract the air-conditioning.

Local knowledge Don't miss the weekend Chocolate Buffet in the lobby salons, or the daily traditional *khim* (a kind of hammered dulcimer) recital.

LOCAL EATING AND DRINKING

At the Metropolitan Bangkok, 27 South Sathorn Road, Nahm (+66 (0)26 253 388) plates up rare, regional Thai cuisine by acclaimed Australian chef David Thompson, a must for serious epicures. Spring Dining Room/Summer Chocolate House (+66 (0)23 922 747), at 199 Soi Sukhumvit 49, has a stunning setting in a glass-fronted modernist home. By night its manicured lawns out front are littered with beanbags and tables where hip expats lounge. Spring has exquisite Thai food; next door, Summer is a chocolate café. Sky Bar (+66 (0)26 249 555) – in the State Tower 1055 on Silom Road in Bangrak – offers some of the most amazing views in town, and a romantic spot to sling a martini. Also on Silom Road, at 21/1 Saladaeng Colonnade in a residential complex, Italian restaurant Zanotti (+66 (0)26 360 002) serves a menu of mostly Piedmontese and Tuscan food. Try the pasta and the selection of 28 types of salami.

GET A ROOM!

For more information, or to book this hotel, go to www.mrandmrssmith.com – our expert team can take care of all your travel arrangements. Register your Smith membership card to enjoy exclusive offers and privileges.

 SMITH MEMBER OFFER A bottle of sparkling wine on arrival.

The Sukhothai 13/3 South Sathorn Road, Bangkok 10120, Thailand (+66 (0)2 344 8888; www.sukhothaihotel.com)

CHIANG MAI

CITYSCAPE Moated walls, market stalls
CITY LIFE Crafty and cultural

There's no place that better embodies Thailand's diverse cultural heritage and modern aspirations than Chiang Mai. This venerable walled city was once the capital of the ancient Lanna kingdom, filled with splendid stupas, saffron-robed monks and dusty tracks. Today, it is a magnificent contradiction, where life's pace ranges from glacial to frenetic: tourists crowd Burmese-style temples and ornately carved teak houses; vendors in hilltribe costumes ply souvenirs beside fast-food outlets; and a raft of cool boutiques and youthful design galleries tempt cosmopolitan denizens. Chiang Mai may have lost some of its somnambulant charm, but if you spend some time wandering the sleepy backstreets, you'll find refreshing remnants of its peaceful past.

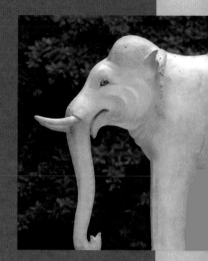

GETTING THERE

Planes Chiang Mai's international airport (+66 (0)53 2702 2233) is 90 minutes from Bangkok by plane, and receives domestic and regional flights from Phuket, Singapore, Hong Kong and Luang Prabang, among others.
Trains Bangkok to Chiang Mai is the most enticing rail journey in the country (www.railway.co.th). Each day, six trains rattle up this 10- or 12-hour route, providing ever-changing landscape views; the sleeper services are excellent, with private two-berth cabins in first class. Train food is poor, but many hotels in Bangkok and Chiang Mai will happily pack you a picnic.
Automobiles Chiang Mai's compact centre is easily navigated on foot, but if you want to venture further afield, it's best to rent a car. Book a luxe tour or hire by the day from Limousine Thailand (www.limousinethailand. com). It's possible to drive from Bangkok, but only the bravest motorists should consider it.

LOCAL KNOWLEDGE

Taxis There are few metered taxis in Chiang Mai. Three-wheeled tuk tuks are ubiquitous, but tend to charge *farangs* (that's you) double fares. There are also numerous *songtaews* (covered pick-ups with two bench rows in the back) that can be rented by the hour or for certain trips – negotiate a price beforehand.

Siesta and fiesta Business hours are between 8 or 8.30am and 5.30pm on weekdays; banks usually close by 3.30pm. Many mall-based shops are open between 10am and 9pm. Some stores in nightlife areas open late.
Do go/don't go The weather is nice and cool between December and February (well, cool by Thai standards). March through May is unbearably hot. The mid-April Songkran water festival might be fun for some, but it's boisterously celebrated here and can be a bit much.
Packing tips Sandals, sunscreen, big sunglasses. Pad for sketching moats, mountains, temples and pandas. Mr Smith might want some long trousers for evenings out.
Recommended reads If you don't know the legend of Jim Thompson, founder of the eponymous Thai silk business (and possibly a CIA agent), who disappeared on an afternoon stroll in the Malaysian jungle, read William Warren's *Jim Thompson: The Unsolved Mystery*. Journeyman Steve Van Beek paddles 1,160km from the province's river Ping to the sea via the Chao Phraya River in one of Thailand's best travel books, *A River Less Travelled: Slithering South*.
Local specialities Fare here is quite different from what you'd experience down in Bangkok or on the islands – most noticeably in northerners' preference for 'sticky' rice (*khao niao*), which locals roll into small balls and

eat with their hands. Curries, which can be deathly hot in central Thailand, are slightly milder here. Everyone goes gaga for pork crackling, typically served with fiery *nam prik* (chilli dip) and the local pork sausages, *sai ua*, which are eaten with raw cabbage and chilli sauce. Also try the region's famous creamy chicken noodle curry, *khao soi*, and spicy Lao-style *larb* (aka Chiang Mai salad).
Also When walking (or driving) around, take plenty of water – sightseeing is thirsty work in these parts.

WORTH GETTING OUT OF BED FOR

Viewpoint Join every other tourist in town and visit Wat Phrathat Doi Suthep (www.doisuthep.com), a mountaintop temple erected in 1383; it's well worth the exodus. More than 915m above sea level and just half an hour outside the city, the temple's vistas are amazing.
Arts and culture Purists will enjoy touring 14th-century Lanna sculptures and San Kamphaeng ceramics at the Chiang Mai National Museum (+66 (0)53 221 308), but we prefer ogling contemporary handmade art in the city's independent galleries. Run by Bangkok-born textile designer Kachama K Perez, Studio Kachama on Nimmanhaemin Road showcases delicate hand-woven fabrics. The silk, hemp, cotton, banana fibre and hilltribe textiles are especially noteworthy because they revive traditional Thai weaving techniques (www.kachama.com). Charoenraj Road is the hub for the city's art scene and home to several boutique art galleries. Our pick is La Luna (www.lalunagallery.com), for its contemporary regional art.
Activities Chiang Mai is a hub for the intrepid: zip across the jungle canopy with Flight of the Gibbon (www.treetopasia.com); scale a few mountains or explore caves with Chiang Mai Rock Climbing Adventures (www.thailandclimbing.com) – they have equipment to hire; or explore the best mountain bike trails with Chiang Mai Mountain Biking (www.mountainbikingchiangmai.com). White-water rafting, horse-riding and *muay Thai* training are also available; ask your hotel for details. Or raid local markets then learn to turn your ingredients into tasty northern-style curries in a traditional Thai home, with Baan Thai Cookery School (+66 (0)53 357 339; www.baanthaicookery.com).
Daytripper Elephant treks are appealing, but you'll find a guided tour of the Doi Inthanon National Park far more edifying: it'll take in dramatic waterfalls, pretty pagodas and hilltribe villages, home to the Hmong, Karen or Shan people (and their reasonably authentic handicraft stalls).

Children A dusk sortie to watch creatures of the night rubbing their eyes and starting their dark day at the Chiang Mai Night Safari (+66 (0)53 999 000) will make bedtime stories all the richer. Catch more nocturnal critters at the Chiang Mai Zoo (+66 (0)53 221 179; www.chiangmaizoo.com): as well as a Twilight Zone, there's an aquarium and a snow dome. Those who still enjoy miniature tea parties might like the Doll Museum at 187/2 Moo 9, Baan Dongkilek (+66 (0)53 837 229).
Walks The jungly reservoir located in the foothills of Doi Suthep offers cool and peaceful respite, along with splendid, unimpeded views of the city. Quench your thirst with a refreshing beer or *manao* soda and drink in the scenery at Galae Restaurant (+66 (0)53 278 655) – we suggest you don't eat there, though.
Perfect picnic Weekending locals head to Namtok Huai Kaew for picnics, and it's easy to see why: this picturesque waterfall near Chiang Mai Zoo is a charming retreat from the city. It's well worth heaving yourselves out of bed early to shop for seasonal, super-fresh food and Thai snacks and drinks at the organic farmers' market held at JJ Market (www.jjchiangmai.com) every Saturday and Wednesday 5.30am and 9am.
Shopping Chiang Mai makes a big bleep on the retail radar. Nimmanhaemin Road is the place to start: the buyers for Armani Casa go specially for Gerard Collection's environmentally ethical bamboo-log tables and chairs (www.gerardcollection.com); Gong Dee Gallery (www.gongdeegallery.com) sells chic wooden

pieces – we love the miniature chests and deco-style handbags; and groovy Ginger boutique is great for girlie gifts, clothes and accessories (+66 (0)53 215 635). Also worth a look is home-set furniture shop AKA (+66 (0)53 894 413; www.aka-aka.com), where you'll find pretty Earth & Fire pottery. Just outside the city, ceramics studio Prempracha's Collection, just off Chiang Mai Sankampang Road (www.prempracha.com), houses a vast array of stoneware in styles you'll have seen at home, for a fraction of the price.

Something for nothing The Sunday Walking Street Market runs the length of Ratchadamnoen Road from Tapae Gate in the Old Town and is the perfect place to people-watch among stalls selling crafts, bric-a-brac and Buddhist mementoes.

Don't go home without... a browse, a buy and a bite to eat at Danish designer Hans Andersen's concept compound the House, at 199 Moonmuang Road (www.thehousethailand.com). As well as super-chic lifestyle store Nomad, the House has a restaurant, a café and a second branch of the fashion boutique Ginger.

CHARMINGLY CHIANG MAI

Although it has become commercialised over the last decade, Chiang Mai still offers a more authentic slice of Thai life than Bangkok, particularly during festivals, where age-old traditions are maintained alongside the modern attitude to *sanook* (fun). If you're happy to get wet, the city's central moat area is quite possibly *the* best place in Thailand to enjoy Songkran (Thai New Year). Here you can enter the spirit of the water fights and bar-hopping, but also sample the more orthodox aspects of the festival, like religious rites, family gatherings and street parades.

DIARY

Mid-February Pale petals and glossy leaves provide a blooming marvellous display for the Orchid Festival. April Chiang Mai is the place to celebrate the Thai New Year's orgy of water-throwing for Songkran. May A candlelit night procession to the summit of Doi Suthep celebrates the life, enlightenment and death of Buddha. November Loy Krathong harks from a 13th-century Sukhothai tradition of giving thanks to the goddess of water and seeking forgiveness for past misdeeds. December Chiang Mai Food Festival sees folk flock to the city to taste tempting traditional treats.

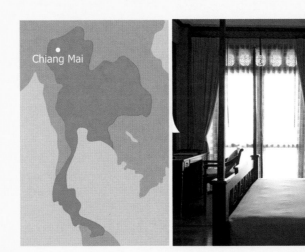

Chiang Mai

Puripunn

STYLE Old-fashioned charmer
SETTING Laid-back historic lane

'It's as if we've strayed into the chambers of a colonial dowager, albeit one with a flatscreen and DVD player and packets of peanuts concealed in ornate wooden boxes'

My lucky number is four. This is according to the elderly Chinese lady kneeling opposite me, who has asked me on which day I was born, consulted a well-thumbed book of horoscopes and scribbled a sudoko-like formula on a scrap of paper. Quite an audience has gathered for my fortune-telling debut: several rows of Buddhas, large and small, as well as several ashen-faced Chinese goddesses, all of whom watch me with benign smiles.

Impulse has brought me here, as it can lead many a man astray in Thailand: a small, handwritten sign sent me down a quiet, flower-scented Chiang Mai street to find Madam Pavinee's cluttered family home. After some shuffling of tarot cards and a brief feng shui lesson I return to the Puripunn, slightly uncertain about my future but clutching a consolation bag, full of fat-fingered bananas and leaf-wraps of sticky rice, that Madam has thrust upon me.

The Puripunn is a hotel you might be lucky enough to stumble upon by chance, but you will find it more easily if you arrange for a car to collect you from the airport. Although the room number lacks a number 'four', our suite feels like an auspicious place; old-fashioned with its dark antique furniture, olive green walls, silk lampshades

and Impressionist oils. The ticking of a grandmother clock further transports us to another era. It's as if we've strayed into the chambers of a colonial dowager, albeit one with a flatscreen and DVD player and packets of peanuts concealed in ornate wooden boxes. There are his 'n' hers silk slippers supplied to skate across the teak floor, which gleams like a polished conker; a balcony from where we watch birds practise swooping from rooftop to rooftop; and a large hot tub filled with water and lotus blossom for our arrival. Directly above, in a composition that brings to mind an oft-repeated scene from *Only Fools and Horses*, is an enormous chandelier.

Our room may be grand but the hotel is small and amiable, and designed to complement the architecture of the traditional homes found throughout the streets of Chiang Mai. You will very likely bump into the owners, a thirtysomething Thai couple, Att and Koy. They've given the Puripunn a personal touch, with him donating Burmese paintings from the family collection, and her designing the garden, which manages to be green and jungly over just a few dozen square metres. Their young son, playing on the small lawn, has yet to contribute anything significant, but is pretty handy with a butterfly net. Att and Koy moved here from Bangkok, and tell us how they fell in love with Chiang Mai, which is cooler and greener, with less shopping malls, and does have people who don't work so hard. 'Lazier?' I ask them. They laugh: 'Well, it took a while to get the hotel finished.'

The Puripunn is a good place to be lazy. There is a gym (although here it's called the 'fitness room') somewhere, but its exact location remains a mystery to us; and, anyway, in this humidity you can break into a sweat simply by turning the pages of your book. Instead, we loll by the pool and order a lunch of spicy minced pork and club sandwiches, watching butterflies flit across the water. The hotel is in a lazy part of town, too, across the Ping River from the city proper, close to the walled Old Town and tucked down a small, almost rustic lane with ramshackle homes for neighbours. In the afternoon we leave our poolside perch to explore, following a little hand-drawn map given to us by our favourite member of staff, Payon, a man so sweet-natured that even a sudden appearance by Chiang Mai's mythical water dragon would probably fail to upset him.

Such serpents coil down carved steps at the nearby temple, Wat Gade (it's more than 600 years old), and a golden puppy statue, garlanded with flowers, smiles up at us. A roof is being replaced, and a group of women sit in the shade of a tree, washing each tile by hand. There's a temple museum, which sounds dusty and dull, but inside we're greeted by a white-bearded wooden head – a Santa of the tropics – and a collection of curiosities. Among ancient bicycles and typewriters is Mrs Smith's favourite cabinet, labelled simply, 'Bits of wood that look like elephant.' We walk out, and on, past age-blackened timber buildings along the river, and cross a footbridge to the Flower Market, where blooms for golden puppies and their owners are painstakingly threaded together. We return to the Puripunn in time for sausages.

As Mrs Smith notes, you can always trust a place that does a good banger, and I have to agree, mentally adding Chiang Mai to Toulouse and Cumberland as trustworthy places. The sausage here is dark and spicy, served with a fiery beef dip peppered with red flecks of chilli, and what look curiously like pork scratchings – they're curls of crispy saltiness. We sit outside in the night air with a bottle of chilled white wine, and wonder what to do with the rest of our time at the Puripunn. There are buggies at hand to take us into town for the Sunday Market, noted for its excellent local handicrafts rather than fake designer buys, and our handwritten map suggests several bars for cocktails. There is Wat Phra That Doi Suthep, the golden hillside temple, to visit, ancient ruins to explore and local noodle dishes to taste. We could, if we so desired, learn Thai cooking at Puripunn or, indeed, take classes in the fine art of carving fruit and vegetables. For the moment, though, we'll just return to our chandelier and bath tub and see where fate takes us.

Reviewed by Rick Jordan

NEED TO KNOW

Rooms **30 rooms.**

Rates Low season, THB4,508–THB26,070; high season, THB5,123–THB26,070, including breakfast.

Check-out Noon, but flexible subject to availability. Earliest check-in, 2pm.

Facilities Spa, gym, library, free WiFi throughout. In rooms: flatscreen TV, minibar, rain shower (except in Deluxe Rooms) in all suites there is also a DVD player and mini stereo system.

Poolside The rectangular jade swimming pool in the middle of Puripunn has a large Jacuzzi at its centre and is surrounded by elegant greenery.

Children In addition to three suites, there is one Puripunn Family Room suitable for those with small Smiths. Babysitting can be arranged in advance, from THB250 an hour. The pool has an integrated children's area.

Also You'll need to book a few hours ahead to experience the hotel's traditional high tea, served daily at 3pm.

IN THE KNOW

Our favourite rooms Bag one of the two chocolate-walled 'Baby' Suites for the most romantic, whirlpool-bath-enhanced stay. All rooms are attractively decked out in Thai-colonial style, with rich greens, calming creams and warm woods. Details such as porcelain-handled taps, ornately framed paintings and brass ceiling fans create a sense of nostalgia.

Hotel bar The over-sized sofas in the Pool Lounge are the perfect spot to settle for a smoothie by day and a cocktail by night.

Hotel restaurant Punna Café is a bright and airy wood-lined dining area on the second floor, where signature northern Thai cuisine is served alongside European dishes and Puripunn's indisputably elegant high tea.

Top table Overlooking the pool and gardens on the upper floor.

Room service Food from the restaurant menu is available in your room from 7am–10pm.

Dress code Loose and laid-back lounge suits for Mr Smith, flowing maxi-dresses or floaty separates for Mrs Smith.

Local knowledge Puripunn offers private classes in Thai cookery and, for more artistic foodies, fruit and veg carving.

LOCAL EATING AND DRINKING

Above the quiet, torch-lit banks of the Ping River, with outdoor tables arranged around a traditional sala, Baan Suan (+66 (0)53 854 169), at 25 Moo 3 San-Phi-Sua, is a magical dining destination – matched only by its moreish menu of northern Thai delicacies such as sweet pork curry with sticky rice balls. Another riverside restaurant is the Gallery (+66 (0)53 248 601), at 25–29 CharoenRat Road. Its tree-shaded terrace is ideal for a sunset cocktail, or try the *laab plan* (minced fish with spices and herbs) – a regional favourite. Not far from Puripunn at 291 Thapae Road, Art Café (+66 (0)53 206 365) is more of a diner than a café. Go for the fantastic breakfasts, or the only decent Mexican food in town, as well as its tempting choice of local dishes. Laid-back drinking hole the Writers' Club & Wine Bar (+66 (0)53 814 187), at 141/3 Rachadamnoen Road, initially opened as a meeting place for journalists and writers – and the scribes in town still congregate here on Friday nights. Supermodels and Hollywood stars are often spotted at casual eatery Mango Tree Café (+66 (0)53 208 292), hidden in the heart of the city's expat enclave at 8/2 Loi-Kroh Road. The *pad thai* and coffee are especially good.

GET A ROOM!

For more information, or to book this hotel, go to www.mrandmrssmith.com – our expert team can take care of all your travel arrangements. Register your Smith membership card to enjoy exclusive offers and privileges.

 SMITH MEMBER OFFER A choice of either a Puripunn Chill or Puripunn Lovely cocktail, and 15 per cent off your first spa treatment.

Puripunn 104/1 Charoen Muang Soi 2, Charoen Muang Road, T Wat Gade, A Muang, Chiang Mai 50000, Thailand (+66 (0)53 302 898; www.puripunn.com)

Rachamankha

STYLE Heritage homage, contemporary courtyards
SETTING Inside the Old City

'It really is one of the most convivial and contemplative hotel libraries in the world'

'There *is* something a little *Matrix* about him,' Mr Smith whispers, peering down the panelled library towards its adjoining study, where a trim, serious-looking man pours over building plans through the kind of over-sized, owlish spectacles only creative folk with good haircuts can wear. We're talking about the Architect – the impossibly suave, linen-suited co-owner and designer of Chiang Mai's Rachamankha hotel. He looks up, sees us huddled at the other end of the long refectory table and stands to close the door with the smallest and most inscrutable of nods.

Mr Ong-ard Satrabhandu is indeed a powerful and influential man in Thai architectural circles, but his pet project the Rachamankha is an alternative reality of altogether more benign proportions. So serene and timeless are its generous courtyards, sweeping temple-like roofs and thick, whitewashed walls that it comes as a genuine shock to discover the whole compound has been built new from the ground up on a previously derelict but fantastically located old city block only within the last decade. Homaging heyday Lanna (15th-century northern Thai) style in its design principles, it is also stuffed full of Chinese and local antiques – scroll boxes, temple paraphernalia, exquisite prints – both inside the cosy, intimate rooms and beyond in the public areas. With Chiang Mai succumbing to some of Bangkok's modern day vices of pollution, traffic gridlock and *Lonely Planet*-toting backpackers, the hotel truly earns the otherwise tired epithet of an oasis of calm.

But we get organised quickly with two wheels and some propulsion, as we're only here for a couple of days (although it's hard to call the 50cc matchbox we rent a motorbike, and while whole Thai families and their pets perch effortlessly on theirs, I spend most of the day hanging on to Mr Smith's love handles with my bum barely off the bitumen).

Chiang Mai is pretty idiot proof – it's a square with a moat – but it does have a complicated one-way system, so there are a few Mr Bean moments before we locate our first destination – an arts and craft shopping street, Nimmanhemin Soi 1, just outside the old city precincts. My favourite boutique is a cavernous gallery space strewn with contemporary textiles purporting to fuse the half-Japanese, half-Thai heritage of the artist with the traditional weaving techniques and fabrics of the area. Mr Smith just thinks it's an overpriced ethnic cushion shop, but the French proprietor is charm personified and soon we are stroking wall-hangings over a fizzy orange drink and wondering about Australian customs.

Emboldened, we explore more – a Burmese art gallery here, a deserted Chinese temple there, a *King and I* municipal square complete with Victorian-looking street lights while we're at it. Eventually we find our way to glam expat hang-out, House, where lime granita cocktails and street Thai finger food quickly assuage the weariness of open-air transport and a million fellow travellers. We return to our Rachamankha paradise rather pleased with ourselves and not a little tipsy; we are asleep in air-conditioned comfort in a nanosecond.

Day Two is the last of our holiday and we wake in a very different frame of mind, barely stirring beyond our room and the long, generous pool other than to stroll across the courtyard for lunch. The Rachamankha's restaurant is well-respected in its own right, and we are pleased to see the Architect holding court as we enter. Pan-Asian dishes reign supreme; we mix piquant Thai fish cakes

with deliciously rich Burmese curry, but guiltily indulge later, outside in the pretty courtyard as the sun sets, in a skyscraper-high club sandwich and the best chips in Thailand. I'm even more ashamed to say tomato ketchup has made its way to the Golden Triangle.

Nightfall — and a slight drop in temperature — stirs a final burst of energy and we venture out again, this time on foot, into the old city. Our slower pace makes clear just how culturally rich this town is. Still outnumbering 7-Elevens, temples lurk on every corner — wooden, brick, gaudy, serene. I pick one with the lights on and the amplified chanting of monks in prayer. Quietly we enter and adopt a lop-sided lotus position at the back, leaving our shoes outside eyed hopefully by the kampong dogs. The young novices turn round to stare but soon rejoin the flow of the repeating mantras. It's wonderfully hypnotic — *Matrix*-like in its own way — and soon even the dogs pad in and collapse in the enveloping sensuality of it all, a string of canine crescents along the wall.

We reinstall ourselves in the library the next morning waiting to transfer to the airport. It really is one of the most convivial and contemplative hotel libraries in the world, largely by virtue of it actually being a library, rather than the designer furniture showroom with expensive coffee-table books beloved of so many other elite retreats. As if to prove the point, the Architect appears, opens one of the glass-panelled cabinets and takes out a tome. He looks sideways at us and tilts his head slowly. This time his nod seems more knowing, almost playful, as if a truth previously withheld is now clear to us all.

Reviewed by Mr & Mr Smith

NEED TO KNOW

Rooms 24, including two suites.

Rates Low season, THB4,700–THB8,360; high season, THB5,100–THB9,100, including à la carte breakfast and selected minibar drinks and snacks. Two-bedroom Suites (sleep up to five), THB12,700–THB19,400.

Check-out 12pm; check-in, 1pm, but both flexible subject to availability. Late check-outs up to 6pm are charged at half the room rate; after 6pm, you'll need to pay for a full extra night's stay.

Facilities Free WiFi throughout, library, art and antiques gallery, massage pavilion, gardens, boutique. In rooms: flatscreen TV with satellite, DVD player, minibar.

Poolside A delectable 20m turquoise-tiled pool with terracotta surrounds has umbrella-shaded day-beds and a massage pavilion for the ultimate in relaxation.

Children The hotel doesn't accept kids under 12; however babies are welcome.

Also Rachamankha is the personal project of interior designer and owner Rooj Changtrakul and his step-father, the famous Thai architect Ong-ard Satrabhandu. The main inspiration for the hotel is 15th-century Lanna architecture, although it also reflects the symmetry of Chinese design. The owner's collection of art and antiquities is on display throughout the hotel and in the upstairs gallery.

IN THE KNOW

Our favourite rooms The Two-bedroom Suites may have the space of an apartment – along with private access to the pool – but our pick would be a romantic Deluxe Room with silk-draped canopy bed.

Hotel bar Rachamankha's bar is a charming spot for a pre-dinner cocktail or a cup of the best coffee in town.

Hotel restaurant The elegant Rachamankha dining room is the only part of the hotel open to non-guests. Small and intimate with white linen–covered tables, Ming-style porcelain, Lanna-period antiquities and heavy silverware, it serves northern Thai and European food. Top tips are the deliciously fragrant *Tai-Yai* prawn soup and earthy lamb masala stir-fry.

Top table One outside in the pretty courtyard.

Room service Light snacks and drinks are served from 6.30am to 10pm.

Dress code Smart but pared down – it's a city hotel not a beach resort.

Local knowledge Staying at the Rachamankha gives you immediate access to the ancient centre of Chiang Mai. There are more than 35 Buddhist temples and it's a short stroll to the night bazaar and the Sunday Walking Street Market.

LOCAL EATING AND DRINKING

Le Crystal (+66 (0)53 872 890), at 74/2 Paton Road, offers fine French dining in sophisticated chandelier-bedecked surroundings overlooking gardens and the Ping River. An old teak house by the water at 9 Charoenrat Road is the location for **the Riverside** (+66 (0)53 243 239), a popular hang-out for locals and tourists with friendly service. The menu is long and includes tasty selections from all over the globe. Get there early to bag a quiet table by the river. There's live music every night, and from about 10pm the place is heaving. The restored colonial villa that is home to **the House** (+66 (0)53 419 011), at 199 Moonmuang Road, was at the forefront of Chiang Mai's renaissance as a style city. The food can be hit and miss, but it has a gorgeous atmosphere and the outdoor bar is a lovely spot for a drink.

GET A ROOM!

For more information, or to book this hotel, go to www.mrandmrssmith.com – our expert team can take care of all your travel arrangements. Register your Smith membership card to enjoy exclusive offers and privileges.

 SMITH MEMBER OFFER A bottle of chilled sparkling wine on arrival.

Rachamankha 6 Rachamankha 9, Phra Singh, Chiang Mai 50200, Thailand (+66 (0)53 904 111; www.rachamankha.com)

HUA HIN

COASTLINE Royal Riviera
COAST LIFE Sassy society sunspot

A couple of hours south of bustling Bangkok, the laid-back resort town of Hua Hin has been a Thai weekender's favourite ever since the royal family started heading here back in the 1920s. Of course, the rest of society followed suit. Enchanted by the feather-soft, white-powder beach, successive monarchs built summer palaces in and around what was once a small village on the Gulf of Thailand's north-west coast. Since then, Hua Hin has grown into a peaceful paradise of seaside chic, with manicured golf courses, world-class spas, sleek hotels and a smattering of appetising seafood restaurants both here and in smaller neighbour Cha-Am. After enduring the frenetic urban hum of Bangkok, it's the perfect escape for some lazy beach-based bliss.

GETTING THERE

Planes Fly into Bangkok's International Suvarnabhumi Airport (www.bangkokairportonline.com), 25km east of the capital. Domestic flights to Hua Hin are currently suspended, so Bangkok's is effectively the closest airport to town, and you'll have to complete the rest of the journey overland.

Trains Rail travel is one of the easiest, albeit slowest, ways to get to Hua Hin. Trains leave from Bangkok's Hualamphong station several times a day, and express trains can cut the journey time to three-and-a-quarter hours (www.railway.co.th).

Automobiles Hua Hin Limousine Services (www.huahin-limousine.com) ferry folk from Bangkok airport or the city centre to Hua Hin and back, and can also arrange day trips around the region. The drive takes two to three hours, but be warned: at times the traffic between Bangkok and Hua Hin gets thundercloud-thick.

LOCAL KNOWLEDGE

Taxis There are usually plenty of taxis and *songtaews* (small pick-up trucks) parked in the centre of town, but you'll need to negotiate a flat rate with the drivers first. If you have the nerve, rattling motorbike taxis are a racier option. However, unless you want to wander further afield, you can easily navigate this small town on foot.

Siesta and fiesta Not wanting to miss the potential custom of the wealthy Thais who flock to Hua Hin, shops and banks open on time, usually around 10am, and close around sunset. Some cafés and restaurants kick off as early as 8am to serve the breakfast crowd, while Hua Hin's Night Market caters to hunger pangs.

Do go/don't go Although it's drier than much of the country during monsoon season (June–October), this region is best visited from November to March, when it's sunny by day and often cool at night. Hua Hin, like Bangkok, gets horribly hot between April and May. Even worse than the heat, though, are the traffic jams on Fridays and Saturdays; head to Hua Hin on a weekday and you'll have the whole place to yourself.

Packing tips Arty agnès B linens for blending in with the smart set.

Recommended reads Since you're lounging where Thai royals like to relax, why not prepare for your trip with a book that features one of them? *Anna and the King of Siam*, by Margaret Landon, is the novel which inspired the famous movie *The King and I*. Don't bring it with you though – it's banned in Thailand for being culturally offensive. *Four Reigns* by Kukrit Pramoj follows the ficticious life of one woman witnessing the rule of successive kings.

Local specialities Like most beach towns in Thailand, Hua Hin boasts tantalisingly tasty seafood, often prepared in simple curries, grilled or deep-fried and served with sweet-spicy sauces. Head to Hua Hin pier or Khao Takiab fishing village further south for the freshest finds. Naresdarmi Road is home to the best authentic Thai; try *hoy tod*, or oyster omelettes. Mango sticky rice (*khao niew mamuang*) is also a highly prized local dish, sold by two warring vendors at the night bazaar.

Also Hua Hin literally translates as 'stone head' – which will make perfect sense to you when you visit the boulder-scattered headland jutting out from the beach.

WORTH GETTING OUT OF BED FOR

Viewpoint Follow Chomsin Road west of town to Khao Hin Lek Fai, otherwise known as Flintstone Hill. This mighty mound offers gorgeous views of Hua Hin, the beach and the nearby mountain range. The most popular time to clamber to the top is sunset, when the vista is particularly camera-pleasing.

Arts and culture Go palace-hopping to savour the royal flavour of Hua Hin. North of town, halfway to Cha-Am, is the teak palace Phra Ratchaniwet Marukhathaiyawan, built by King Rama VI in 1923. Its split-level living areas (the royal quarters are on stilts), covered boardwalks and beachy elegance make it an exquisite example of tropical architecture. In 1926, King Rajakhipok (Rama VII) commissioned a summer palace in Hua Hin for his wife, Queen Rambhai Barni. He named it Wang Klai Kangwon, which means 'far from worries'. When the royals are away, the palace is open for public viewing.

Activities Combining parasailing and surfing, the high-energy, adrenalin-pumping sport of kitesurfing is all the regional rage. Get hooked up and take to the waves at one of the local schools: try Kite Thailand (www.kitethailand.com) or Kiteboarding Asia (www.kiteboardingasia.com).

Best beach About 6km south of Hua Hin, Khao Takiab is the ideal seaside spot. Fringed with palms and adorned with a 20m-high golden Buddha statue, this wide stretch of soft white sand is now dotted with a dozen small beach-shack restaurants offering cheap, simple yet scrumptious food.

Daytripper To see 'the mountain of three hundred peaks', drive about 45km south of Hua Hin to Khao Sam Roi Yot National Park. The scenery here is breathtaking – beautiful beaches, limestone cliffs, a picture-perfect mountain range, and a vast network of ancient caves, including famous Tham Phraya Nakhon, which contains a royal sala, or 'open room', bathed by sunlight from above. There's something for wildlife-lovers, too – endangered animals such as antelope-like serows, dusky langurs (a species of monkey) and Irrawaddy dolphins can be spotted in the park.

Children This being the beach, there's plenty to keep kids occupied. Seaside pony rides are prolific and, in most cases, the animals are well looked after, but be sure to check before you mount up. For more animal action, take a trip north-west to Kaeng Krachan National Park (Thailand's largest) home to waterfalls, a lake, birds and wild elephants.

Walks The sandy 5km stretch of Hua Hin Beach is heaven for strolling, running, horse-riding and the best spot for people-watching.

Perfect picnic Take a trip west of town to the Hin Lek Fai viewpoint, which has a lofty platform from which to enjoy a sunset picnic and a bottle of wine as you gaze at the gorgeous views. There's also a restaurant there should you need extra provisions.

Shopping No one comes to Hua Hin to shop. In fact, many probably head here to escape the mega-malls that dominate much of Bangkok. Nonetheless, there are several small boutiques around town. The Hua Hin Bazaar, about 100m west of the beach at the corner of Naresdamri and Damnoen Kasem roads, is a good place to hunt for shell trinkets, wood carvings and

fab Thai pop CDs. During the day call in at Chatchai Market, off Phetkasem Road, to pick up fresh, inexpensive foodie treats for picnics. Come evening, hit the adjacent Night Market along Dechanuchit Road for fresh-cooked stall fare, and, if you're there on Saturday night, drop in for a bite and live jazz at Cicada Market, in the park close to the Hyatt.

Something for nothing For a right royal freebie, admire some courtly local architecture at Hua Hin's train station, one of the oldest in Thailand. This charming building, complete with royal waiting room, was commissioned by King Rama VI and built in the same exuberant style as his palace.

Don't go home without... paying a visit to Hua Hin Hills Vineyard (www.hauhinhillsvineyard.com), west of town, where elephants are employed to help cultivate the vines. The Sala restaurant is a smart spot for lunch with fabulous vistas over the winery.

HOLEY HUA HIN

Spend any time in Hua Hin and you'll realise that, apart from the beach and the spas, the real reason so many people flock to the city is its great golfing. Hua Hin has not one, nor two, but eight world-class golf courses, all open to the public (for a small greens fee, naturally). The oldest is the 18-hole Royal Hua Hin Golf Club (+66 (0)32 512 475), located very centrally behind the station. If you want something newer, head to the Springfield Royal Country Club (+66 (0)32 593 223). Its Jack Nicklaus–designed course is a favourite among pros and passionate amateurs alike.

DIARY

March Look skywards in Cha-Am during the Thailand International Kite Festival. **Mid-April** Songkran is the water-flinging Thai New Year celebration. **Mid-May** Visaka Bucha Day celebrates the life, enlightenment and death of Buddha and is the holiest day of the year in the Buddhist calendar. **June** The Hua Hin Jazz Festival (www.jazzfestivalhuahin.com) brings world-class performers and visitors to the city. **August** Every day during the month, you can play at courses participating in the Hua Hin Golf Festival for THB800 a round. Also during August, about 300 yachtsmen compete in the colourful Hua Hin Regatta. **December** Petrolheads flock to the Sofitel to show off their motors during the Hua Hin Vintage Car Rally.

Aleenta Hua Hin

STYLE Salubrious honeymoon hideaway
SETTING Secluded Pranburi sands

'Private space is the big thing here... And the sea! The sea, right there! ... Being this close to the elements is super-sexy'

Taking a taxi to Thailand beach hotel Aleenta Hua Hin as night falls, we haven't a clue what lies ahead. As we twist and turn into remoter-looking backwaters, we keep expecting the hotel to loom up like a glittering casino round every next corner, so we're surprised and pleased when we pull up outside a discreetly glowing doorway on the roadside.

We learn eventually that we're not in the town of Pranburi itself, but in a coastal neighbourhood called Pak Nam Pran, which has always been a favourite beach-house spot for rich Thais, and has latterly become a strip of boutique hotels. Well, 'strip' isn't quite right; it's still relatively undeveloped and, if you take a walk at night, you're more likely to meet an owl than a hen party.

Reception staff are charming and welcoming, and we're guided quickly to our room after a brief explanation of what's where. Aleenta Hua Hin seems the antithesis of the luxury big-hitters, with its cosy bar and restaurant

(for grown-ups only) and pretty little swimming pool – the only communal spaces in the main resort. Private space is the big thing here, and we're thrilled with what we've been given. Outdoors, we get a little square of lawn, a plunge pool, day-beds for sunbathing and a breakfast table. And the sea! The sea, right there! I mean, we never actually have breakfast on the little lawn, because we'd get wet, but being this close to the elements is super-sexy, it must be said.

Inside, the room has been done out in simple, almost rustic-chic style, with a dark-purple bedspread and lots of cushions, a thoughtful array of lighting, a bamboo unit with all the amenities – fruit, water, books and iPod dock – and a smooth stone floor. We hardly leave the room. No one bothers us while we're here, apart from when we ring for room service, and the staff always wait until we open the door ourselves. Tonight, though – our first night – we sally forth to dine in the hotel restaurant, curious to see who else is staying here.

The clientele, we determine astutely, is very honeymoon, Aleenta's breezy beach bungalows providing a backdrop for paired-off chilling out. It's hard to imagine coming here not as a couple, even though the hotel has a family-oriented annex down the road. It's late, so we order just some good *tom kha kai*, the classic Thai coconutty chicken soup, and vegetable tempura. Mr Smith notices some hilariously 1980s-looking cocktails arriving at the next table; we've been on a bit of a health kick, so we hold back. For now.

The crashing ocean lulls us to sleep, and nothing wakes us apart from our physical incapacity to sleep forever. Even when we do 'get up', it's hardly a rush for the shower. We call room service for a spot of breakfast and investigate the iPod that comes with the room. It looks promising to start with, but I'm sad to find there's a surfeit of chart jazz on there, and not even a whole Beethoven symphony. Still, we know next time to bring our

own iPods, which will give us a bit more to get fractious about. At the moment, all is harmony between Mr Smith and me; we're contentedly quiet, but the nuzzle count is way up. Sorry if that's too much information, but it's important to convey that the 'romantic atmosphere' at Aleenta is effective.

I can be curiously churlish when it comes to 'romantic atmosphere', and I loathe the scent of the essential-oil burner that has been lit in a corner of the room. 'Why don't you ring reception and complain that the room smells too nice,' suggests Mr Smith. 'And ask if they can bring something more fetid and dungy to waft around us?' 'Ha,' I say, and pick up the oil burner in order to pop it outside, so it can waft its aromatherapeutic potion towards the surging waves. Alas, it is very hot, and I swiftly up-end it onto the floor. After that, everything goes a bit menthol. I decide I'd better learn to love the smell and crawl humbly into bed with Mr Smith. 'Don't worry, love,' he soothes. 'Now we know what it's like to be really minted.'

When the sun reaches its height, we decide to do our duty as English roses, and head to the pool to sunbathe, covered in factor 30. The pool and deck are very relaxing; and we are joined by an older Canadian couple, who chat quietly and take dips in the sparkling pool. When the hour is right, we fall happily off the wagon, with a pair of creamy tropical cocktails replete with cherries and those ageless little paper parasols.

Aleenta Hua Hin is utterly charming and, somehow, quite quirky, though I can't put my finger on why that is. It might be the deadpan restaurant mâitre d', or the fact that the bicycle Mr Smith takes for a twilight spin has no brakes. It might be the lack of corporate gloss. Or it could just be that you're so removed from the hurly-burly here – it really does feel like the back end of beyond – that you loosen up and start to find almost everything quite amusing. As every tropical lovebird knows, there's no use crying over spilt mint.

Reviewed by Sophie Dening

NEED TO KNOW

Rooms 21, including six rooms at Frangipani, the family-oriented annex up the road.

Rates Low season, THB5,480–THB12,800; high season, THB6,797–THB12,800, including breakfast. Rates exclude seven per cent tax and 10 per cent service charge.

Check-out Noon. Earliest check-in, 2pm.

Facilities Two spas, yoga area, free WiFi. In rooms: private balcony or veranda, minibar, books, iPod dock (but no TV).

Poolside Adjacent to the bar and restaurant, a beautiful little teacup-shaped infinity pool looks out to sea.

Children Aleenta is divided into two sites: one smaller, child-friendly wing called Frangipani, and the main adults-only resort. Extra beds are available in all rooms except the Pool Suites for THB1,500 a night. Under-fives stay free.

Also There is a two-night minimum stay at weekends.

IN THE KNOW

Our favourite rooms The panoramically endowed Penthouse is an obvious choice, with its rounded bedroom, rooftop lounge and sunken stone tub (ideal for aromatherapy baths; the Ocean View Suite has one too). We also like the bathroom in Frangipani 3; and Palm 5 for its picture-perfect entrance.

Hotel bar The little open-air bar is excellent, turning out tasty tropical cocktails.

Hotel restaurant Aleenta's simple, colonial-style restaurant serves Thai and Western dishes, with nightly themes, such as pasta or barbecue, masterminded in the open kitchen by Rose the chef. The intimate indoor/outdoor dining room catches sea breezes and the sound of the waves. At Frangipani, there's a small and convenient alfresco restaurant.

Top table It's all good but, forced to choose, we'd say poolside outdoors or by the window indoors.

Room service The restaurant menu can be ordered any time from 7am to 10.30pm.

Dress code High fashion or factory outlet – no one's really looking.

Local knowledge Golf trips can be arranged, as can cookery classes, over in Frangipani. The hotel offers guests a different excursion every day, whether it's a trip down the River Kwai, or a bob around the floating markets. Aleenta's KA spa uses its own blend of natural ingredients to make wonderfully sensuous body scrubs and massage oils; there's also a steam room. The Sky Spa offers open-air treatments above the restaurant.

LOCAL EATING AND DRINKING

It's a 30km drive to Hua Hin, with all its cafés, restaurants, bars and nightlife. Book at ever-popular pavilion restaurant Supatra by the Sea (+66 (0)32 536 561), 122/63 Soi Mooban Takiab, Nongkae, and secure a table in the seaside gardens, then order the mouthwatering Modern Thai dishes. La Villa (+66 (0)32 513 435), at 12/2 Poolsuk Road is a small, very casual joint, which serves delicious Italian fare. Their speciality – an outstanding crab pasta – has fans among many of Bangkok's glitterati. Sleek, chic WiFi café I Talay (+66 (0)32 531 268), at 39/4 Petchkasem Road , boasts a great smoothie selection and impressive art gallery. Elephant Bar (+66 (0)32 512 021) at the historic Sofitel Hotel, 1 Damnernkasem Road, brings a dose of colonial cool to your holiday. Try one of their signature cocktails and relax to the smooth sounds of the in-house pianist.

GET A ROOM!

For more information, or to book this hotel, go to www.mrandmrssmith.com – our expert team can take care of all your travel arrangements. Register your Smith membership card to enjoy exclusive offers and privileges.

SMITH MEMBER OFFER A bottle of Aleenta label wine and a gift set from the Galleria Aleenta Luxury collection; a bottle of champagne for five-night stays; a three-course meal for 10-night stays.

Aleenta Hua Hin 183 Moo 4 Pak Nam Pran, Pranburi, Hua Hin 77220, Thailand (+66 (0)25 148 112; www.aleenta.com)

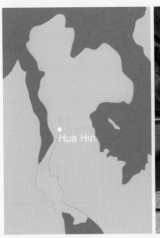 

Alila Cha-Am

STYLE Asian austerity
SETTING Seaside serenity

'It might not be the most obvious of settings, but we settle into our bathroom for a nightcap. Mr Smith flicks on the intimate lighting, music and quite possibly the most impressive rain shower known to man'

Minimalism and babies, I fear, are two concepts certain to collide. Speeding out of a chaotic Bangkok, in a taxi crammed with enough infant paraphernalia to keep Mini Smith going for a fortnight, we three were headed – just for the weekend – towards tranquillity, designer architecture and all things stylish at the Alila Cha-Am, near Hua Hin. Two hours later we arrive, gasping in awe of the colossal marble stairway leading up to the resort, but also in nervousness at the thought of tackling it with a pushchair. Within seconds, however, our mountain of luggage (and pushchair) has disappeared and we are being led up to check-in heaven: an expansive reflection pool and ocean views welcome us in.

'There's music coming from the walls,' whispers Mr Smith as we're led past futuristic structures of mesh and stone towards our room. Sure enough, gentle vibes are seeping from somewhere. A couple of staircases later we enter our Horizon Room, and are again met by mellow music. This time it's emanating from the Apple TV system. Mini Smith immediately flails her arms around, signalling approval.

The thing about designer minimalism, I begin to realise after surveying our spacious room, is that aside from looking fabulous, it's actually rather baby-friendly – there's simply less to grab, poke, pull and destroy. As Mini Smith scoots across the beautifully bare floor and high-fives the sleek concrete walls I wonder why we've bothered to childproof our once fashionable home with an unsightly explosion of rainbow-coloured play mats. In the meantime, Mr Smith is eyeing the 'study area' subtly hidden behind the bed. In a matter of minutes he's fitted the travel cot rather snugly under the lengthy slab of wood. Out of sight, out of mind...

I heard a rumour there's an adults-only Chill Pool here. 'I suppose I better try it out, darling,' I sigh, rather unconvincingly, as I usher my significant others in the direction of the 'other' pool. Flanked by the cocktail-shaking Red Bar and sunloungers, it is the perfect spot to swim in solitude. After a time, however, I wonder how the other Smiths are getting on and pack up my magazines.

Thankfully, it turns out the Active Pool is not going to disappoint us. Ocean views and the neatest of lawns provide a soft backdrop and pretty, pruned hibiscus hedges still grant me lots of privacy. 'Ahh, look, Mummy couldn't bear to be without us,' Mr Smith quips as he catches me sneaking behind a hedge and onto a sunlounger.

After a dose of sun-kissed snoozing, Mr Smith informs me there's a Thai couple having their wedding photographs taken on the beach. I bolt upright and move in closer for a prime spectator perch. Three photographers, two stylists-cum-petal throwers and a handful of assistants: this is better viewing than any Thai soap opera. I take a sneaky snap of my own, mainly because I'm loving the stylist's electric blue drainpipe jeans and fluttering hand fan (for himself not the bride, might I add). Any plans of joining the hotel's afternoon excursion to the nearby Khao Luang cave sanctuary are quickly forgotten. Why leave when there's live entertainment right here?

Eventually, I pry myself away to join Mr Smith for an early evening apéritif at the rooftop bar, Clouds Loft. As Mini Smith sets about making friends with the affable bar staff we lounge on day-beds, sipping on Alila Sundowners, a delectable mix of vodka, ginger, passionfruit, watermelon, basil, martini and ginger ale.

An hour later we return to Clouds Loft for dinner and try our luck getting Mini Smith to fall asleep under the stars. We're not sure if it is the soothing sounds hailing from unidentified hotel orifices, the pushchair-friendly paths or simply all that fresh sea air that does it, but she drifts off in record time. Now we can get on with enjoying a cosy dinner for two. Highlights include the prime Australian beef tenderloin and a trio of juicy scallops sitting in cracker bread boats on purple waves of herb sauce.

It might not be the most obvious of settings, but we settle into our bathroom for a nightcap. Mr Smith flicks on the intimate lighting, music and quite possibly the most impressive rain shower known to man as I marvel

from the bath tub at the heavenly vision of water and light falling in front of my eyes. This is, unarguably, the best bathroom we've ever been in.

Another day, another wedding shoot. This time it's an antipodean beefcake and his glamorous Asian beauty. Again, there's an entourage of stylists and photographers. And more costume changes than a John Galliano collection parade. After tucking into a hearty breakfast we return to our room suitably stuffed and Mr Smith sprawls across the bed. 'It's not time for a nap yet,' I gently chide. 'I'm not napping,' purrs Mr Smith, 'I'm relaxing.' It's hard to argue with him and we're soon snuggling.

When naptime finally does roll around I tiptoe from the room and head to the spa for 90 minutes of uninterrupted 'me' time. Carrying around a small child for the past nine months – make that 18 if you factor in pregnancy – has left my limbs screaming for refuge. Thankfully, they find it here. The Alila signature massage – a fusion of long Balinese strokes, deep-tissue Swedish techniques, acupressure and traditional Thai movements – proves the perfect tonic for a weary mama.

Ah, Alila Cha-Am, thank you; not just for allowing us an unexpected romantic respite but for proving that minimalism, high-end design and babies can live happily together after all. I can't wait to ditch the multicoloured mats as soon as we get home.

Reviewed by Ellie Brannan

NEED TO KNOW

Rooms 79, including seven pool villas.
Rates THB5,060–THB24,000, including à la carte breakfast.
Check-out Noon, but flexible subject to availability. Check-in, 2pm.
Facilities Free WiFi throughout, library with books, DVDs and board games, internet-linked computers, spa, gym, gardens. In rooms: flatscreen TV, Apple TV with music and films, DVD player and preloaded iPod (on request), minibar.
Poolside Little ones in tow? Splash around in the black-tiled beachfront Active Pool, overlooking the ocean. The walled sanctuary of the Chill Pool near the spa is a child-free zone, and a sun trap in the heat of the day.
Children Alila may seem a tad trendy for smudgy fingers, but children are welcome. Baby cots and high chairs are provided for free, and extra beds for older kids (THB1,000) and babysitting (THB300 an hour) can be arranged.
Also Built like a Roman bath, Spa Alila's cool limestone treatment rooms encase you in silence as pretty psychedelic 'colouramas' are projected onto walls. The Alila signature massage blends Thai, Balinese and Swedish styles.

IN THE KNOW

Our favourite rooms For a fine romance, book one of the secluded Pool Villas by the beach. They share the uncluttered but serene design of all the rooms (care of Thai talent Duangrit Bunnag), but are more spacious and ensure total privacy. Dornbracht rain showers with soothing mood music make for seductive bathing.
Hotel bar The Red emulates fashionable city bars with its moody lighting, red Perspex bar, ambient soundtrack and heady cocktail list. Chilled-out by day, when it offers wellness-boosting elixirs, it comes to life on weekend evenings when Bangkokians rock up at the resort.
Hotel restaurant Motion is a relaxed, poolside retreat, with tables both on the deck and inside where concrete, glass and bamboo add to the air-conditioned comfort. Chef Siam Kaewcheerat has blended the best of local dishes with global cuisine. For something more atmospheric, saunter upstairs to rooftop Clouds Loft where you can sip a tropical cocktail alfresco as you gaze up at the stars, with a seasonal menu featuring Mediterranean-style seafood, pizza and pasta.
Top table Enjoy an intimate dinner, designed specifically for you, in one of the candlelit beach cabanas.
Room service An edited version of Motion's café-style menu is served until 11pm.
Dress code While transferring through Bangkok, stock up on Thai label Greyhound to fit in with the surrounds.
Local knowledge Take your pick from activities including private early-morning yoga classes, a champagne picnic for two, culinary tours of the local market, a mountain bike ride to the nearby fishermen's village or watersports.

LOCAL EATING AND DRINKING

Fishing village Cha-Am is a good bet for fresh seafood, but head south to Hua Hin, its more cosmopolitan neighbour, for wider dining options. Set in an atmospheric two-storey colonial-style building, **Monsoon** (+66 (0)32 531 062), 62 Naresdamri Road, serves Thai and Vietnamese dishes and classy cocktails – we fell for the caprioskas. Take an upstairs table for breezy street views. For a low-key local with authentic Thai cuisine, clued-up travellers head to **Moon Smile & Platoo** (+66 (0)32 511 664) on Poolsuk Road, for stir-fried and curried seafood.

GET A ROOM!

For more information, or to book this hotel, go to www.mrandmrssmith.com – our expert team can take care of all your travel arrangements. Register your Smith membership card to enjoy exclusive offers and privileges.

 SMITH MEMBER OFFER A mixology class for two.

Alila Cha-Am 115 Moo 7, Tambol Bangkao, Amphur Cha-Am, Petchaburi 76120, Thailand (+66 (0)32 709 555; www.alilahotels.com/chaam)

KHAO YAI

COUNTRYSIDE World Heritage wilderness
COUNTRY LIFE Safaris, spas and shiraz

A couple of hours from Thailand's pulsating capital, Khao Yai National Park is quite literally a breath of fresh air. Dominated by the monsoon forests of the Dong Phaya Yen mountains, this lush hilly landscape offers more than 2,000 square km of Unesco-protected jungle, waterfalls and wildlife – a diverse habitat that's home to creatures great and small, from hornbills and hoopoes to lizards and leopards. Beyond the park gates, fertile farmland and fashionable weekend retreats lend the 'Provence of Thailand' an air of sophistication not found in other rural areas – complete with vineyard vistas and verdant fruit orchards. Leave Bangkok to spend a few days here and you'll find a mix of tropical adventure and tranquillity that's hard to find elsewhere.

GETTING THERE

Planes Khao Yai's nearest international airport is Suvarnabhumi in Bangkok, about 175km south-west (www.bangkokairportonline.com).

Trains It's a slow-going four- to six-hour train ride from Bangkok to Nakorn Ratchasima, or you can hop off a tad earlier at Pak Chong. Both are handy for the park region.

Automobiles It can take three hours to motor up from Bangkok, but, once you leave the city suburbs, it's a scenic drive. The brave may choose to hire a car (Avis, Budget, Europcar and Hertz all have desks at Bangkok airport), but a more sane choice would be to organise a transfer with your hotel.

LOCAL KNOWLEDGE

Taxis Hire a car and driver or use your hotel's car service: taxis are few and far between in these remote reaches.

Siesta and fiesta The park is open every day from 6am to 9pm. Most shops and restaurants open from 9am to 6pm (shopping malls and convenience stores stay open until 9pm). Banks open weekdays, 8.30am–3pm.

Do go/don't go The cool season (November–February) is the best time to visit, when the May–October rains have left the jungle lush and fresh and migrating birds fill the skies; expect warm sunny days and cool evenings. The mercury hits the mid-30s in March/April, but Khao Yai is still one of the coolest spots in Thailand. Midweek visits will be rewarded with solitude: weekends and public holidays see an influx of escapees from Bangkok.

Packing tips Binoculars and zoom lenses for close encounters of the bird kind; mudlark trainers for trekking; long trousers to keep leeches at bay on waterfall walks.

Recommended reads Craig Robson's beautifully illustrated *Birds of Thailand* will help you identify the country's feathered residents. *Sightseeing* by Rattawut Lapcharoensap is an illuminating, poetic series of short stories about Thai life. Philip Cornwel-Smith's *Very Thai* is an entertaining insight into local popular culture.

Local specialities North of the park is the country's agricultural heartland, so scour menus for locally sourced beef, cheese and organic produce. *Som tam* – green papaya salad in a sweet, spicy and sour dressing – is particularly relished in the north. Stalls at the fruit market at Klang Dong are heaving with locally grown jackfruit, custard apples, mangoes and grapes. There's also a growing wine industry in this part of Thailand; hey, it's no Napa Valley, but the vineyards are worth a visit, and the wines – shiraz, cabernet sauvignon, chenin blanc and tempranillo – are interesting. PB Valley (www.khaoyaiwinery.com) and GranMonte (www.granmonte.com) are the two most sophisticated producers.

Also Getting lost in the jungle might make your trip memorable, but not in a good way: hire a guide if you plan to explore deeper into the wilderness.

WORTH GETTING OUT OF BED FOR

Viewpoint You'll drop your jaw for the canopy-skimming panoramas from atop Khao Luk Chang (Baby Elephant Mountain), just outside the park's northern boundary.

Arts and culture In these parts, a day-trip to the Khmer temples comes second to a day on the dairy farm for most Thais: maybe it's all that fresh air and cattle, but there's a vibrant cowboy subculture in Khao Yai. Drop in on Farm Chokchai on the Friendship Highway (+66 (0)44 328 386; www.farmchokchai.com) and watch kitschly clad farm hands roping Friesian steers or make your own ice cream. There are several cowboy bars dotted around the area and, if you're really lucky, you might even happen upon a local rodeo.

Activities Birdwatching, elephant trekking and night safaris (your best chance to eyeball wild elephants) are the park's bread-and-butter pastimes, but sportier explorers can also try mountain biking, white-water rafting and kayaking – ask your hotel to arrange outings for you. Put in some effort and you'll get a gourmet pay-off on a customised wineries bike tour with Spice Roads Asia (www.spiceroads.com). Your guide will take you on an easy-ish ride to the GranMonte and Khao Yai vineyards, stopping off for tastings and lunch. At tee time, test your handicap at the scenic 18-hole Jack Nicklaus–designed golf course at Smith hotel Kirimaya; its clubhouse is perfect for post-round G&Ts.

Daytripper About 220km from Khao Yai, Phimai is home to prehistoric archaeological site Ban Prasart, where excavations have uncovered 3,000-year-old remains. It's also the location of 12th-century Khmer temple Prasat Hin Phimai. At the end of the ancient highway to Angkor, Prasat Phimai is smaller but older than the legendary Cambodian site by a couple of centuries. Extend your trip further afield to neighbouring province Buriram to see Phanom Rung, another grab-your-camera Khmer temple complex on the rim of an extinct volcano.

Children There's only one thing more appealing to kids than tiger-hunting, waterfall-climbing and elephant-riding: a trip to the Bat Cave at Khao Luk Chang. Bruce Wayne won't be there, but a million wrinkle-lipped bats pour from its mouth every day at dusk.

Walks There are 50km of park trails, ranging in difficulty from amble to expedition – just take plenty of water: even a short hike can be challenging in the heat. Once you've giggled at the stuffed animals and pickled snakes in the main visitor centre (open 8.30am–4.30pm), follow the signs to Nam Tok Kong Kaew waterfall, an easy 10–15-minute walk. Continue along the same path and you'll get to the first tier of the three-tier Nam Tok Haew Narok, the park's highest set of falls (in rainy season, mud and fallen trees may sometimes prevent you reaching the top).

Perfect picnic In surroundings this splendid, there are almost too many places to name, but our favourite spot is the Nong Pak Chee look-out shelter near the salt lick, where you can play hide and peep with Khao Yai's park life while you picnic. You might be lucky enough to spot a hornbill or even an elephant.

Shopping You don't come to Khao Yai to shop, but you can browse stalls and try local delicacies (fried grasshopper, anyone?) at Pak Chong Night Market. Not so keen on cooked insects? Roast pork is another speciality that is well worth a try. Retail addicts can get their fix in the nearby town of Pak Thong Chai, one of Thailand's foremost silk-production centres; you can also watch weaving demonstrations at Machada Thai Silk (+66 (0)44 441 684). Do you remember *Toy Story*? You can pick up fun neckerchiefs, straw stetsons and milk sweets from the Farm Chokchai shop for the (big) kids in your life.

Something for nothing Drive through the park's southern entrance and enjoy screensaver-perfect mountain views as you creep upwards. It is particularly jaw-dropping at sunset, and there are several observation points along the road. Keep an eye out for elephants, hornbills and tigers (if you do happen to see one, buy a lottery ticket immediately because it's your lucky day).

Don't go home without... a piece of pottery by the artisans at Ban Dan Kwian, famous for their textured, rust-hued ceramics. The village's kilns turn out utensils, chimes, vases, jewellery and cutesy figurines made with fired clay from the Mun River.

KEENLY KHAO YAI

Khao Yai National Park is Thailand's oldest, third largest and most popular national park, well deserving of its Unesco World Heritage status. The magnificent mountainous terrain rises to 1,351m at its summit, covers five vegetation zones and contains one of the biggest untouched monsoon forests on earth. It is home to more than 300 types of bird, and hundreds of species of other wildlife, including elephants, bears, bats, gibbons and tigers.

DIARY

January–February Chinese New Year brings holidaying nationals to Khao Yai. **April** The Songkran water extravaganza for Thai New Year sees most shops and businesses close. **November** On the first full moon of the 12th lunar month, tiny handmade boats (*kratong*) lit with candles float along waterways to honour the river goddess during the beautiful Loy Kratong festival. The start of the cool season makes Khao Yai a popular place for 'winter' open-air music events. If you fancy cutting yourself a slice of the Thai music scene, the Bonanza Khao Yai hosts a slew of local pop, bossa, ska, reggae and indie bands at a number of grand gatherings, including the Big Mountain Music Fest in February.

5 December The timing of Thailand's Father's Day pays respect to the country's head of state; it's also the King's Birthday and an important public holiday.

Kirimaya

STYLE Grown-up rustic retreat
SETTING Forested foothills

'Mrs Smith slopes off for an in-room massage while at Mist bar I enjoy a vodka tonic and endless vistas of the golf course and mountains'

With two children under the age of three years old, our Smith slip-away to Kirimaya has been guiltily highlighted on the calendar for four long months. But now, parting demonstrations by the Red Shirts to escape Bangkok is looking tricky. Luckily, we're rescued by the Thai New Year water festival. Songkran's splashes have temporarily cooled any drawn-out political rallying as we set off north to what some have nicknamed 'Thailand's Tuscany', a few hours beyond the capital.

Denying our inner alcoholics a tour of the various local vineyards en route proves extraordinarily tough, but in our guise as semi-responsible grown-ups, Mrs Smith and I opt instead for tender, organically grown, superbly sweet corn being steamed by leathery ladies in battered straw hats at makeshift roadside stalls. At just THB20 for three ears, we guzzle down the golden grain before grabbing a bag to go.

We would have sped right past Kirimaya but for the scrub's sudden metamorphosis into manicured lawn. There's something about sweeping, tree-lined driveways that makes me realise I've been scrunching my shoulders ear-wards, and Kirimaya's verdant valley descent swiftly unknots any city-induced hunch. Rolling down the blacked-out windows of our Land Rover, Mrs Smith lets in a whoosh of sunny-grass scent and out a bluster of brunette bob.

We've barely managed to get a be-sandalled foot out of our SUV and through the antique teakwood portico before our bags are being neatly stacked on a golf cart that is all ours to potter about in for the weekend. Ushered by a squad of smiling, silk-suited staff, we hasten with an electric hush past minimalist wood-and-concrete buildings that house the genteel riffraff and onward to one of only four Tented Villas. As we clatter across a creaky wooden bridge over a river of reeds and into a cacophony of cicadas and frogs, Mrs Smith gestures at the Jack Nicklaus–designed greens. With a cheeky grin, I whisper that the only teeing off I have in mind for this weekend will take place between the sheets. Mrs Smith swats me like a mosquito, of which there seems to be a welcome lack for such an aquatic setting.

We pull up at the most distant and obviously jammiest tent on the property – the enormous deck boasts a private view of the largest pond. Mrs Smith flits about gushing over the accoutrements of our cavernous canvas cocoon: 'Ooh, look darling, a Nespresso machine! *Loving* the living-room sofa-bed – that's just what we need in our home theatre so the four of us can curl up together. OMG, the bathroom's bigger than our apartment, and – wow! – just how big can a tub be? The kids would go splash-happy swimming in it!' I gently remind her that this weekend is all about the two of us and celebrating the fact that we don't have to worry about little people drowning. On cue, our private butler deftly offers lemongrass-infused chilled towels and watermelon juice, before beating a hasty retreat.

A tropical downpour and a steamy siesta later, Mrs Smith and I saunter out in shades and sarongs to cool off in the infinity pool. Now wherever there's a pool, there's a childhood comfort-food craving for French fries, right? Alas, my little mermaid pouts when she is told the

restaurant only serves Thai food, since the resort is promoting a truly 'authentic experience' (as opposed to the ubiquitous wannabe Italian or cowboy outlets in this region). But Khun Su, the super waitress, suggests crispy crab spring rolls instead and disappoint they do not. Skinny sticks the circumference of my pinkie and length of my forearm arrive filled with juicy crabmeat and a delicate whisper of chopped chives and coriander. They don't last long and are perfectly paired with icy glasses of local red grape juice.

Post-dip, Mrs Smith slopes off for an in-room massage while at Mist bar I enjoy a vodka tonic and endless vistas of the golf course and mountains. After an hour, I head back to indulge in a pre-arranged, complimentary milk and rose petal bath drawn by our butler. Lights dimmed and candles flickering, Mrs Smith shyly slips in and I follow suit.

Our appetites now reaching a ravenous crescendo, we decide to order in. Mrs Smith, now craving red meat,

almost pulls a diva when she's told that the Western room-service menu, which the staff has neglected to remove, is no longer available. Once again super Su comes to the rescue and offers to golf-buggy over a steak from the grill at sister property Muthi Maya. It takes a while, but we snack on more crispylicious spring rolls and pop open some champagne in the interim while watching neon-green fireflies on the terrace. When the steak arrives, it is sublime.

The next morning, we awaken to the sound of angels' trumpets falling on our canvas roof. We peek outside and giggle like coy newlyweds when we see that Mother Nature has strewn our path with white blossoms. The ensuing day is a blur of bliss.

Before we know it, our Smith stay is drawing to an end. We never did go on that highly recommended night safari in the Khao Yai National Park, nor did we trek the hills. And forget about the local markets, we couldn't get enough of our tent! If you're looking for a clandestine escape, Kirimaya scores a hole in one. We'll certainly be back, both with and without the kids. Actually, after our 48 hours here, I've a growing concern that we might be returning with two plus one next year.

Reviewed by Krissada Clapp

NEED TO KNOW

Rooms 64, including 11 suites.

Rates THB9,000–THB33,000, including buffet breakfast. Excludes seven per cent tax and 10 per cent service charge.

Check-out Noon, or any time until 6pm for an extra half-day rate, subject to availability. Check-in, 2pm.

Facilities Jack Nicklaus-designed 18-hole golf course with clubhouse, locker rooms, pro shop, personal butler, WiFi throughout, CD/DVD library, gym, spa. In rooms: flatscreen TV, CD/DVD players, minibar.

Poolside The infinity pool with lush mountain backdrop is serenity itself.

Children They're more than welcome, and will adore forays into the national park to spot exotic wildlife. Baby cots are free and extra beds for older kids cost THB1,400 a night.

Also The rustic surrounds of Maya Spa are a sensual backdrop for pampering treatments. If you're seeking peace, book a stay during the week, as weekends are popular with city-weary Bangkokians and things can get busy.

IN THE KNOW

Our favourite rooms Play *Out of Africa* in one of the romantic Tented Villas. The canvas exterior belies the elegant luxury within. Decor is a simple yet comfortable mix of natural textures and colonial-style furniture, with a massive sunken spa pool at its centre. With a private deck and mountain vistas, this is safari-chic at its sexiest.

Hotel bar Inspired by a wildlife hideout, but with sleek leather chairs and charcoal sofas, the Mist bar is a minimalist, masculine spot for afternoon tea or an evening cocktail, with killer views of the national park. Try the resort's own take on a lychee martini, called the Smile of Khao Yai.

Hotel restaurant Graze on a menu of modern Thai and international food at the open-sided, high-ceilinged Acala Restaurant, overlooking the lake and golf course. Above is the Mist, an intimate venue serving Japanese cuisine. At the clubhouse, T-Grill is a safari-style steakhouse, complete with faux leopard-skin seats.

Top table The corner table closest to the golf course at Acala is best for views and a cool breeze.

Room service 6am to midnight (last orders at 11pm), with a range of tasty Thai treats.

Dress code Ralph Lauren khakis and Nicole Farhi linens to get into safari mode.

Local knowledge Under three hours' drive from Bangkok, the jaw-dropping scenery and wildlife of Khao Yai National Park aren't to be missed. Look out for elephants (your best chance of seeing them is on a night safari), deer, Asiatic bears, gibbons, macaques and four varieties of hornbill. There are even tigers, although they are rarely seen. The concierge can organise guided hikes, safaris, mountain biking, birdwatching and elephant trekking, either in the park or close by.

LOCAL EATING AND DRINKING

Guests at Kirimaya can also eat at sister resort Muthi Maya's Italian eatery Myth Bar & Restaurant, a five-minute drive away, and charge it to their room. It might be casual but the inspired menu blending Thai and Western cuisines at Khrua Khao Yai (+66 (0)44 297 138) is extraordinarily popular. It's hard to believe that Thailand has a burgeoning wine industry, but around Khao Yai a couple of wineries exist growing chenin blanc and syrah. Have lunch overlooking the vineyards at PB Valley Winery's Great Hornbill Grill (+66 (0)36 226 415/416). International and Thai dishes are served either on the terrace or in the air-conditioned restaurant.

GET A ROOM!

For more information, or to book this hotel, go to www.mrandmrssmith.com – our expert team can take care of all your travel arrangements. Register your Smith membership card to enjoy exclusive offers and privileges.

 SMITH MEMBER OFFER A bottle of wine; 20 per cent off all food, drink and spa treatments; and 50 per cent off green fees.

Kirimaya 1/3 Moo 6, Thanarat Road, Moo-Si, Pakchong, Nakorn Ratchasima 30130, Thailand (+66 (0)44 426 000; www.kirimaya.com)

KOH SAMUI

COASTLINE Beloved bays and beaches
COAST LIFE Sun-worshipping, bar-hopping

Cellophane-clear waters, pastel coral beds, beaches overhung with impossibly green palm fronds... With raw ingredients like these, it's no surprise that Koh Samui is considered one of the world's best holiday destinations. Phuket's more relaxed sibling is a sun-blessed, moon-struck altar to carefree living: once a party-pleasure centre for the backpacker crowd, Samui has grown into a sophisticated tropical retreat. And while a stay here is all about admiring aquamarine seascapes and monolith-strewn shores, there are outlying islands, picturesque waterfalls and densely forested hills to refresh the beach-bored. Thailand's third largest island may come to regret its popularity, but with a little effort, it's still possible to find that idyllic paradise beach.

GETTING THERE

Planes Largely open-air and with a flower-lined runway, Samui's teak-beamed airport is certainly one of a kind. Operated by the hip, Hawaiian-shirt-wearing people at Bangkok Airways (www.bangkokair.com), it receives the airline's regional jets from Bangkok, Phuket, Singapore and Hong Kong, among others. Thai Airways also flies from Bangkok (www.thaiairways.com).

Trains There's a comfortable sleeper service, with two-person first-class cabins, from Bangkok to Surat Thani, which links up with a bus-and-boat connection to Samui (www.railway.co.th).

Boats If you have time to spare, you might want to take a Seatran Ferry (www.seatranferry.com) from the mainland to one of three ports on Koh Samui, but be prepared for confusing timetables and the possibility of a rather long trip (it takes between one and three hours in dry season, depending on the boat). Once on Samui it's easy to get ferries and longtail boats to neighbouring islands.

Automobiles A car or jeep is essential if you want to explore; the Tawee Ratpakdee ring road follows the island's perimeter, so getting around is child's play. If you prefer two wheels, there are plenty of cheap motorbikes to hire, but there are also plenty of injured tourists: get a helmet, don't wear flip-flops, and take things slowly.

LOCAL KNOWLEDGE

Taxis Cabs cruise around the more populous areas of the island. Meters are installed but their purpose seems to be primarily decorative, so agree on a fare beforehand.

Siesta and fiesta As on most tropical islands, regard for timekeeping is scant. Most hotels and large restaurants will operate regular hours, but you'll find the more local establishments open late in the afternoons.

Do go/don't go Koh Samui has two high seasons – from May to November and from January to March – both producing a high number of sunburnt bodies and motorbike mishaps. It's still pleasantly sunny during the off-peak periods, but be prepared for rain.

Packing tips Bermudas, singlets, bikinis and sundresses are de rigueur. Flip-flopping is acceptable everywhere. Make sure you're armed with insect repellent: Samui has some very single-minded mosquitoes.

Recommended reads You'll have heard of Alex Garland's paradise-lost tale, *The Beach*, much of which is based on nearby Koh Phan Ngan. Try sci-fi escapism with *The Chronoliths* by Robert Charles Wilson, or track down a copy of Carol Hollinger's *Mai Pen Rai Means Never Mind* for an engaging insight into Thai culture through the eyes of a 1960s expat.

Local specialities As you'd expect from any fishing community, flipping-fresh seafood is particularly noteworthy; look out for sour and spicy fish soup, prawns with tamarind, and local oysters from mainland Surat Thani. There's also an abundance of coconuts thanks to the prolific palms – delicious when paired with chilli, chicken, coriander and lemongrass in *tom kha gai* soup. The dining scene is diverse and surprisingly sophisticated, owing much to the diligence of the Samui Culinary Circle, an association of idea- and ingredient-sharing chefs and caterers (www.siamdiningguide.com).

Also If the fantastic fresh Thai food whets your appetite, learn how to cook or take a fruit-carving class at the Samui Institute of Culinary Arts (+66 (0)77 413 434; www.sitca.net).

WORTH GETTING OUT OF BED FOR

Viewpoint Charter a private boat with Tours Koh Samui (www.tourskohsamui.com) and discover the hidden coves and dramatic limestone caves of Ang Thong Marine National Park, a 42-island archipelago north-west of Samui. Stop at Mae Ko Island and make the 40-minute climb to Thale Noi, an inland saltwater lake on the mountainside: dramatic views make it worth the effort.

Arts and culture Koh Samui's indigenous population has a strong Muslim background, so the characteristic Buddhist architecture that defines much of the mainland is less in evidence here. That said, Samui does boast the 12m-high 'Big Buddha' at Wat Phra Yai, an enormous golden statue of the seated Buddha: cross the footbridge to the tiny islet (although you may even be able to spot it as you fly into Samui airport).

Activities Take the pachyderm express to the top of a waterfall: water cascades over purple rocks at Samui's tallest and most impressive cascade, Na Muang, and an elephant trek with Na Muan Safari Park (+66 (0)77 424 098) provides a breezy shortcut to the falls' upper tier. For the even more adventurous, Canopy Adventures in Bophut can take you on a treetop-to-treetop tour of the jungle, swinging along 500m of cable (+66 (0)77 414 150; www.canopyadventuresthailand.com).

Best beach Choeng Mon is possibly the prettiest and most romantic beach in Samui, with none of the chaotic commercialism of popular sunspots such as Chaweng. The waters are among the calmest around the island.

Daytripper Wonderful watersports are in plentiful supply here, but snorkelling and diving top the bill: explore the scintillating under-sea scene at Ang Thong or Koh Tao on a boat trip with 100 Degrees East (+66 (0)77 246 936;

www.100degreeseast.com) or the Dive Academy (+66 (0)77 427 339; www.thediveacademysamui.com).

Children Most of the snorkelling or kayaking trips are suitable for over-eights. There is plenty more to do and see, including the Samui Aquarium and Tiger Zoo (www.samuiaquariumandtigerzoo.com) and the nearby Na Tien Butterfly Garden. The bowling alley and cinema at Tesco Lotus (+66 (0)77 245 400) offer air-conditioned respite and Jungle Minigolf at Choeng Mon is fun for a couple of hours (+66 (0)81 787 9148).

Walks Skip the tourist haunts and gain a peek into traditional island life at Laem Set on Samui's relatively undeveloped southern tip. From this quiet stretch of sand, you can meander through coconut plantations and visit the Muslim fishing community of Ban Hua Thanon, before sampling fresh-as-you-like seafood.

Shopping Samui wasn't made with shoppers in mind. The usual beach garb, pirated DVDs and souvenirs are easily available along the Chaweng stretch. Cute bikini boutique Life's A Beach (+66 (0)77 422 630) carries a wide range of Aussie brands, including Wahine and Seafolly. For more upmarket spending opportunities, Lara Shopping Plaza (+66 (0)77 231 631) houses international brand outlets such as Lacoste, Geox and Nautica. Siddharta at the Fishermen's Village in Bophut (+66 (0)77 245 014) sells hippie-luxe fisherman's pants, beach dresses, jewellery and bags. Visit the Naga Pearl Shop in Thong Krut and they'll take you to see their pearl farm on Matsum, just offshore, but if you go you will be expected to buy.

Something for nothing A quaint air of bohemia still lingers at Bophut's Fisherman's Village, once a favoured backpacker haunt and now one of the most perfectly preserved places on the island. Take a leisurely stroll down the street lined with old wooden Chinese shop houses now home to fashionable bars, restaurants and tiny stores selling quirky knick-knacks. **Don't go home without...** treating your body as a temple: Samui is Thailand's holistic haven and if you're looking to spa, detox or enjoy your best-ever massage, this is the place to do it. Bliss out at Kamalaya Spa (www.kamalaya.com); the site is built around an ancient spiritual cave-retreat for Buddhist monks. Spend the day recharging and then fill up on the fresh organic cuisine from in-house restaurant Soma. Alternatively, hit the Alchemy tea bar and treat yourself to one of the ambrosial tonics based on ancient Taoist, Thai and Ayurvedic recipes.

CHAOTICALLY KOH SAMUI

It's impossible to miss the posters for the Full Moon Party when in Samui. Once a lunar month, nearly 20,000 visitors take the 50-minute ferry ride to neighbouring Koh Pha Ngan, disembarking into a hedonistic party whirlwind. It's an experience in itself, whether you're young at heart or just plain curious. Smart hoteliers have also begun chartering boats to take you out and back for a short glimpse of the party – long enough to have a little fun, but not so long that you feel stranded; we recommend one of these abbreviated journeys for those who want to see what all the fuss is about without your fun turning into a feat of endurance.

DIARY

April Songkran, the Thai New Year, sees revellers making merry by throwing water at each other. **May–June** The Koh Samui Regatta draws the world's top yachtsmen for a week of passionate sailing (www.samuiregatta.com). **July** The Avis Samui Tennis Open brings keen racketsmiths to the courts. **August** The Fisherman's Village Festival is the focus of five days of festivity, with live musical performances by Thai bands in the spirit of Woodstock. **5 December** HM the King's birthday, which is celebrated nationwide as a public holiday and Thai Father's Day.

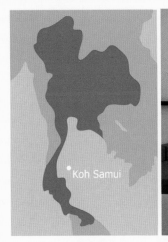 

Koh Samui

The Library

STYLE Novel beach hideaway
SETTING Swinging Chaweng

'Believers that the first meal of the day is the most important will especially love the Library. "Breakfast culture" is its official label, but no eye-rolling please – this mighty spread is worthy of a marketing-spiely big-up'

'What's black and white and red all over?' I ask Mr Smith in our taxi on the 10-minute ride from Koh Samui airport to our beachside retreat. He groans. 'I'm referring to the decor,' I tell him. 'Bet you can read me like a book...' Mr Smith is bored with my puns and we're not even at the Library yet.

Blood-red pool, sleek Macs and monochrome suites referred to as 'pages' are just some of our destined den's design headlines. I'm a sucker for the witty literature theme, but will too many book-related gimmicks relegate the hotel to Mr Smith's form-over-function folder? I suggest a round of word association. 'When I say "library", you think...?' 'Hushed,' mutters Mr Smith looking out the window at Chaweng's main drag, a scrum of DVD, Hello Kitty T-shirt and knock-off Havaianas stalls. 'Full of bookish types...' he says ogling bar girls and good-time seekers. Another sigh.

Seasoned seen-it-done-it travellers might sniff at the mention of Chaweng Beach; as someone who stayed

here in a few-bahts-a-night beach hut two decades ago it is undeniably developed. Ducking signs for Häagen-Dazs and Starbucks, we swerve around a couple of parked mopeds and into a discreet grey driveway. Spying the pin-drop-peaceful lobby and one of the beachside sanctuary's white reading figurines, it's as though we've been teleported to a modern art gallery. At the risk of facing a travel writers' tribunal under cliché charges, I declare it an oasis.

'Sawadee,' chorus three gentlefolk at reception before handing us refreshing chilled facecloths and tiny bowls of orange sorbet. Given our 'page' key (with its pencil-like attachment – nothing humdrum here), we head past the tall grey wall and follow the discreet decking through bright green grass to our quarters in the lower half of one of the shuttered white cubes. Beyond, a ruby pool glistens, backdropped only by sparkling sapphire sea.

Pausing in our sleek black-floored suite just long enough to fling on swimwear, we manage to transform it from

minimalist to ransacked. Yelps of delight are elicited
by the huge sexy white computer, a shiny espresso
machine and a giant flatscreen TV, and we concur it's
more *American Psycho* film set than the ensuite-less
shack we last bunked in on this beach. Mr Smith
wonders what director Mary Harron would make of
that blood-coloured pool. Bret Easton Ellis–inspired
serial-killer scenes may sound a tad jarring when
celebrating a boutique paradise in a Buddhist
country, but that crimson tide is pretty bonkers.

Our next debate is less controversial. Should we
beanbag it poolside or on white powdery sand?
Sun-creamed and flopped on a Fatboy, another perk
to our Chaweng location is revealed: the people-
watching. Mr Smith is distracted by a pert, well-
endowed Signora Smith – wow. She's oblivious to the
notion that it's not terribly Thai to bust out naturist
tendencies in flagrante. Meanwhile, I'm ogling a
sunburnt couple – ouch! Frolicking in the crystal-
clear sea a few hotels down, they're redder than our
pool. A few two-for-one glasses of happy-hour rosé
later and we're still glued to our big black beanbags,
but by now it's the pastel-hued sunset that has our
eyes on stalks.

Now, what's not an obvious complement to this
grown-up library-themed playground? Try adding
a boisterous toddler. Nervous that we're busting the
relaxing vibe for the pairs of Mr and Mrs Smiths
either side of us, instead of irritated glances, we are
treated to an excellent kids' menu and sandcastle-
building pool boys. We succumb to our giant poolside
cushions and paperbacks while Junior Smith splashes
in the shallow end. The purchase of fresh coconuts
from beach sellers is the only activity to winch us
from our prone state.

Sure we came to Koh Samui with great plans to
visit the Big Buddha at Wat Phra Yai, Bophut fishing
village and take elephant rides in Lamai, but with
the Library's sleek gym and book- and DVD-lined
relaxation rooms, we're spoiled for distractions.
Simply finding all the inspired touches in our
bedroom keeps one afternoon occupied. (Top of
the attention-to-detail league table are magnetic
icons as do-not-disturb signs, secret snack jars in

the outdoor living room and his 'n' hers monochrome flip-flops to keep.) Little wonder our fellow guests – a mixture of European arty types and friendly well-to-do Asian families – stray from their parasol-shaded, red-towel-covered beanbags only to pad over to Page restaurant for some of the island's finest Thai cuisine. (The evening take on tapas is particularly inspired.) Feeling intrepid, on our second night we take those two steps to the beach, turn right and end up at flower-filled Eat Sense for aromatic *kaeng* (curries) and spicy *nams* (sauces) all as prettily presented as the restaurant and its gardens.

Believers that the first meal of the day is the most important will especially love the Library. 'Breakfast culture' is its official label, but no eye-rolling please – this mighty spread is worthy of a marketing-spiely big-up. A slender tray with creatively cut fruit, a dainty basket of pastries and shot glasses of smoked salmon and artichoke tips and delicately diced fruit salad have me reaching for my camera. With this to look forward to, we don't even mind our little one waking us up early. All this (plus cooked-to-perfection eggs) is washed down with a first-class cappuccino and a view of that gorgeous blonde beach. So smug are we, that we actually enjoy an occasional plane overhead – it's a welcome reminder some poor blighters are off home while we're only a few chapters into our epic boutique break. OK, Mr Smith, I'll pack the puns in. But you have to admit, this trip's been a proper page-turner. I'm just not sure I ever want to get to the ending...

Reviewed by Juliet Kinsman

NEED TO KNOW

Rooms 13 suites (ground floor) and 13 studios (upstairs).

Rates Smart Studios, THB12,600–THB14,000; Exotic Suites, THB14,400–THB16,000, including breakfast; excludes taxes at 18 per cent.

Check-out Noon, but flexible subject to availability. Earliest check-in, 2pm.

Facilities Spa, gym, library (naturally), DVD/CD selection, free WiFi in the restaurant, library and pool area. In rooms: huge flatscreen TV, CD/DVD player, wireless headphones, coffee maker, minibar. Suites have Macs with broadband.

Poolside Looking out over the beach and the bay, the Library's eye-catching pool is lined with vivid scarlet Italian tiles, coloured to match the parasols and loungers on the wooden decking that surround it.

Children Under-12s stay free in their parents' room; cots (free) and extra beds (THB2,500 a night) can be provided. There's a children's pool, and an assortment of beach-based activities on offer. Babysitting costs THB250 an hour.

Also After check-out, guests can leave their luggage in storage and use the shower facilities at the Fit (fitness unit) to go sandlessly from beach to airport.

IN THE KNOW

Our favourite rooms The Bookmark Suite is closest to the beach and affords fabulous views of the sea and the ruby swimming pool from the comfort of the bed. All suites have Jacuzzis to bliss out in.

Hotel bar The Page restaurant's beach bar is a modern-minded chill-out zone, serving mean mojitos and zingy, zesty lychee caprioskas to a soothing soundtrack of Buddha-Bar-esque tunes.

Hotel restaurant The Page restaurant sources organic, seasonal ingredients to produce a sophisticated range of Thai and Western dishes, which you can savour alfresco on the deck, or in the high-ceilinged, soft-grey indoor dining area.

Top table Secure a spot on the terrace, as close to the sea as you can.

Room service A variety of snacks and meals from the restaurant menu are served between 7am and midnight daily.

Dress code Lazy beach garb all the way – with perhaps a summer dress or shirt upgrade for dinner.

Local knowledge Leave your holiday reading at home. The Library lives up to its name, with hundreds of titles available to leaf through, as well as a wide selection of DVDs.

LOCAL EATING AND DRINKING

Charming Italian chef Francesco Vitagliano cooks up a fine selection of traditional rustic dishes at elegant Chaweng restaurant Bellini (+66 (0)77 413 831), at Soi Colibri, Chaweng South, 46/24-26, Moo 3, Tambon Bo Phut. Pizzas, pastas and seafood are all rendered with flair. At Chaweng South 43/04-5, cool, casual Betelnut (+66 (0)77 230 222) is run by an American chef who likes to cook a collision of Thai and Californian cuisine. Check out stylish restaurant Guapa (+66 (0)897 230 222), at nearby 46/12, has an impressive wine selection, quality cocktails and an innovative tapas menu created by Betelnut's chef. Eat Sense (+66 (0) 77 414 242) for an exquisite menu of authentic, healthy Thai food. Starfish & Coffee (+66 (0)77 427 201) – not the most obvious bedfellows – but this quirky café at 51/7, Moo 1, in Tambon Bo Phut, makes them seem the most natural of marriages, recreating Mediterranean chic within its brick walls. Nosh aside, this inimitable joint offers massages and boasts an attached boutique.

GET A ROOM!

For more information, or to book this hotel, go to www.mrandmrssmith.com – our expert team can take care of all your travel arrangements. Register your Smith membership card to enjoy exclusive offers and privileges.

 SMITH MEMBER OFFER A bottle of sparkling wine on arrival. Members booking a suite will also get free airport transfers; members staying five nights will be treated to a romantic dinner for two at the Page.

The Library 14/1 Moo 2, Bo Phut, Chaweng Beach, Koh Samui, Suratthani 84320, Thailand
(+66 (0)77 422 767; www.thelibrary.co.th)

Koh Samui

YL Residence No. 17

STYLE Miami meets Samui
SETTING Secluded south-east

'Is it just me or does everything taste better when you have an uninterrupted view of an azure ocean and the morning breeze is heavy with the smell of frangipani?'

Being hit on the noggin by a two kilogram coconut hurtling to earth is not an event you want happening on your tropical vacation. At YL Residence No. 17, management has a unique method of ensuring that such unfortunate incidents never occur. Every three months or so, a specially trained simian hit squad scampers up the coconut palms on command to wiggle free any possible projectiles. Junior Smith's jaw drops at the idea of such aerial monkey business, but unfortunately the palms have been recently denuded and aren't due for their next stripping for some time. We can't believe our bad luck at missing the primate performance.

Thankfully, that's the only thing this happy band of Smiths is going to miss out on for the next couple of days. YL is an architecturally designed estate that covers almost six hectares of prime beachfront on the island of Koh Samui's least developed stretch of the south-east coast. Less a hotel than an extensive luxury home, its original media mogul owner relaunched it as a superb example of the ultimate luxury holiday digs. You see, although there are 10 exquisite villas that can quite easily accommodate 20 adults, YL Residence only takes one booking at a time. Usually it's for weddings, ultra-special private events or parties, but here we are – Mr Smith, our nine-year-old daughter and myself – with the mind-blowing room in which to run riot and a staff of 16 to carry out our every wish. Is it too late to phone our friends and have them join us?

On arrival, having swept past a saluting guard and manicured lawns, we're greeted with a bottle of chilled Piper-Heidsieck, partnered with fresh dragon fruit, by the pool. Followed by an hour-long massage, our entry to YL World is stupefyingly special. The place is chic but informal, elegant but intimate.

Dawn breaks the next day and, from the comfort of our bed, Mr Smith raises the electronic blinds to unveil the sunrise. We snooze – there is some early-morning chatter about taking a dip in the pool or a possible stroll along the beach, but we default to flop mode – before sending for breakfast in bed. Is it just me or does everything taste better when you have an uninterrupted view of an azure ocean and the morning breeze is heavy with the smell of frangipani?

Food is certainly one of the highlights at YL. Within 20 minutes of our arrival, we'd had our first of several meetings with head chef Reuben, who wanted to know our likes, dislikes, preferred meal times and the style in which we wish to dine. There are both à la carte and bespoke options available. The former is particularly useful if your over-relaxed brain will only allow you to point at words on a page. If you are hankering for something more off-piste, however, all you need do is ask.

One evening, Junior Smith decides all she fancies for dinner is a ham sandwich. It arrives with real ham and cheese, fresh local lettuce, ripe tomato and home-made mayonnaise piled atop thick freshly baked bread. Held together with miniature spears bearing tiny seashell knobs, the edible artwork is accompanied by crisp fries carefully arranged into a sculptural grid and tomato sauce for dunking. It is declared excellent; pretty enough to impress, but not too intimidating to scoff. If you're a gourmet traveller, you can also cook for yourself and your villa guests – there's a full stainless-steel kitchen with temperature-controlled wine cabinet – or you can learn to prepare a meal with one of the resident chefs. We are now dab hands at whipping up *tom yum goong* (lemongrass and prawn soup), *gaeng kiew wan gai* (green chicken curry) and Thai spring rolls.

It may come as no surprise that water is a key theme in these parts. The beachside infinity pool with conveniently located pool house – and Tong, the fabulous barman – becomes an overwhelming magnet for us. It is long enough for laps but takes on a new life at night when tiny fibre-optic lights embedded within the tiles assume the illusion of a constellation.

The service is understandably impeccable and, this being Thailand, the team are friendly, relaxed and always smiling. A glass of chilled water is never further than arm's length away and our needs are anticipated well before we're even aware of them ourselves. Given almost no warning, staff can arrange yoga and pilates classes, tantalising massages and spa treatments, trips on quad bikes or Sea-Doos, kite surfing, sea-kayaking and just about any other activity you can imagine. We are, however, content to relax in barefoot bliss around the resort. This is just too good...

During the two days we spend at YL, my awareness of many things – minimal flower arrangements and banana, coconut and peanut butter mocktails, for example – is enhanced. Most important, though, is my rediscovery of the idea of bespoke. The service at YL epitomises the best of the 'b' word – with everything from food to tunes tailor made to suit our desires. Other 'b' words that spring to mind are beautiful, blissful and boutique. Apart from missing out on the monkeys, our stay at YL Residence just couldn't be any better.

Reviewed by Helen Bodycomb

NEED TO KNOW

Rooms 10, including one suite, for exclusive hire.

Rates US$3,000 a night, for YL Suite and one Deluxe Studio (up to four guests) up to US$5,000, for YL Suite, three Deluxe Studios and six Studios (up to 20 guests). Excludes seven per cent tax and 10 per cent service charge.

Check-out As long as you're not clashing with other guests, check in and out when you please.

Facilities Personal butler, free WiFi throughout, library with CDs, DVDs and books, kayaks and snorkelling gear, cars with driver, clubhouse, picnic lawn. In rooms: flatscreen TV, stereo, Bose DVD player, minibar and Urb toiletries.

Poolside An inky lap pool stretches between the lawn and beach.

Children Small guests are given the same attention as older ones.

Also Minimum two-night stay. Rates include à la carte breakfast, a bottle of champagne in each bedroom, a massage, complimentary minibar, fruit, flowers, turndown treat, airport transfers, staff and services. Pets and smoking are allowed.

IN THE KNOW

Our favourite rooms When you book, the luxe YL Suite comes as standard (if arriving with friends, put dibs on it early.) With its sumptuous four-poster, separate living room and Smeg kitchen, it's the grandest room. Wherever you sleep, though, the all-white, indoor–outdoor beach-house design and pared-down style will invoke calm, with a contemporary mix of natural rattan, seagrass and reclaimed teak. Revel in the delectable oval bath tubs.

Hotel bar The bar opens at 11am and stays that way until all guests have drifted off to bed. Order any drink you like (mojitos are a must), plug in your iPod or check out the Residence's tunes supplied by friends including Gilles Peterson, Phil Asher and Aaron Ross. For parties or weddings, you can even organise a DJ.

Hotel restaurant The airy beachfront Clubhouse is simply furnished with grey rattan chairs, teak tables and a gourmet kitchen. Slide back the glass doors and let the sea breeze waft in as you graze upon a menu concocted by ex-Necker Island chefs Graham Brundle and Reuben Kimber. Using local and homegrown organic produce, including fresh seafood, they can cater for any diet. The smaller Pool Room has its own bar and is a more intimate spot for lunch or dinner.

Top table With five kitchens, you can choose where to dine: on the beach, lawn, the Clubhouse main suite or your room.

Room service 24 hours. Just ask for whatever you want.

Dress code Bikini, sarong, shorts or linen shirt… wear whatever you would at home if home was a mansion in the tropics.

Local knowledge Water babies rejoice: YL has ocean-going vessels from Sea-Doos to kayaks (a trip to Ang Thong Marine Park, featured in *The Beach*, is our top tip). Snorkel or dive with the Residence's own dive master, or there's kite surfing for adventurous types. On land, enjoy yoga, pilates, bespoke picnics or a massage in the nearby spa.

LOCAL EATING AND DRINKING

At nearby Thai restaurant **Sabingrae** seafood is barbecued on the beach. YL staff will point you in the right direction. Further north the Bophut Fisherman's Village is home to **the Shack** (+66 (0)77 246 041), at 88/33 Moo 1, Tambon Bo Phut. Owned by former New Yorker Larry Snyder, it's known for great steaks, jazz and blues. Glam global club **Nikki Beach** (+66 (0)77 914 500) pulls in the island's beautiful people for all-day dining and waterside lounging at sunset.

GET A ROOM!

For more information, or to book this hotel, go to www.mrandmrssmith.com – our expert team can take care of all your travel arrangements. Register your Smith membership card to enjoy exclusive offers and privileges.

 SMITH MEMBER OFFER A cocktail and a Thai tapas party, and an Urb spa gift for all guests.

YL Residence No. 17 117 Moo 2, Tambon Maret, Koh Samui, Suratthani 84310, Thailand (+66 80 519 2988; www.ylresidence.com)

PHANG NGA

COASTLINE Andaman marineland
COAST LIFE Ducking and diving

Imagine the perfect beach and Phang Nga can probably beat it.
This postcard-spectacular south-western Thai province hugs the
Andaman Sea, with crystal-clear waters and jaw-dropping bays
giving way to sheer limestone cliffs and dense tropical jungle.
On land, the region nurtures mangrove ecosystems and ancient
primary rainforest; offshore, the Similan and Surin islands
beckon with some of the world's most gasp-worthy dive spots.
Exuding a laid-back vibe, Phang Nga's hub – and diving jump-off
point – coastal Khao Lak lacks the razzle-dazzle of Phuket
and Krabi, but that's just the way visitors like it. Sun-soakers,
nature-lovers and thrill-seekers won't fail to be awestruck.

GETTING THERE

Planes Fly into Phuket International Airport (www.
phuketairportonline.com), just south of Phang Nga
province, on Phuket island. Connecting from Bangkok is
a cinch due to the many domestic and regional carriers
plying the route. Arrange a transfer north to the mainland
with your hotel: Khao Lak is about an hour and a half's
drive up Highway 4; Phang Nga Bay is around an hour
to the north-east.

Trains Thailand may have a natty rail service but this
region has been sadly neglected. You can catch an
overnight train from Bangkok (www.railway.co.th) to
Surat Thani, but you'll then need to grab a bus west
into Phang Nga (it's a 150km drive to Khao Lak).

Boats If you're arriving from Phuket, you can grab a boat
to Ko Yao Yai and Ko Yao Noi islands in Phang Nga Bay:
hop aboard at Bang Rong pier on the north-east coast.

Automobiles It takes a steady 11–12 hours to drive from
Bangkok to Khao Lak but there are plenty of scenic
stop-offs en route. There's only one road to follow so
it's hard to get lost – or hire a driver to take the strain.

LOCAL KNOWLEDGE

Taxis Outside of resort areas, you're more likely to find
motorcycle taxis (for short hops), tuk tuks and shared
jeep-style pick-up trucks rather than regular taxis. You

can rent motorbikes too – owing to strict fines for not
wearing a helmet, Khao Lak has a lower accident record
than elsewhere, although you still ride at your own risk.

Siesta and fiesta Most folk come to Phang Nga for
adventure or to unwind, so it's all about early nights
and dawn starts. Shops, bars and restaurants follow
suit – it's rare to find anywhere that stays open much
later than 10pm.

Do go/don't go Sunshine is an everyday occurrence from
November to April, when waters are clear and calm. Low
season (May–October) can be a little stormy and wet on
the Northern Andaman Coast, but you'll find it much
quieter – to the point where it can seem a tad deserted.
If you're diving at the Similan Islands National Marine
Park aim for December to May (it closes mid-May–early
November due to rough seas).

Packing tips If you plan on flopping beachside, stock
up on books and magazines before you arrive as they're
quite rare in these parts. The laid-back diving culture
extends to the dress code.

Recommended reads Edited by Robin Nagy, *Children
of the Tsunami: Khao Lak – A Story of Hope* is an
absorbing and often heart-wrenching collection of
stories, poems and pictures by kids who were affected
by the region's 2004 tragedy.

Local specialities The Andaman Sea is awash with delicious seafood – whether you order it grilled, steamed or fried, your tastebuds will thank you. Southern Thai cuisine tends to be sweeter and spicier than that found in the rest of the country, with a distinct Muslim influence. One popular dish is earthy *massaman* curry, usually made with beef, potatoes and peanuts. *Khao yum* is a healthy mix of cooked rice, lemongrass, chilli, lime, dried coconut and a syrupy fish sauce – it's a traditional breakfast, but makes for an equally desirable lunch.
Also Phang Nga province is a melting pot of Buddhist, Muslim, Chinese and sea gypsy communities and, unlike further south in the country, they coexist here with very little angst.

WORTH GETTING OUT OF BED FOR

Viewpoint Phang Nga Bay's Koh Phing Kan, dubbed James Bond Island, made a splash with 007 in *The Man with the Golden Gun*. The sheer limestone cliffs are a breathtaking sight. That also means it's on the tourist trail, so avoid the crowds by chartering a private boat.
Arts and culture There is little in the way of museums and galleries in these parts, but the Ao Phang Nga National Park has several prehistoric rock art sites featuring images of humans, crabs, elephants and other motifs reflecting the region. Khao Khian, also known as Inscription Mountain or Writing Hill, sports drawings of people, crocodiles, dolphins and sharks thought to be around 3,000 years old.
Activities Float or swim, it's all about getting wet in Phang Nga. West coast Khao Lak is the destination for snorkellers and divers who head straight for the nearby Similan Islands. Dive centres outnumber hotels, allowing scuba converts of all skill levels to experience newly discovered reefs and perhaps glimpse rare species. Inland water antics can be found at waterfalls in the surrounding national parks: Namtok Ton Chong Fa, Namtok Lam Ru and Namtok Ton Sai can be reached on foot, or by kayak.
Best beach Please, don't make us choose! In a region that's defined by its glorious beaches, everyone can find their idea of seaside heaven. South of Bang Sak, the fine coral-sand strip of Cape Pakorang – loved by surfers for its reef break – is quieter than its neighbours, and Koh Kho Khao, just off the coast near Takuapa, offers the quintessential desert island escape. In Ao Phang Nga, you'll find unspoilt shorelines, plus great bay views.

Daytripper Similan Islands National Marine Park is one of the world's top dive sites and its amazing topography makes it an aquatic adventure for both beginners and experienced divers. Its nine islands, 60km west of Phang Nga's coast, offer pristine beaches and snorkelling. Organise a daytrip or longer 'live-aboard' foray (try Sea Dragon: www.seadragondivecenter.com).
Children Older kids will get a kick out of jungletastic Khao Sok National Park, east of Takuapa, which will wow with ancient rainforest and sheer limestone mountains. Eco Khao Lak (www.khaolakholiday.com) and Phuket Trekking Club (www.phukettrekkingclub.com) both accompany adventurers into Khao Sok, with activities from elephant safaris to canoeing on the Sok River.
Walks Khao Lak-Lam Ru National Park, south of Khao Lak, has walks suitable for all ages and energy levels, with lush vegetation, hidden beaches, sea cliffs and striking peaks reaching up to 1,050m. Bring your camera for close-ups of the local inhabitants including flying lemurs, macaques, hornbills and tapirs.
Perfect picnic Sitting on the fringe of the Khao Lak-Lam Ru National Park is a restaurant shaded by a canopy of tropical green with peek-a-boo views of limestone cliffs. BYO picnic and perch nearby or dine on some of the freshest seafood around.
Shopping Phang Nga is more about beach-hopping than hot shopping, but the street market held in the charming town of Takuapa every Sunday, between November and April, offers a water-free diversion.

Something for nothing In the aftermath of the Boxing Day tsunami in 2004, it soon became obvious that the Phang Nga coastline was the worst hit in Thailand. Around 6,000 people were killed, mostly in the Thai Muang, Khao Lak, Bang Niang and Ban Sak regions. There's a fitting memorial to those who lost their lives at fishing village Ban Nam Khem north of Khao Lak that is worth a look.

Don't go home without... visiting the turtle sanctuary at Thai Muang National Park (www.thailandecoportal.com), south of Khao Lak, which monitors the region's four species of marine turtles. Dating back to pre-dinosaur times, these creatures are among the oldest and rarest to inhabit the planet, but their existence is threatened by over-fishing and development. From December to February, you can visit the beach after dark, accompanied by a ranger, to watch females lay their eggs in the sand. Then, for seven magical days during March, hatchlings are released back into the sea.

PEACEFULLY PHANG NGA

There are few places left in Thailand that retain an untouched, undiscovered air, yet the Khao Lak coast in Phang Nga is far less developed than other Andaman hotspots, and any recent building work has been carefully monitored. Although it's beginning to make a bigger bleep on the tourist radar, this gorgeous southern province still offers a tranquil escape from modern life.

DIARY

January/February Chinese New Year is celebrated by Chinese-Thai families in the region. March For seven days, usually the first week of the month, hundreds of baby turtles are released into the sea at Thai Muang Beach. April The Songkran water festival – Thai New Year – brings partying to Phang Nga. The Chao Ley (sea gypsy) village on Ko Surin Tai Island holds the three-day Loy Rua (floating boat) Festival during the full moon of this month to honour their ancestors. October The local Chinese community forgoes meat during the Vegetarian Festival.

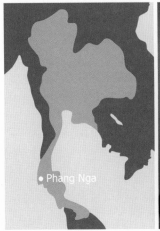

Phang Nga

Aleenta
Phuket-Phang Nga

STYLE Sleek seaside sugar cubes
SETTING Sultry Siam shores

'By itself on a beautiful, empty coastline, this
hotel places the accent firmly on privacy...
no need to mingle with anyone other than your
very own Mr or Mrs Smith unless you want to'

Dear reader, a warning: this review is not going to be a whirlwind of adventurous escapades or filled with non-stop activity; in fact, the next few pages are going to be about mostly doing nothing. If doing nothing, however, sounds ideal to you, I can recommend no better spot to do it in than Aleenta Phuket–Phang Nga.

By itself on a beautiful and completely empty stretch of coastline just north of Phuket, this inviting hotel places the accent firmly on privacy. There's no central pool area, no buffet breakfasts – no need to mingle with anyone other than your very own Mr or Mrs Smith unless you want to. Aleenta has been designed so that, even if the hotel is full, you feel as though it's your own special place.

And a bit of seclusion is what this stressed-out Mr and Mrs Smith were desperately in need of after a particularly long period of holiday- and sunshine-free time in our hectic working lives. From the moment we hopped into a smart van (the hotel lays on transfers for those who are staying

for three nights or more) to our arrival at the resort, where we were greeted with chilled water and cold scented towels, we knew this would be the perfect place for the two of us to unwind and find some peace. A sunglasses-clad and sunblock-lathered Mr Smith immediately started looking around for the loungers.

First, though, we checked into our room. We were staying in a Beachfront suite – a freestanding villa that comprises one-third of what the resort terms its 'residences'. The other two suites weren't occupied, however, so Mr Smith and I had both the private pool and the spacious communal living area, with its comfy day-beds and huge flatscreen TV, entirely to ourselves. We spent the next half an hour poking around our suite (might as well get the hard work out of the way before we do absolutely nothing for the next 48 hours). Two and a half of the four walls are made entirely of glass, and retract fully to provide instant access to a private beach-facing deck at the front and the secluded pool to the side. Glass is also a feature of the spacious bathroom-cum-dressing room, with enormous windows that allow the sun to bathe the room in glorious orange light. Clever planting outside ensures our modesty is protected at all times. Thank goodness.

The clean, contemporary style of the room certainly appeals to this Mrs Smith (known to everyone in her office – hopefully with affection – as 'the neat freak'). Despite all the transparence and white surfaces, the light wood and natural tones keeps the space from feeling too chilly – Aleenta Phuket–Phang Nga definitely avoids the can't-find-the-door-to-the-bathroom brand of minimalism – and beautifully concealed lighting emphasises the balance of the decor. Despite all the out-and-out luxury, there's also absolutely nothing ostentatious, OTT or 'gold taps' about it all, which sets it apart from plenty of other resorts and hotels in this part of the world.

Though there's a turtle sanctuary, national parks and other such adventures an easy drive away, I'm ashamed to admit we didn't leave the resort. Not once. We lazed by our pool during the day and, on the occasion it got cool enough in the late afternoon, we wandered up the beach with our feet in the surf. In the evenings, we drank Singha beer and played *Jenga* (borrowed from the small library) on our deck. We were spectacularly slothful. The closest we got to 'frenetic' was booking a massage and a yoga lesson in the same phone call.

There are a few local seaside restaurants close to Aleenta that you can head out to for a meal, but there's no need to wander off piste. The hotel's stylish Restaurant offered a small but perfectly formed menu of Thai, international and well-being focussed food, prepared beautifully by a French chef who was happy to adapt dishes for my fussy vegetarian Mr Smith. He still talks about the handmade spring rolls he devoured on two consecutive nights. We lingered over the wine list and chatted to the lovely staff, all happy to practise their English (Aleenta makes a point of hiring local people, and the resort hosts daily language classes).

Hotel workers have the power to turn a good holiday into a great memory, and the people who brought our drinks, turned down our beds and flapped napkins over our knees at Aleenta were unfailingly accommodating and helpful. The resort claims its staff can guess your future needs. They're not wrong. On arrival, I found myself fretting in that very British way – ie, getting worked up but not daring to complain – about the lack of sun-beds beside our pool. A few minutes later, I looked through our window to see that two panels, complete with towels and cushions, on the deck have been ingeniously lifted to create lounging pads in which Mr Smith and I can stretch out. Amazing: they'd managed to anticipate our plans for our entire stay...

Reviewed by Mr & Mrs Smith

NEED TO KNOW

Rooms 30 – including 15 villas and 15 suites.

Rates THB9,900–THB31,900, including breakfast and a daily yoga lesson; excluding 17 per cent tax and service charge. Check-out Noon. Earliest check-in, 2pm.

Facilities Spa, yoga pavilion, gym, library of CDs and books, boutique, free WiFi throughout. In rooms: preloaded iPod, fridge, minibar, yoga mat, TV and DVD player.

Poolside The Ocean View Lofts have access to a 30m infinity pool overlooking the Andaman Sea. All other suites and villas have private pools.

Children All ages are welcome in the Ocean View Residences and Beachfront Villas, but other villas are for over-12s only. Free baby cots are available upon request.

Also Christmas bookings require a minimum seven-night stay. All year round, Aleenta requests and matches donations of THB40 a day to support the local turtle sanctuary. Ask the hotel to arrange a trip to see hatchlings and rescued turtles.

IN THE KNOW

Our favourite rooms The Ocean View Loft Suites have two floors, double-height ceilings and private sun-decks. For the pinnacle of pampering, go for the presidential Spa Villa, which includes a private pool and Jacuzzi, outdoor lounge and spa treatment room. To lay the luxury on even thicker, engage the services of a private butler and a personal chef.

Hotel bar The relaxed beach bar is an essential stop-off for an alfresco cocktail, and plays chilled-out lounge and jazz music.

Hotel restaurant Choose from Thai and international fusion at the Restaurant, fine-dining with gourmet seafood by the waves at the newer Chef's Table, or light meals and drinks at the Beach Lounge. All vegetables come from the hotel's organic garden.

Top table Request a table on the beach and dine within inches of the ocean.

Room service A selection from the restaurant menus can be served in your room throughout the day until 11pm. After this time until 6am, a smaller menu of drinks and snacks is available.

Dress code Assured but unfussy – light linens and flowing summer dresses; flip-flops or sandals – leave the heels at home.

Local knowledge Swot up on your culinary skills with Aleenta's daily Thai-cookery course, which starts with a chef-led tour of local vegetable markets and culminates in sampling your creations. There are cocktail mixology courses, too. Detox after at Spa IV, where treatments revolve around the sun – and the moon, earth and sea – with ocean views to match. Yoga and thai chi are also favourite pastimes around Aleenta.

LOCAL EATING AND DRINKING

This part of Khao Lak isn't overly endowed with eateries. Rather than upmarket bistros, you're more likely to find roadside shacks nearby, serving up authentic (pretty darn spicy) Thai dishes. Phuket to the south is a different story: try Sunday brunch at the bright and buzzing Oriental Spoon (+66 (0)76 316 500) on Surin Beach Road – you'll need to book. In Surin Beach itself, at 121 Srisonthorn Road, Weaves (+66 (0)76 270 900) is a romantic evening option, with a pan-Asian menu: dine poolside or in the comfort of a private air-conditioned room. Or, discover cool interiors and fantastic fusion-modern Thai food at gastro favourite Lim's (+66 (0)76 344 834), 28 Phrabaramee Soi 7, Kalim Beach. Along the street at number 223/3, Joe's Downstairs (+66 (0)76 618 245) is a sunset-cocktails stop where the crowd are so fashionable, it smarts.

GET A ROOM!

For more information, or to book this hotel, go to www.mrandmrssmith.com – our expert team can take care of all your travel arrangements. Register your Smith membership card to enjoy exclusive offers and privileges.

 SMITH MEMBER OFFER A romantic breakfast with bubbles and a red rose; a magical bath experience for five-night stays; a candlelit dinner for two for seven-night stays.

Aleenta Phuket–Phang Nga Natai Beach, Phang Nga, Phuket, 82140, Thailand (+66 (0)25 148 112; www.aleenta.com)

PHUKET

COASTLINE Mighty mountains, silvery sands
COAST LIFE Farangs, flip-flops and fishing boats

Dropped like a giant pearl into the azure Andaman Sea, Phuket is a textbook tropical paradise of perfect beaches and rainforest-coated cliffs. Jetting in by plane, you'll spy jungle-clad hills twisting across the island like green dragons' spines, and the fringes of development where Phuket is expanding around – and even up – the mountains. Away from the beach, the island's towns and temples offer their own thrills, from the unique Sino-Portuguese architecture of Phuket Town to the hectic tuk tuk-travelled streets of Patong Beach, home to some of Thailand's most dynamic – and infamous – nightlife. Whether you come here for a party, an insight into Buddhist culture, or just the healthy trinity of sand, sun and serenity, you'll find what you're looking for.

GETTING THERE

Planes 30km from Phuket Town, Phuket International Airport (www.phuketairportonline.com) is Thailand's second busiest after Bangkok, with charter flights connecting to dozens of destinations.

Trains There are no trains to Phuket. Buses travel from the Southern Bus Terminal in Thonburi, Bangkok, but the journey is a back-straining 14 hours; it makes far more sense to hop on a one-hour no-frills flight.

Automobiles Navigating Phuket by car is manageable with the help of a decent map. Roads can be treacherous though, so don't scrimp on insurance. Motorbike rental is also a possibility, if you can stomach the statistics (10,000 accidents a year).

LOCAL KNOWLEDGE

Taxis Flagging down taxis in Phuket is relatively hassle-free; fares start at THB50. Three-wheeled tuk tuks are everywhere in Patong and Phuket Town, but are becoming expensive. Negotiate a round-trip rate if you'd like one to wait for you while you shop or sightsee; be prepared to pay upwards of THB150 an hour. A cheaper, but slower, option are *songthaews*, which run between the main resort areas and Phuket Town.

Siesta and fiesta Phuket's enthusiastic mercantilism means shops open on time, and will stay open until late into the night. Some cafés and restaurants open as early as 8am to serve the breakfast crowd; and some bars stay open until the wee hours.

Do go/don't go Phuket is most alive during the sunny season, from November to March. Be prepared to pay significantly higher prices for rooms in this period, and make that dinner reservation promptly. When the monsoon lull hits, expect slower service and more irregular opening hours at shops and eateries.

Packing tips Yoga-wear for seaside stretchers. Swimwear, sarongs and sandals will be fine for those who don't plan on anything more strenuous than moonlit strolls or sunbathing on the sand; ocean-going explorers may want to bring kayak-friendly footwear.

Recommended reads Explore Thailand's hidden depths further while you lie supine on the beach: try the excellent *Travelers' Tales Thailand* anthology, or Steve Rosse's short-story collection *Thai Vignettes: Phuket and Beyond*. Adventuring seafarer Fernão Mendes Pinto recalls his 16th-century pan-Asian odyssey in *The Travels of Mendes Pinto*, translated by Rebecca D Catz.

Local specialities Succulent seafood from the Andaman Sea characterises Phuket's menus. Dishes are likely to be barbecued, marinated, and garnished with a medley of herbs and spices. Locally grown pineapples and cashew nuts also feature prominently; stir-fried chicken with cashews (*gai pad med mamuang himmapan*) is a particular favourite. Southern Thais like their food spicier and often add fresh turmeric to curries, giving them a distinctive yellow hue. *Khanom cheen nam ya* – rice noodles soaked with spicy fish-flake soup and served with a plate of fresh vegetables and fruit – is a popular breakfast dish, while the item that most often crops up on beach-bar menus is *pad thai*: egg-fried noodles with chicken or prawns, *nam pla* (fish sauce), chilli, spring onion and a scattering of toasted peanuts.

Also For a true taste of Thai hawker food, head to the colourful night market surrounding the new Robinson's Department Store, where sumptuous spreads of fresh Islamic, Thai and Chinese snacks titillate the palate.

WORTH GETTING OUT OF BED FOR

Viewpoint Perched on a hilltop, the beautiful Wat Chalong, Phuket's most important temple, is located in the south of the island (off bypass road 4021). Alternatively, a seaplane tour with Destination Air (www.destinationair.com) to Krabi or Phi Phi provides breathtaking views of the Andaman Sea.

Arts and culture Phuket Town's Sino-Portuguese architecture is the island's cultural claim to fame, a charming legacy left behind by wealthy Chinese tin miners in the 19th century. Phuket's Town Hall, Provincial Court and Nakorn Luang Bank building are among the most magnificent examples. Along Thalang Road, you'll find Thalang National Museum, the island's most important repository of history and culture. Pay your respects at Wat Prahong in Thalang, where a huge golden Buddha is half-buried in the temple floor – supposedly bestowing a curse on anyone who attempts to dig it up.

Activities Phuket is a water babe's paradise and offers world-class snorkelling, sailing and fishing. You can also kayak around Phang Nga Bay's semi-submerged sea caves with Sea Canoe (+66 (0)76 528 832; www.seacanoe.net). Horse-riding is also a great way to explore the island – try the Phuket Riding Club in Chalong Bay (www.phuketridingclub.com). If horses just aren't big enough, follow in the footsteps of Sir David Attenborough and take an elephant trek in the Chalong highlands at Siam Safari elephant camp (www.siamsafari.com).

Best beach Little hand-painted signs mark the trail down to Laem Singh beach on the island's west coast. This superlative sand-stretch may just be Phuket's most

beautiful – blissfully free of hotels. While it used to be a secret spot for local residents, these days the word is out: go early to mark your territory. The best restaurant is Ali's, which was also the first.

Daytripper Learn to dive by taking the plunge in one of the top 10 dive spots on the planet: Similan Islands National Marine Park (+66 (0)76 453 273), off the coast of Phang Nga north of Phuket, is suitable for both beginners and experienced divers alike.

Children There are kid-friendly monkey, elephant and crocodile shows at Phuket's zoo (www.phuketzoo.com), along with a butterfly farm. If they're too small to snorkel or scuba dive, the recently renovated aquarium at Cape Panwa (www.phuketaquarium.org) will give toddlers an up-close view of Thailand's underwater world.

Walks A stroll around the elegant Sino-Portuguese quarter of Phuket's Old Town is a must-do, peeking into the colonial-style shophouses along the way. While you're there, browse the bookshelves and grab a coffee at Bo(ok)hemian Arthouse and café at 61 Thalang Road (www.room2521.com); or stop for respite at the China Inn Café restaurant at number 20 – if only to see the beautifully restored interior of what was once a bank.

Perfect picnics Wat Chalong, one of the most ornate of Phuket's monasteries, is a good place to work up an appetite. Stroll through the grounds, get your fortune told, then find a peaceful spot in front of the spectacular ocean view to enjoy a picnic. There's a restaurant close by if you've forgotten your hamper.

Shopping Central Festival Phuket (+66 (0)76 291 111) and the Surin Plaza (+66 (0)76 271 241) are the only two malls worth a trawl. For more selective shopping, Lola (+66 (0)76 271 619) stocks the choicest beachwear. To feather your nest, fly by 'Bypass Road' (Chalermprakiat 9 Road), home to dozens of furniture and home interior shops, including Chan's Antique (www.chans-antique.com), an Aladdin's cave of bronzes and teak carvings. For quirkier finds from Burma and beyond, head for Thalang Road; Colonial Influences (+66 (0)76 214 801) has a stylish selection of stock.

Something for nothing The southernmost point of Phuket, Cape Promthep is the best place to grab an uninterrupted view of the heavenly Andaman Sea sunset. There's always a crowd waiting with their Nikons; get there an hour or so beforehand to commandeer a good spot.

Don't go home without... tasting a durian. This large, spiky-shelled fruit is notorious for its frankly repellent odour (hence the nickname, 'stinky fruit'). Although less intrepid stomachs may baulk at the custardy pulp within, many regard durian flesh as a delicacy and, among Thais, its aphrodisiac effects are the stuff of legend.

PECULIARLY PHUKET

Phuket embraces a strong sense of eco-friendly entrepreneurship and opportunistic ingenuity: look out for crafty DIY-versions of everyday items around the island. Chances are you'll see roadside rubbish bins fashioned from old truck tyres, sunloungers built out of leftover piping, and dumbbells shaped from spare concrete slabs.

DIARY

February The Old Phuket Town Festival brings lively traditional music, dance and spicy food to the streets, which are closed to traffic. April Phuket Bike Week welcomes Hondas, Harleys and more roaring engines for charity (www. phuketbikeweek.com). July Yachting on the high seas at Phuket Race Week (www.phuketraceweek.com). October Local Chinese go vegetarian amid the bustle of processions at Phuket Vegetarian Festival (www.phuketvegetarian.com). November Phuket Carnival on Patong Beach offers plenty of kitschy fun and floats to welcome the start of high season. 5 December The King Cup Regatta is Asia's biggest regatta, held in honour of the King's birthday (www.kingscup.com).

Anantara Phuket Resort & Spa

STYLE Refined, rustic and romantic
SETTING Blue lagoon

'Like a moment in a film when the hero, who has been struggling through dense jungle, parts the leaves to unveil an idyllic village'

The entrance is so discreet you wonder if a Special Ops team would be able to locate it (though why one would want to is quite another matter). Imagine the pain, then, of our taxi driver. He manoeuvres the vehicle down a narrow laneway flanked by high stone walls before pulling up at a modest gap in the bricks. The only sign that this is indeed a doorway to a friendlier world is the appearance of a smiling bellboy. As Mr Smith and I breach the fortress-like walls, the Anantara Phuket Resort & Spa's interior reveals itself like a grand cinematic experience. My eyes pan across a large waterlily-covered pond, inhabited by schools of fish, paddling ducks and hovering dragonflies, all edged with lush flora.

We are tired and famished, having arrived on a hot, breeze-free late afternoon. Not even gulping down the chilled welcome drink in the open-air *sala* during check-in can stop me from staring at the fluffy white ducks in the pond and imagining them roasted in honey, their glazed crispy skins and plump dark meat gently laid slice by slice on a white plate...

My culinary daydream is interrupted by a softly spoken woman bearing a nametag simply stamped with 'A' – she has come to guide us to our private Pool Villa. Hidden from the prying eyes of passers-by, the villa's tall wooden fence conceals a glassy green pool, a waterside *sala* and a well-stocked wine fridge, all of which hold promises of drunken skinny-dipping sessions with Mr Smith.

As Miss A leads us to the bedroom, I am intrigued by a strange terrycloth origami arrangement – 'towel-a-gami', if you will – placed atop a wooden chest at the foot of the bed. At first glance I think it odd to shape white hand towels into two croissants placed side by side, pointy tips facing outwards and fat mid-sections bound together. But as we explore the villa further and find turtle mascots everywhere – a turtle-shaped shower knob in the bathroom, an iron turtle perched on the pool's edge – we realise the towel-a-gami is, in fact, a sea turtle.

Because Anantara is located on a protected sea turtle nesting area, the shelled creature is an important motif.

We read with interest from the Mai Khao Marine Turtle Foundation pamphlet that the resort is set at a specific distance away from the beach to protect the sand and its lighting is designed to be invisible from the beachfront so as not to disturb the female turtles as they come lumbering out of the water to lay their eggs.

A door slides silently open to reveal our spacious dark-wood walk-in wardrobe complete with floor-to-ceiling mirror. I unpack and hang my colour-coordinated holiday attire neatly so that when I'm done it looks like a display rack straight out of a hip fashion boutique. Mr Smith takes the more avant-garde option of strewing his clothes dramatically both in and around his open suitcase.

The Phuket sunset is famously over in under half an hour. Blink and you'll miss it. So, after exploring every nook and cranny of our villa, Mr Smith and I literally run to the beach just in time to catch the

glowing saffron egg yolk slide down behind the horizon. Vast swirls of strawberry, lemon and blueberry stretch across the sky above ripples of a rapidly darkening sea as night falls. And Anantara at night is simply magical.

Making our way back to the heart of the resort is like a moment in a film when the hero, who has been struggling through dense jungle, parts the leaves with his quivering hands to unveil an idyllic village: secluded villas emanate glowing light; trees and flowers rustle lushly around a lily-padded lagoon; guests recline on plush cushions in pavilions set over calm ponds. The cool night air pulses with a meditative chorus of baritone bullfrogs. Look up, and the black silhouettes of slender coconut trees frame a clear sky sprinkled with a dusting of stars.

The key element that gives this Shangri-la the wow factor is its fabulous use of lighting. Bright enough to see yet dim enough to tease, it is of the soft,

warming variety – it glows from damask lampshades or from iridescent fibre-optic chandeliers that resemble fine jellyfish tentacles dangling from the ceiling. Spotlights add dramatic contrast, highlighting strategic parts of trees and buildings, while rows of flickering fire torches along wooden boardwalks set off faint tribal chants in my head.

However, of all the features at Anantara, the one that captures my imagination (and holds it to ransom) is the Tree House tapas bar. No, let me rephrase that. It is the *entrance* to the Tree House. A grand, spiralling wooden staircase wraps around an age-worn Banyan tree lit with floating lanterns, as if it had been ripped from the pages of Enid Blyton's *The Enchanted Wood*. My dream retirement home is a tree house by the sea. That night, I get a preview of its charms.

The resort has a timetable of activities – yoga lessons, Thai language classes, even specific Rainy Day Activities – designed to entertain guests throughout their stay, but Mr Smith and I decide to create our own special Nighttime Activity and invent a version of the Turkish bath within our villa. In the outdoor tub, right beside the pool, we sit sipping wine and soaking in a hot bubble bath until we are just about cooked, then we swing our legs over and plunge into the chilly pool. A few more repetitions ensures our circulation is pumping rather nicely, thank you very much.

In ancient Sanskrit, the word 'anantara' means 'without end'. With all the relaxation and light-hearted fun Mr Smith and I were experiencing, I was sort of hoping to be absolutely over all the loveliness and luxuries, so that when the time came I wouldn't mind if it ended. Of course, there's no such luck.

Reviewed by Jo Soh

Rooms 83 private pool villas, including the two-bedroom Similan Suite.

Rates THB13,000–THB81,000; THB65,000–THB144,000 for the Similan Suite (sleeps four); includes buffet breakfast. Tax is extra at 18.7 per cent.

Check-out Noon, but flexible subject to availability. Check-in, 2pm.

Facilities Free WiFi throughout, spa, gym, tennis courts, library with books and DVDs, boutique, gardens. In rooms: flatscreen TV, DVD player, preloaded iPod, espresso machine, wine fridge, minibar.

Poolside Stretching the length of the beachfront, the pool covers all options: swim for as long as you like, lounge on a day-bed or paddle up to the Infinity bar for liquid refreshment.

Children The Turtle Club provides fun, artistic and cultural adventures for over threes. The hotel supplies free baby cots and extra beds for older children for THB3,600 a night.

Also The Anantara supports the Mai Khao Marine Turtle Foundation, which protects sea turtles that lay their eggs on the local beach, donating US$1 a room a night.

IN THE KNOW

Our favourite rooms The gorgeous Lagoon Sala Pool Villas share the same elegant dark teak and pale linen of the other room categories, but include private outdoor salas around the lagoon. This rustic setting is a world away from urbanity and the ideal spot for yoga, a massage or romantic dinner.

Hotel bar Perched above the resort, the Tree House is a magical hideaway. Choose a cleansing juice, coffee or sorbet tea by day or a retoxing cocktail by night. Infinity is the swim-up pool bar offering juices, shakes and cocktails.

Hotel restaurant One of three eateries, La Sala evokes the feeling of a casual colonial-style club, with grey rattan chairs and potted palms. The blue glass light installation and crisp, modern interior at poolside Sea.Fire.Salt turns heads, but sit outside to enjoy the sea breeze. Open-fire barbecue cooking with seafood and salt is the speciality here (there's even a salt sommelier). Anantara is proud of its wine collection: discover why with an individually designed menu matched to tipples at the Tasting Room.

Top table Book a private dining experience in your room, at your *sala*, by the beach or beside the pool.

Room service An extensive selection of dishes is available 24 hours.

Dress code Relaxed but chic is the way to dress for any of the Anantara restaurants: work that white linen.

Local knowledge The hotel can arrange a multitude of tailored trips, based on land or sea, including jungle exploring, wildlife watching, sailing and sea cruises, rafting, diving, elephant trekking, art tours and even private surfing lessons.

LOCAL EATING AND DRINKING

The tropical sophistication and jazzy soundtrack at Siam Supper Club (+66 (0)76 270 936) attracts the island's more discerning expats. It serves an easy-going menu of pizzas, grilled fish and meat, and cocktails. Lotus (+66 (0)81 797 8110) is a casual beach restaurant with a modern-rustic vibe and jaw-dropping views at sunset. Book ahead as it's extremely popular. If you fancy getting out of the hotel for breakfast or a snack, head to Paula's Retro Café (+66 (0)76 270 283), a local favourite. For lunch, quiche, home-made bagels, fresh sandwiches and salads are on the menu.

GET A ROOM!

For more information, or to book this hotel, go to www.mrandmrssmith.com – our expert team can take care of all your travel arrangements. Register your Smith membership card to enjoy exclusive offers and privileges.

 SMITH MEMBER OFFER An hour's unlimited Anantara signature cocktails for two.

Anantara Phuket Resort & Spa 888 Moo 3, Tumbon Mai Khao, Amphur Thalang, Phuket, 83110, Thailand

Phuket

The Racha

STYLE Luxed-up nature
SETTING Fantasy Island

'While Mr Smith basks on the sand, Long Island iced tea in hand, I head to a reef on the other side of the island for snorkelling'

Mermaids have always fascinated me, I once confessed to Mr Smith. Sometimes I wonder if, with my intense love of the ocean, I might actually be one (or at least a related species). Perhaps that's why, for our first holiday in many years, he's chosen to take me to the Racha, located on its very own secluded island just off Phuket in Thailand.

The island sun is beating down on our white BMW 520d as we head south to Chalong Pier in Phuket. This is the location of the Racha's office and the place where we are to leave the mainland and catch a speedboat to the resort. I've been warned that, since it's December, the journey across may be quite, well, rough. My one previous experience on a dive boat was absolutely horrendous – by the end of it, I couldn't have been less like a mermaid, curled up on the deck feeling sick and sorry for myself (although if mermaids are green, at least I had that part right).

I am contemplating this memory in the moments before stepping aboard. Thankfully our host has a pill for me that should help with any feelings of seasickness during the 35-minute transfer. Its effects are soon felt and the whole world seems to be floating around me. I'm then asked to choose a fragrance for our villa. In my enlightened state, it seems like an odd request, but then scent is so subjective – what works for one person might make another turn up their nose, quite literally. Given a choice of lemongrass, jasmine and lavender, I go for the latter.

Perhaps it is the medication, the tamarind lollies provided on board the boat, or my excitement at getting so close to our destination, but the ride isn't too bad. In fact, I even nod off for a while and am only woken by the change in the engine sound of the speedboat as it slows down. As I open my eyes, the first thing I see is Mr Smith, my prince, on a boat, just like in *The Little Mermaid*. I smile to myself before taking a peek outside to check on the colour of the water and the quality of the sea. What can I say? I'm a picky mermaid. It is perfect – icy blue and so clear I can see the sand five metres below the surface.

When we jump onto the white sandy beach, someone is already waiting to lead us to our beachside palace. We pass the gym, spa, a couple of restaurants, a cosy library with a few computers (although why would anyone want to know what was going on in the real world?), three swimming pools and a tennis court. Our Grand Deluxe Villa is spacious with a stylish, minimal white-on-white fit-out. It even has a spirit-lifting view of the sparkling blue Andaman Sea.

For me, the bathroom in any room I stay at is very important and the Racha doesn't disappoint. There's a deep tub and separate shower, as well as a rain shower out in the courtyard. Is there anything better than bathing *au naturel* in the tropics? What impressed music-obsessed Mr Smith, however, was the Bose iPod dock sitting right near the bed. He can DJ while I bathe.

If adventure is your middle name, then the Racha should definitely be on your dream destinations list. The resort offers all-terrain vehicle tours around the island, cycling, hiking, windsurfing and sailing. To satisfy my inner mermaid, however, I decide to go snorkelling. While Mr Smith basks on the sand, Long Island iced tea in hand, I head to a reef on the other side of the island with one of the guides. The water is deep – between five and eight metres – and the current quite strong, but there is a huge array of corals and fish to be seen. When I'm

back on shore, I've still got the urge, so I drag Mr Smith to the front beach. Here, the sea is calmer but still a living aquarium. I spot rainbow-hued parrot fish, and a moray eel comes out from its rocky hiding spot to say hello.

All that underwater activity has caused my stomach to groan. There are a few dining options to choose from at the Racha, but the Sunset Beach Restaurant, a casual affair that serves a barbecue buffet each night, sounds like the best way to counter all my cravings. I'm not disappointed – there's a choice of grilled seafood, Thai dishes and Western options. Mr Smith and I are highly amused by the resort's choice of entertainment at the restaurant. Anyone who's been to Thailand will know of the country's great affection for a cheesy cover band, and there's one rocking out for the punters tonight. They crank out hit after hit, from Elvis to Beyoncé and Michael Jackson, and as we tuck into our meals, we play a spirited game of 'guess the next song'. It's not quite the romantic meal by moonlight we'd anticipated but it was definitely memorable – and fun.

With the night still young, we head to Ice Bar for a cocktail. It's a really chic spot and here the music is more what we'd anticipated – a Café del Mar-style soundtrack playing in the background. We choose an overstuffed sofa to lounge by candlelight and the bartender makes me a very moreish Cosmopolitan. Really, what more do you need to unwind?

Even after just a couple of days, this little mermaid feels like she's had the holiday she's been longing for – relaxing, peaceful and fun. But, unlike at the end of the movie, I actually get to go home with my prince.

Reviewed by Pam Chiang

NEED TO KNOW

Rooms 70 villas, including nine suites.

Rates THB11,500–THB65,000, including buffet breakfast. Excludes eight per cent tax and 10 per cent service charge.

Check-out Noon. Check-in, 2pm.

Facilities Library with WiFi, tennis and basketball courts, spa, yoga studio, gym, five-star Racha dive centre, beach club, mountain bikes, gift shop. In rooms: broadband internet, flatscreen TV, CD/DVD player, preloaded iPod, minibar.

Poolside Swim to the beat of underwater music in the sublime infinity pool by the beach or the secluded garden pool.

Children Kids are welcome, but this is more of a grown-ups playground. Baby cots are free and extra beds for older kids cost THB600 a night. Staff can babysit for THB300 an hour with a day's notice.

Also The Racha is on just-remote-enough Racha Yai Island, 20km south of Phuket island, so getting here is a bit James Bond. A private limousine from Phuket airport and thrilling 35-minute speedboat transfer cost THB9,600 each way, excluding 17 per cent tax and service charge. A cheaper scheduled speedboat service is also available.

IN THE KNOW

Our favourite rooms All villas are serene and clutter-free, with whitewashed walls, dark shutters and streamlined teak furniture. Suites 101 or 102 are more secluded and have the most spectacular sea views, along with their own plunge pools. Splashing out? The Lighthouse is a five-storey, two-bedroom 'villa' with 360-degree island views.

Hotel bar Nurse a mojito as you watch the sun set over the sea at the smart Lobby Bar. Ice Bar is a late-night perch for drinks, live music and karaoke. The Club del Mar Beach Club is the go-to spot for nocturnal quaffing, with a DJ spinning tunes (it also boasts a pool, spa and dishes up a mean buffet lunch).

Hotel restaurant The Racha has restaurants to suit all food moods. The relaxed, contemporary Earth Café serves breakfast and dinner indoors and alfresco. Opening onto the pool deck, the romantic Fire Grill plates up pizzas, pastas and salads during the day and gourmet offerings at night. Casual Sunset Beach Restaurant lets you sink your toes into the sand as you graze on Thai food, burgers and sandwiches at lunch and barbecued seafood and steak in the evening. On the eastern side of the island, chic daytime café Gerardo's Beach Club offers Thai-Western fusion dishes and killer cocktails.

Top table Private dinners are encouraged – we suggest a candlelit dinner on the Star Deck.

Room service Available 7am–midnight, or book a private chef for a barbecue on your terrace.

Dress code Hippie chic (those designer dip-dye vests and maxi-dresses are so Racha).

Local knowledge With turquoise water and a powdery white beach Batok Bay, in front of the resort, is fantastic for snorkelling. If you want more isolation, Siam Beach is a five-minute walk over a small hill. There are also first-rate dive sites close by. Arrange diving courses or trips at the five-star Racha dive centre (which boasts its own instruction pool). Work the kinks out afterwards at the resort's Anumba Spa, which includes treatment rooms for couples.

LOCAL EATING AND DRINKING

There's a Thai restaurant at the opposite end of the beach to the Racha – ask resort staff for directions. If your flight arrives in Phuket after 3.30pm in the afternoon, you will have to stay overnight in either Phuket town or Chalong. In the former, Siam Indigo (+66 (0)76 256 697), 8 Phang Nga Road, serves Thai fusion in a charming historic building; in Chalong Kan Eang@Pier (+66 (0)76 381 212), at 44/1 Viset Road, whips up seafood and Thai fare overlooking the bay.

GET A ROOM!

For more information, or to book this hotel, go to www.mrandmrssmith.com – our expert team can take care of all your travel arrangements. Register your Smith membership card to enjoy exclusive offers and privileges.

 SMITH MEMBER OFFER A bottle of wine and a fruit basket.

The Racha 42/12–13 Moo 5, Rawai, Muang, Phuket 83130, Thailand (+66 (0)76 355 455; www.theracha.com)

Phuket

Trisara

STYLE Understated glamour
SETTING Private bayside

'Keen to start exploring, we call the concierge to send a buggy and take us to Trisara's private beach. As if by magic, two beach boys are already arranging sunloungers and covering them with white beach towels when we arrive'

Driving along the highway, my mind is trying to reconfigure memories like a jigsaw puzzle. It has been eight long years since my last visit to Phuket. The things I remember? A narrow road, a long deserted coastline with dark rubber-tree forests set back from the beach. A sea the colour of emeralds. The hot and sour flavours of *kang som*, a local version of bouillabaisse. I have to confess that I was afraid all this may have changed in the intervening time.

Already, as Mrs Smith and I cruise towards our destination – it has been almost a decade since I was last in this part of Thailand, but it's also five years since we married, so this is like a second honeymoon – there is cause for concern. The highway has grown more lanes with more cars travelling along them and far fewer trees at its edge. Sadly, it seems, the enemies of nature and solitude have already taken their toll.

Off the main road though, there are hopeful signs. Beautiful Nai Thorn beach is quiet and gentle waves roll in from the ultra-green sea to the sand. Past the beach, I direct the car up a steep, narrow road where we find the gates of Trisara. At reception, we're welcomed by a sea breeze and a 180-degree view of the ocean. Really, it wouldn't take much more than this to make me happy. However, Elle, one of the managers, has prepared chilled jasmine-scented towels and two glasses of cold honey-ginger tea – she explains it's good for settling stomachs after the long, winding drive. Then she places a gorgeous garland of flowers around a delighted Mrs Smith's wrist. I get the feeling that at Trisara there will be impressive attention to detail and warm hospitality.

For the next two nights, our home will be a spacious Ocean View Pool Villa. It's very contemporary Thai, with teak floors and an enormous king-size bed dominating the bedroom. The bathroom makes my jaw drop – his 'n' hers vanities, a bath big enough for the both of us and a rain shower (there's another sexy one outside, as well). But my favourite feature is the private infinity pool overlooking the ocean. During our stay here, I can see myself and Mrs Smith languidly floating between long stretches of reclining on the poolside sunloungers.

While Mrs Smith makes herself a cup of tea and satisfies her sweet tooth with some crunchy cookies and home-made dark chocolate truffles, Elle shows me all the villa's facilities. I flick through the channels on the flatscreen TV and pop my iPod in the dock. This is some place.

Keen to start exploring, we call the concierge to send a buggy and take us to Trisara's private beach. As if by magic, two beach boys are already arranging sunloungers and covering them with white beach towels when we arrive. By this time, it's approaching 6pm and the sun is about to set. It couldn't be more romantic. We walk hand in hand along the sand to the jetty, and it's as if we've turned back the clock to when we first met.

The following afternoon, after a lazy morning in the villa – French toast with red berries and eggs, bacon, sausages, tomatoes and hash browns served promptly at 8am, followed by plenty of lolling by the pool – we decide to go snorkelling in the resort's private bay (no jet skis, thank goodness). By the floating jetty we feed what seems like thousands of friendly fish in a technicolor underwater world.

Have I mentioned that I'm a chef? So far, both Mrs Smith and I have been greatly impressed with Trisara's cuisine. There's been nothing too elaborate – although Phuket lobster club sandwiches by the beach did feel quite posh – but flavours and presentation have proved sensational.

It all adds up to high hopes for what will be our anniversary dinner. We've arranged to dine on a deck by the beach under the moon, with just the lapping waves and chirruping crickets as a soundtrack. That alone would have been special enough, but dinner was perfect. I chose to go native – fresh spring rolls and sweet pork with rice and Thai-style salsa – while Mrs Smith decided on a trio of fish tartare and duck egg carbonara. For me, the combination of spice, acid and sweetness was spot-on, and the selections from the Western menu were creative, elegantly displayed and well balanced.

All too soon, our visit was at an end. Much to our disappointment we hadn't managed to fit in a proper trip to the spa, although Elle did walk us up there on our arrival and the ocean views are absolutely sublime. Throughout the resort, nothing was overlooked – the decor is subtle and well executed, and the service was incredibly thoughtful right until our last minute. Surprisingly, I found out what 'trisara' means without having to ask anyone – the word is Thai for 'three heavens'. Mrs Smith and I definitely found ours in the surroundings, the people and the cuisine. We were truly in three heavens, right here on earth.

Reviewed by André Chiang

NEED TO KNOW

Rooms 39 pool rooms, suites and villas.

Rates Low season, US$630–US$2,260; high season, US$790–US$3,200, including breakfast (except during peak season) and airport transfers. Excludes 18.7 per cent tax.

Check-out Noon, but flexible subject to availability. Check-in, 2pm.

Facilities Free broadband internet in rooms and some public areas, library of books, CDs, DVDs and board games, spa, gym, tennis courts, gift shops, gardens. In rooms: flatscreen TV, CD/DVD players, minibar, own-label natural toiletries.

Poolside A fabulous 45m saltwater lap pool stretches along the resort's beachfront.

Children Welcome: baby cots provided and under-12s stay for free; extra bed and breakfast for over-12s, US$125. Trisara also offers a kids club and babysitting with staff for US$10.50 an hour.

Also 21 December–10 January, a 10-night minimum stay applies, and breakfast costs extra (US$25.50 a person, or half price for children).

IN THE KNOW

Our favourite rooms Each super-tasteful suite or villa has a jaw-dropping ocean view and its own pool. If pushed to choose one, Ocean Front Pool Villa 407 sits right on the seafront, so you have undisturbed vistas and utter privacy. Bathrooms throughout are divine: surrounded by leafy gardens with huge baths, sofas and sexy outdoor showers.

Hotel bar Overlooking the pool and beach, Trisara's bar exudes masculine chic and a laid-back, clubby atmosphere. Its charcoal and aubergine palette is funked up with dusky pink hanging lanterns and a chill-out soundtrack.

Hotel restaurant The people at Trisara are reluctant to brag, but the restaurant really is one of the best on Phuket. An elegant space, it's set to one side of a cascading waterfall, with the bar on the other, but sit on the palm-shaded deck to lap up the beachfront ambience. The first-rate menu spans ultra-fresh Thai and international food, and arguably the best *pad thai* you'll ever taste. There are also beach barbecues in the cool season.

Top table The middle table of the front row has a picture-postcard view, but arrive early as you can't book ahead.

Room service Available 24 hours, mirroring the menus, wines and drinks on offer at Trisara's bars and restaurants.

Dress code Tory Birch kaftan, Zimmerman swimwear and Havaianas by day; Missoni at night.

Local knowledge Trisara's spa is drop-dead gorgeous, offering private treatment suites with sea views that open out to breezy pavilions and gardens. Indulge in a signature, six-handed 'Royal Trisara' massage, which involves pampering by three therapists. Active types can also enjoy tennis coaching on two floodlit championship courts, hire a jet ski, kayak or dive gear, or charter one of Trisara's yachts for a romantic cruise around Phuket and the local islands.

LOCAL EATING AND DRINKING

Baan Suan, five minutes' drive from the hotel, whips up tasty Thai in a pretty garden setting (ask staff for directions). Raise the romance quotient several notches at chichi **Weaves Restaurant** (+66 (0)76 271 050), at Surin Beach, where you can opt to dine poolside or in the air-conditioned comfort of a private room. Soak up panoramic horizons as you sip cocktails and sample East-West tapas at fashionable **360°, The Lookout** (+66 (0)76 317 600) at the Pavilions, Phuket.

GET A ROOM!

For more information, or to book this hotel, go to www.mrandmrssmith.com – our expert team can take care of all your travel arrangements. Register your Smith membership card to enjoy exclusive offers and privileges.

 SMITH MEMBER OFFER An exclusive gift of handmade chocolates and fruit, plus 25 per cent off all massages in the spa.

Trisara 60/1 Moo 6, Srisoonthorn Road, Cherngtalay, Thalang, Phuket 83110, Thailand (+66 (0)76 310 100; www.trisara.com)

HOW TO... GET AROUND

If you're getting your tuk tuks and cyclos in a twist or feeling flummoxed about how you pay for your xe om, gen up on our guide to getting around, south-east Asian-style...

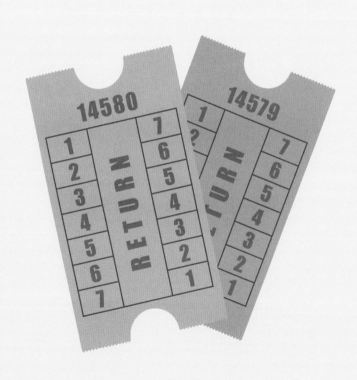

CARS

Street signs are usually in English and most roads in south-east Asia are in decent shape, although off the beaten path in Cambodia, Laos or Bali things can get bumpy. Given that some licences are bought rather than earned, driving can be haphazard, and only the very brave – or foolish – would hire a car to navigate Bangkok. Self-drive is not possible for foreign visitors in Cambodia and Vietnam, and rarely allowed in Laos, but this is a blessing given the novel approach to road rules. Why bother, when you can hire a private car with driver to take the strain? If you do drive, adopt a defensive strategy and keep off rural roads at night.

TUK TUKS

The brightly coloured – and noisy – three-wheeled tuk tuks are synonymous with Bangkok, as are the scams drivers try on their passengers. Agree on your price before you hop on and unless you're aiming to look bedraggled and reek of petrol, save tuk tuks for short, backstreet journeys. The Cambodian remorque moto is similar: it has a motorbike and small carriage, which somehow accommodates an entire Khmer family.

CYCLOS

There is no finer way to explore Indochine than from the recumbent comfort of an authentic cyclo. The passenger sits in a bucket seat at the front with commanding (read terrifying) views of the traffic while the rider pedals behind. They're being edged out by motorbike taxis in some big cities, but hail one and you can pat yourself on the back for minimising your carbon footprint (but this might be offset by your guilt that the 75-year-old driver is having a hernia along the way).

MOTOS AND XE OMS

Do as the locals do and ride pillion on a motorbike taxi, or perch sidesaddle for added elegance (ideal if Mrs Smith has donned a dress – or Mr Smith a sarong). It's a convenient and cheap way to weave around busy urban hubs such as Bangkok and Ho Chi Minh City. Known as moto in Cambodia and xe om ('bike hug') in Vietnam, the ride can be hair-raising, so stick to the quieter backstreets. Hang on tight and don't part company with your flip-flops.

MOTORBIKES

Doing the *Easy Rider* thing, by hiring your own motorbike, is an exciting way to explore the region off-the-beaten track. Sleeping dogs, cavorting chickens, crazy cows, grumpy buffaloes and drunken villagers make for challenging obstacles. The Thai islands have the highest road accident records in the country, and the spectacle of tourists with 'scooter rash' is all too familiar. Reduce your chances of joining them by avoiding midnight jaunts when drunk drivers let loose. Oh, and definitely make sure you have insurance.

BUSES

You might happily hop on a city bus in Singapore or Bangkok, but unless you relish reliving your backpacker years, it's best to avoid long-haul bus journeys in south-east Asia. Buses are mostly modern, comfortable and air-conditioned, but drivers love cranking up the karaoke volume to 11 on most routes. A *songthaew*, or covered pick-up truck, is however, a natty way to get around Thailand's islands and less congested cities.

BOATS

Low-rise and surprisingly speedy, longtail boats are a real buzz when zipping around the back *khlongs* of Bangkok, discovering the rivers of upcountry Laos or bobbing between Indonesia's tropical islands. However, the novelty might wear off once you've been drenched by mucky canal water and deafened by engine noise. Keep trips short and protect your valuables from a soaking. Speedboat drivers tend to be unpredictable and cavalier, so watch out for overloading and avoid travelling late at night, when most accidents happen.

TRAINS

Travelling by train can be slick (in Singapore or Bangkok, where rapid rail systems and skytrains rule) or enchanting. Thailand's extensive railway network is a little slow and cranky, but comfortable if you're wrapped up against the arctic air-con. Vietnam's railway is fast improving, although still not that fast. Trains in Cambodia are notoriously decrepit, but spare a thought for Laos which doesn't even have any.

Time zone GMT +7 hours.

Dialling codes Country code for Vietnam +84:
Hanoi (0)4; Hoi An (0)510; Nha Trang (0)583 –
drop the zero if calling from overseas.

Language The official language is Vietnamese,
although English is widely understood. French is
still spoken, mainly by older people in the south.

Currency Vietnamese dong (VND), although the
US dollar (US$) is accepted.

Tipping culture A 10 per cent tip is appropriate
unless already added to the bill.

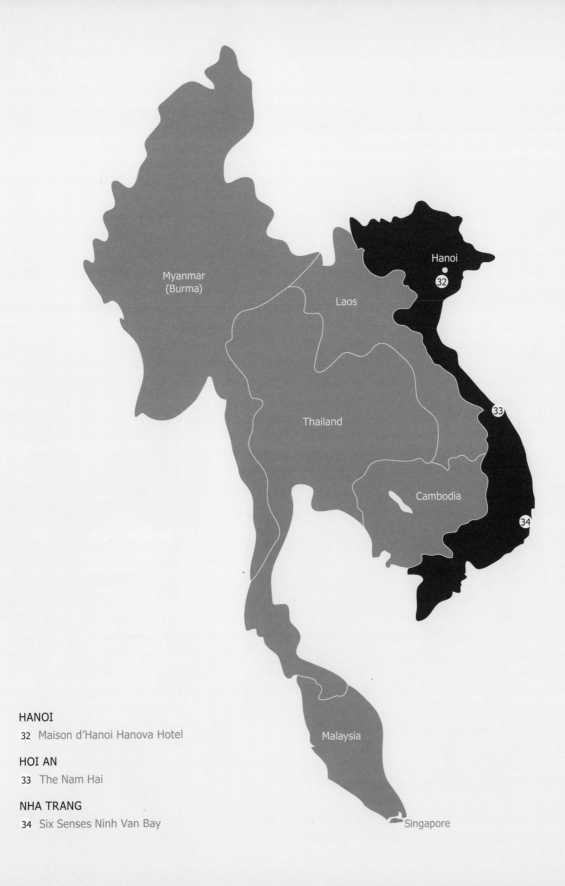

Myanmar
(Burma)

Laos

Hanoi
32

Thailand

33

Cambodia

34

Malaysia

Singapore

HANOI

32 Maison d'Hanoi Hanova Hotel

HOI AN

33 The Nam Hai

NHA TRANG

34 Six Senses Ninh Van Bay

HANOI

CITYSCAPE Ancient landmarks, buzzing boulevards
CITY LIFE Colourful culture clash

Ho Chi Minh City may have the pace, but capital Hanoi has the grace. The French influence lives on in the city's grand architecture, tree-lined boulevards and parks, just-baked baguettes and bohemian coffee shops throughout the former first city of Indochine. This northern outpost, however, has a thousand-year history that dates back long before the colonial era and its more recent communist past. Nowhere is this more palpable than in the Old Quarter, the historic heart of Hanoi. Follow your feet down sidestreets or let a cyclo take the strain while the neighbourhood's rich tapestry weaves its magic around you. With its designer dining, bold boutiques and buzzy bars, Hanoi is going places fast.

GETTING THERE

Planes The main airport, Noi Bai International Airport (www.hanoiairportonline.com), serves Hanoi and is about 45km from the downtown area. Direct flights route here from Asian capitals and a few cities in Australia and Europe. Domestic flights connect Hanoi with most Vietnamese cities.

Trains Hanoi is home to the Reunification Express (www.vr.com.vn) connecting the north and south of the country, hugging the coast to and from Hué, Danang and all points south; nightly sleeper berths are available. There are also luxurious night trains to Lao Cai, gateway to the popular northern hill station of Sapa.

Automobiles Self-drive is not possible in Vietnam, but that will come as a relief when you see the heart-stopping Hanoi traffic. A car with driver can be arranged if you are planning an epic odyssey south.

LOCAL KNOWLEDGE

Taxis There are lots of taxi firms in Hanoi, but ensure you hire one with a meter. There are still cyclos (three-wheeled pedicabs) and xe oms (motorbike taxis) roaming the streets, but overcharging is the norm.

Siesta and fiesta This is Hanoi, where they do things by the book. Banks and government agencies take a little break during the day, so hours are usually 8am–11.30am and 1pm–4pm, plus Saturday mornings. Shops keep longer hours and will usually be open 8am to 8pm. Most restaurants dish up until about 10pm and a few bars will rumble on into the wee hours.

Do go/don't go Hanoi is prone to wet, chilly winters so you might want to avoid November to February, although this is the best time to travel in the south, where it's warm and dry. The summer monsoon brings hot, humid weather. April, May and October are the ideal times to visit. A lot of businesses shut up shop during Tet (Vietnamese New Year), which falls in January or February depending on the lunar calendar.

Packing tips Mr Smith, don't take the pith – helmet we mean. The pith helmet is universally known as the Ho Chi Minh hat here and can be picked up for just a few dollars, so don't cart your designer one from home. Mrs Smith, don't pack much, as then you'll have the perfect excuse to raid the designer boutiques of Nha Tho Street and the Old Quarter.

Recommended reads *The Sorrow of War* by Bao Ninh offers a poignant insight into the Vietnam conflict from the northern perspective. *Derailed in Uncle Ho's Victory Garden* is legendary war photographer Tim Page's account of his return to Vietnam to establish a memorial to fallen correspondents on all sides.

Local specialities Cooking is elevated to an art form in Vietnam, with more than 500 regional dishes to sample along the way. *Pho*, the noodle soup that built a nation, is a popular snack at any time of day. *Bun cha* is a delicious dish of rice noodle vermicelli, grilled pork and herbs adored by northerners and southerners alike. Fresh ingredients and delicate flavours rule.

Also The Old Quarter is a city within a city, crammed into a claustrophobic warren of alleys to the north of Hoan Kiem Lake. Each street is named after its original trade, footpath cafés spill onto the roads, hawkers jostle with hustlers to make a sale, motorbikes and cyclos fight for territory, and visitors try to make sense of it all while browsing the boutiques and bars. The Old Quarter is where mediaeval and modern Hanoi collide and it makes for a pulsating ride.

WORTH GETTING OUT OF BED FOR

Viewpoint An early morning stroll around Hoan Kiem Lake will have you charmed. Dawn is exercise time and you can witness the hypnotic moves of mass t'ai chi as folk gather to practise this ancient art. Finish with a lakeside cuppa at Hapro Coffee on the south-western tip of Hoan Kiem. Or explore pretty Ngoc Son Temple on an island in the north-eastern corner of the lake, reached by ancient red bridge, the Huc (Rising Sun).

Arts and culture The Temple of Literature, 2km west of the lake, was established in 1070 and is one of the best-preserved historic buildings in Hanoi, housing the oldest university in Vietnam. Fans of Confucian architecture (rather than the confusion architecture that reigns in some parts of the city) will appreciate the harmonious gardens and pavilions.

Activities If Vietnamese cuisine has really tickled your palate, then sign up for one of Hanoi's excellent cooking classes. Highway 4 (www.highway4.com) offers half-day courses that include a visit to a local market, several popular recipes and a hearty lunch.

Daytripper It's a three-hour drive east to Halong Bay, one of the must-see natural marvels of Vietnam. This World Heritage site is home to about 3,000 limestone islands, soaring skywards like stone sentinels from the aqua sea, as well as captivating caves and floating fishing villages. A day trip doesn't do it justice, so book a night aboard a luxury junk such as the Bhaya (www.bhayacruises.com) and let the bay work its wonders – you may be tempted to stay even longer.

Children To experience true kitsch, take smaller Smiths for a ride on a swan pedalo on Truc Bach Lake or neighbouring Ho Tay (West Lake). Fans of *Top Gear* will enjoy the fact that one of these very swans was converted into an amphibious vehicle to transport Richard Hammond's pink Minsk motorbike. Warning: do not try this at home. For an alternative aquatic entertainment kids will love, book a pew at the Thanglong Water Puppet Theatre (www.thanglongwaterpuppet.org).

Walks Head into the heart of the Old Quarter to discover Hanoi at its exuberant best. Start at St Joseph Cathedral and amble along hip Nha Tho Street while you work out which boutiques or cafés merit further investigation later on. Then navigate your way through the maze of streets – look out for the silk boutiques of Hang Gai, the Buddhist paraphernalia of Hang Quat, the herb sellers of Lan Ong, the ghost money of Hang Ma, the bar strip of Ta Hien and the marble gravestones of Hang Bac. Finish up on the north shore of Hoan Kiem Lake for a refreshing ale at microbrewery Legends Beer.

Perfect picnic Not so much a picnic as a rolling food fest, the Taste of Hanoi tour with Onbike Vietnam (www.onbikevietnam.com) takes you to all sorts of local eateries, as well as pagodas, temples and more.

Shopping One of Hanoi's headline acts is shopping. Popular purchases include silk clothing, embroidered lace and old propaganda posters. Craft Link at 43 Van Mieu Street (www.craftlink.com.vn) is a fair-trade shop

specialising in minority handicrafts and textiles. Khaisilk, at 96 Hang Gai Street, is Vietnam's best-known fashion house offering dressy designer silks. When in town, Hillary Clinton stopped by to get some threads at Ha Dong Silk, 102 Hang Gai Street. We're not sure that's an endorsement, but we like the collection.

Something for nothing Pay your respects at the restored One Pillar Pagoda, set in a park behind the Ho Chi Minh Mausoleum. Originally built by Emperor Ly Thai Tong in the 11th century, it is an elegant design representing a blossoming lotus rising from a sea of sorrow. The French weren't so impressed and wantonly destroyed it before quitting Hanoi in 1954.

Don't go home without... sampling a *bia hoi*, the world's cheapest beer at just 15 cents a glass. It's not a brand, more like the local moonshine.

HIGHLY HANOI

No trip to Hanoi is complete without a pilgrimage to the Ho Chi Minh Mausoleum Complex. Humble Ho was embalmed against his dying wishes for a simple cremation and lies in a glass sarcophagus in the heart of this foreboding marble structure (he takes a holiday in Russia around October or November for essential maintenance). This is the holiest of holies for many Vietnamese so no talking or giggling, and absolutely no photographs.

DIARY

January/February Tet, aka Vietnamese New Year, means much of the country is on holiday. April The slithery traditions of snake-catching and breeding are celebrated at the Le Mat Snake Festival, held in a village just outside town. Processions, music and food are highlights. 30 April Liberation Day commemorates the fall of Saigon to the north in 1975. It's popular with Hanoians, as it marks them getting one over the southern oiks. 1 May International Workers' Day falls in May, so it's very much 'up the revolution'.

Maison d'Hanoi Hanova Hotel

STYLE Colonial hipster
SETTING 21st-century Old Quarter

'Below street level is the hotel's restaurant, the Hanova Café, and it's a good place to begin the day. But after that it seems almost criminal not to go on a culinary adventure in the neighbourhood'

One of the promises I made to my children at the time they entered the world was that their education would consist not only of school but travel, too: discovering differing cultures, climates and geographies. When I made one of those vows I was staring deep into the eyes of a tiny, unopinionated baby, not an attitude-riddled teenager.

So it's with a mix of anticipation, and not a little trepidation, that we – Mr Smith, our 15-, 12- and five-year-old sons and me – board the plane to Vietnam for a family holiday. We've not been in Hanoi long, however, when I realise my older kids' idea of adventure is almost completely restricted to surfing the internet. Thankfully, the hotel offers the feature that matters most to them (give them a free wireless connection and they'd likely be happy stranded in a cabin in Antarctica for months on end).

Of course, it wasn't the complimentary technology that made us choose this particular destination. There were two things that appealed to Mr Smith and me from afar. One, Maison d'Hanoi is not a faceless, enormous chain hotel that could just as easily be found in Helsinki or Hong Kong. The second reason is that it's located in the historic Old Quarter of the city, which is vibrant and

eclectic and packed with art galleries, colonial architecture, handicraft markets and restaurants of all description just begging to be explored.

The hotel itself is what the locals refer to as a 'tube house', a tall, narrow terrace that makes the most of the tiny plots of land in the Old Quarter. The design blends French colonial style with Asian motifs. Polished timber floors in the rooms are sleek against trims of red, gold and black and contemporary bedheads that are upholstered to make them a feature.

As we need plenty of space to accommodate our brood, we have booked two rooms: a Classic Standard Double for us and a Deluxe Twin with an extra bed for the kids. While not the largest rooms you'll ever stay in, both tick all the necessary boxes. One of the more unusual features of these types of buildings is that they have very few windows, so natural light comes through skylights and walls made of glass bricks. The boys' room, with its twin beds, is a little more spacious than ours, but they're happy to simply have some privacy (and free internet). Don't get any ideas about romantic sojourns in the bathroom though – even solo, the shower curtain wants to wend its way around your naked torso. Since we're at the budget end of the boutique business such idiosyncrasies seem quite trivial.

Below street level is the hotel's restaurant, the Hanova Café, and it's a good place to begin the day. But after that it seems almost criminal not to go on a culinary adventure in the neighbourhood. Particularly appetising is a little spot called Green Tangerine, on Hang Be Street. During the lunch hour, it is packed with expat corporate types enjoying French dishes in the gloriously restored colonial house and courtyard. Thankfully, there are meals that appeal to all our boys as well. Elsewhere, the street food is spectacular – simple, delicious and incredibly cheap. Don't miss the action on 'chicken' street (real name: Ly Van Phuc Street) where you'll find every part of the bird barbecued at a seemingly endless string of outdoor stalls.

During the days, in an attempt to retain their attention, we give the older boys one of the two city guides we've brought with us and let them direct explorations. In the mornings, we ramble through the Old Town and head

towards Hoan Kiem Lake. A dawn stroll around its edge is what most Hanoians count as exercise, although you'll also see some practising their t'ai chi. At its centre is a tiny island housing the serene Ngoc Son Temple, a respite from the hustle and bustle. By lunchtime, though, the Junior Smiths are ready to get back to their laptops. It's not hard to understand where they're coming from. Walking can be exhausting, especially when you're continually jumping on and off the footpaths to avoid either the makeshift kitchens of street vendors or the hundreds of mopeds heading straight for you.

We have a trip to breathtaking Halong Bay planned, just three hours' drive away, promising sailing on an intimate junk, kayaking, trekking and cave-hopping, but it's a distraction of an altogether girlier kind that gets our vote in Hanoi. And it's one aspect of our trip that I can assure you will never make any of the boys' Facebook pages. We wake one morning to rain falling outside and, unable to stand the thought of spending all day in the hotel, decide on a family excursion to a local beauty parlour. Not the swish rooftop spa at the hotel, you understand, but a humbler place patronised by locals. The Cherry Beauty Salon is a few doors up the road from the Maison d'Hanoi and it's incredibly cheap – only US$5 for a manicure and a few bucks more for a pedicure. For the first time in their lives, my two elder sons have a facial, manicure, pedicure and a four-hand massage, the latter sending them into fits of giggles. So, from our centrally located base camp, Mr Smith and I have introduced our sons to the tastes of Vietnamese food, the fundamentals of Buddhism and the joys of pampering. You can't learn that from Google.

Reviewed by Lee Manton

Rates US$86–US$220, including buffet breakfast, excluding 10 per cent tax and five per cent service charge.
Check-out Noon, but flexible subject to a half-night's fee before 6pm. Check-in, 2pm, unless rooms are available earlier.
Facilities Free WiFi throughout, computers for guests' use, travel desk (for advice on surviving, or even thriving, in Hanoi), small rooftop spa. In rooms: standard and flatscreen TVs, DVD players in suites, minibar.
Children Welcome, but avoid entry-level Classic Standard rooms which don't have space for an extra bed (US$20 a night). Baby cots are free. The lift only operates to the 10th floor, so be prepared for a gentle climb if your room is above.
Also The rooftop Royal Spa is a nice touch, with three treatment areas separated by screens, plus a Jacuzzi and sauna. It's not a resort spa, as Hanoi is space-sensitive, but then it's not resort prices, with massages from just US$12.

IN THE KNOW

Our favourite rooms Decorated in vibrant colours with oversized silk bedheads, contemporary art, lanterns and parquet floors, rooms are a graphic modern take on Vietnamese design. At the lower end of the price scale, most Classic Standard rooms don't have a window, so we suggest opting for at least a Deluxe. Given the reasonable rates, go the whole hog and take a suite. 801 is a Classic Suite with a big balcony. 1201 is a stylish Deluxe Suite with views over St Joseph's Cathedral.
Hotel bar The Piano Bar is part of the restaurant and features a pianist playing romantic tunes most evenings. Wine starts at less than US$20 a bottle, spirits from just US$30.
Hotel restaurant Located beneath the lobby, Hanova Café Restaurant continues the contemporary Vietnamese feel with geometric silks on the ceiling. The menu includes trad local and international dishes.
Top table All tables are equally enticing as the restaurant layout is symmetrical.
Room service A leaner room service menu is available 24/7, but unless you're staying in a suite, it might be too cosy to dine in your room.
Dress code Something you really like, as there are a lot of mirrors on the walls. Those old Che Guevara T-shirts are sure to go down well in the home of the revolution.
Local knowledge The hotel is located in the beating heart of Hanoi's Old Quarter, just a gentle stroll from trendy Nha Tho strip and the iconic Hoan Kiem Lake. Join the fray from a safe distance with a cyclo ride, urban Vietnam's traditional form of transport – it's still a romantic and relaxing way to get around.

LOCAL EATING AND DRINKING

At 48 Hang Be Street, Green Tangerine (+84 (0)438 251 286) offers French food with a Vietnamese twist in a leafy courtyard. More local institution than bar, Minh's Jazz Club (+84 (0)438 287 890; www.minhjazzvietnam.com), on Luong Van Can Street, is the longest-running live jazz venue in Hanoi, hosted by father and son duo Minh and Dac. Another popular Nha Tho stop, Moca Café (+84 (0)438 256 334) is perfect for people-watching thanks to its full frontal windows. If you're a shop-till-you-drop type, scour the boutiques before settling down here for assertive coffees and home-brewed beers.

GET A ROOM!

For more information, or to book this hotel, go to www.mrandmrssmith.com – our expert team can take care of all your travel arrangements. Register your Smith membership card to enjoy exclusive offers and privileges.

 SMITH MEMBER OFFER A margarita cocktail for each guest.

Maison d'Hanoi Hanova Hotel 35–37 Hang Trong Street, Hoan Kiem District, Hanoi, Vietnam (+84 (0)439 380 999;

HOI AN

CITYSCAPE History-steeped harbour town
CITY LIFE Sailors and tailors

Hoi An will charm your pants off, but that's fine – this is the tailoring capital of Vietnam, so it's easy to find another pair. Nose around 19th-century merchant houses, explore old temples or just browse the cafés and galleries of this river-straddling former trading port. It's a small coastal city to be savoured, slowly. Just beyond town is China Beach, one of the most alluring stretches of sand in the country, hugging the coast all the way to Danang. Culture cravers won't be disappointed either, as the surrounding hinterland cradles the vestiges of an older empire, including the Cham temples of My Son. Add to the mix diving around the Cu Lao Cham Marine Park and the excuse to replace your wardrobe for a steal and you'll find Hoi An is the real deal.

GETTING THERE

Planes Danang International is the closest airport to Hoi An, a 45-minute drive away, with regular connections from popular Vietnamese destinations including Hanoi, Ho Chi Minh City and Nha Trang. Currently direct international flights are fairly limited, but Silk Air (www.silkair.com) offers links from Singapore and Siem Reap in Cambodia.
Trains 30km from Hoi An, Danang is a major stop on the daily Reunification Express train connecting north and south Vietnam. Sleeper berths are available to and from Ho Chi Minh City, Nha Trang and Hanoi. Go for first class with air-conditioning (www.vr.com.vn).
Automobiles A car is not necessary for visitors to pedestrian-friendly Hoi An, but if you want to explore further afield, your hotel can organise a car with a driver for you.

LOCAL KNOWLEDGE

Taxis There are several metered taxi firms in Hoi An and it costs about US$6 to travel to the beach resorts. Xe oms (motorbike taxis) also patrol the streets, but prices are not fixed. A taxi from Danang to Hoi An will set you back about US$15.
Siesta and fiesta The Vietnamese observe a siesta during lunch, so banks and businesses tend to trade 8am to 11.30am and 1pm to 4pm, as well as on

Saturday mornings. Shops keep longer hours and will usually open 8am to 8pm. Restaurants serve up until about 10pm and a few bars rumble on after midnight.
Do go/don't go April and May are usually ideal for hitting Hoi An, with China Beach's seas at their calmest from May to July. Despite its location in the tropics, Hoi An experiences a wet winter monsoon (October to March), when it can be cool at night; the summer monsoon (April to September) brings hot but breezy weather. In October and November typhoons regularly slam into the central coast; the city floods and the only way to get around is by boat.
Packing tips Everyone has that favourite item of clothing they just can't bear to part with but, try as they might, can't replace either. Now you can: bring along your desert-island dresses and dinner suits and the legendary tailors of Hoi An will whip up a copy for you. This is not bodged 'Kevin Clein', Bangkok-style, but a bespoke copy, uniquely crafted.
Recommended reads The Quiet American by Graham Greene captures the flavour of 1950s Vietnam before the American armada arrived. Greene lived his books as much as wrote them, blending journalistic experience with fiction. The 2002 film starring Michael Caine is also a must, as much of it was filmed in the alleys of Hoi An.

Local specialities The city has its own regional speciality in the shape of *cao lau*, short noodles with bean sprouts, croutons, greens and pork slices. It is said to be best prepared with water from the Ba Le Well in the centre of town, but most restaurants have adopted purified water as a wholesome alternative. Another favourite is white rose, a steamed dish of prawns in rice paper. Sample local dishes in the restaurants along Bach Dang Street, or try some original creations in the more sophisticated surrounds of Nguyen Thai Hoc Street.

Also Every full moon (the 14th day of the lunar month), the residents go traditional to celebrate Legendary Night. As much electrical light as possible is extinguished, and houses are lit up with enchanting silk lanterns. Motorbikes are banned from the Old Town and there are food stalls, cultural performances and games.

WORTH GETTING OUT OF BED FOR

Viewpoint Experience life on the other side of Hoi An's Thu Bon River. Cross over the bridge to the An Hoi Peninsula, where Nguyen Phuc Chu Street offers a panoramic view back over the Old Town, miraculously spared the ravages of the American War. Nab a balcony pew at the River Lounge (at number 35) and wash the vistas down with Italian coffee and pastries.

Arts and culture The Handicraft Workshop, in a centuries-old-Chinese merchant's house on Nguyen Thai Hoc Street, offers demonstrations of traditional skills such as lantern making, embroidery and soap stone sculpture. There's also a performance of folk music and dancing twice a day (except Monday).

Activities If Vietnamese cuisine has really tickled your palate, then sign up for one of Hoi An's excellent cooking classes. Highway 4 (www.highway4.com) offers half-day courses that include a visit to a local market, several popular recipes and a hearty lunch.

Best beach It's had a TV series named after it and its white sand stretches for a whopping 30km. Do you need to be told anything else to be sold on China Beach? It's fringed by palms, has beachfront seafood restaurants and you can walk forever. The waves provide boisterous bodysurfing, but do pay attention to the flags, as currents along this stretch can be strong.

Daytripper The old imperial capital of Vietnam, Hué is located 140km north of Hoi An. Explore the old Citadel complex and remains of the Forbidden Purple City, the emperors' hideaway modelled on the more famous Forbidden City in Beijing. If you are feeling a little adventurous, take the coastal railway from Danang to Hué in one direction. The track wraps itself around the shoreline, delivering spectacular coastal scenery.

Children Cham Island is actually seven smaller bumps in the ocean, surrounded by a marine park; organised boat trips can pick you up from your hotel and speedboat you to these tropical isles in 25 minutes, before revealing local fishing villages and dropping you off for a bit of snorkelling. For more serious scuba action with older kids, try Rainbow Divers (www.divevietnam.com).

Walks Lose yourself in the heart of old Hoi An. Phan Boi Chau Street has some elegant French architecture and easily connects with fashionable Nguyen Thai Hoc Street, home to cafés, bars and restaurants. Cross the historic Japanese Covered Bridge and browse the art galleries on the other side. For a ramble further afield, make for the craggy karst formations of the Marble Mountains, north of Hoi An, which are dotted with temples and shrines. Its five peaks are named after the elements; Thuy Son (Water Mountain) is the most famous, with caves and killer views.

Perfect picnic Lush Thuan Tinh Island is just 3km from the centre of Hoi An, but it's a bit of a secret. Hire one of the river boat skippers to take you there, then visit the organic market to grab supplies for lunch. Alternatively, book a Thuan Tinh Island Cooking Tour (+84 (0)906 477 770) where you choose produce from the market then learn how to cook up four dishes.

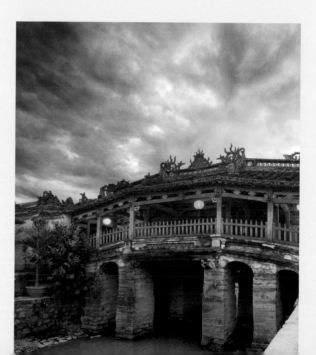

Shopping Warning: Hoi An can be seriously challenging for recovering shopaholics. Tailormade clothing, handcrafted shoes, embroidered linens, contemporary art, exquisite lanterns and antiques... the temptations are endless. Yaly Couture (www.yalycouture.com) is one of the most successful of the city's 500-odd tailors, with numerous branches in the Old Town. Also don't miss the gorgeous silks on sale at the Hoi An Cloth Market on Tran Phu Street. There are tailors on site if you want bolts of fabric turned into something special within 24 hours.

Something for nothing Ideal for walking or bike rides, the countryside around Hoi An is pancake flat, which goes some way to explaining the annual floods that visit the town. Explore the emerald green rice paddies that stretch as far as the eye can see, criss-crossed by canals. Kids career around on water buffaloes or take cooling dips while elders tend the fields. Timeless, magical, eco-friendly and it won't cost you a cent.

Don't go home without... catching sunrise or sunset at the ruins of My Son, a striking jungle-set temple complex 55km inland from Hoi An. Once the heart of the ancient Champa kingdom, it's like a mini Angkor or Bagan.

HISTORICALLY HOI AN

Hoi An is the best preserved ancient town in Vietnam and is a Unesco World Heritage site. Several historic houses are open to visitors and offer a time capsule of life in the 19th century. Tan Ky House is still occupied by the Tans (either the fifth or seventh generation – no one seems entirely sure) and was built by their Vietnamese merchant ancestor. The architecture blends Chinese and Japanese influences, and the rooms are packed with interesting antiques.

DIARY

23 March Strictly speaking, it's a Chinese festival but the whole community participates in the goddess of the sea ceremony, meant to protect the city's fishermen and help them prosper. **15 July** The Long Chu Festival (meaning 'royal barge') is celebrated with parades, processions and a common feast to ward off ghosts and other evils. **August** The Mid Autumn Festival revellers, on the 14th and 15th days of lunar August, give thanks to the moon, with much dancing, singing and partying by Hoi An's children.

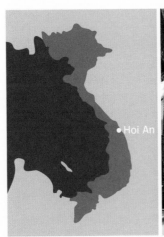 

The Nam Hai

STYLE Seaside design shrine
SETTING Iconic China beach

'Exquisite is the word that springs immediately to mind as we explore'

I wouldn't want anything less than perfection for my blushing bride, but when we're shown around our villa at the Nam Hai I do worry that Mrs Smith may have raised expectations about what her newly appointed husband might come up with for future romantic sojourns. We've been buggied from reception to our room by a friendly fellow with a wide grin (perhaps anticipating our reaction upon arrival) and because we're on our honeymoon, we've been upgraded to a One-Bedroom Beachfront Villa. 'Welcome home!' calls our driver, and as we enter, from the look on Mrs Smith's face I can tell she is ready, willing and able to call this place home for now. And maybe for ever more.

Exquisite is the word that springs immediately to mind as we explore. Neutral tones abound, and opportunities for lounging surround us. A raised platform in the centre of the villa is draped with white muslin and houses our king-size bed, a sunken eggshell-lacquered bath tub faces an LCD TV screen, an iPod plays the chilled sounds of Café del Mar, and there's a cosy lounge area for two. And then we find the bottle of Moët on ice and chocolate cake left for us in celebration of our recent nuptials.

Having arrived after sundown, the true splendour of our surroundings isn't revealed until we wake at sunrise the next day. Sweeping aside the muslin drapes at the foot of our bed, we open the French doors and take in the vista – the South China Sea stretching out to the Cham Islands in the distance.

Honeymoons are renowned for certain activities, but perhaps not early starts. We decide to kick off our stay with a swim in the ocean followed by one of the daily yoga classes conducted in an open pavilion. Afterwards, it's off to the restaurant, overlooking one of the three gorgeous pools – for tropical fruit and freshly cooked omelettes. Sated, Mrs Smith chooses our sunloungers and one of the ever-helpful Nam Hai staff immediately rolls out fresh towels and proffers chilled face flannels and water. It's a ritual that will be repeated many times during our visit and by the end of our stay Mrs Smith has fulfilled her ambition to spend half a day beside each pool.

Extracting ourselves from the prone position, Mrs Smith and I take a table at the Beach Restaurant. You won't need to stretch your imagination too far to imagine the scene: tables by one of the large pools, under a cloudless sky and overlooking the ocean. The food is simple and local and we enjoy a delicious lunch of grilled fish.

Apparently, according to Mrs Smith, no tropical holiday – in particular, no tropical honeymoon – is complete without some pampering in the spa. Complete? We only just got here. But I am a willing participant in this relaxation game, and so dutifully follow. We are met with iced lemongrass and ginger tea and, after selecting a massage oil from a choice of five, are led to a treatment room set over a serenely beautiful reflection pond. The session kicks off with a foot therapy performed while we sip tea and stare into the water. The massage itself is divinely relaxing and we float back to our villa to sup on rum and soda and watch the sky turn pink as the sun goes down.

Filling your days at the Nam Hai isn't too tricky, given the seemingly limitless distractions. For the activity-inclined, there are tennis courts, a gym, golf courses, organised beach volleyball games and trips to the Cham Islands just for starters. Having discovered the local cuisine and a taste for it, we enrol ourselves in another of the hotel's offerings, a Vietnamese cooking class. Early in the morning we cycle into a local village with one of the

resort's chefs, who guides us around the market showing us the tropical fruits and inviting us to taste each one. He is full of energy and fun and it's a great chance for us to experience a little slice of local life. On return to the Nam Hai, we are given time for a quick swim before we are led into one of the restaurant kitchens to cook up a feast of rice-paper rolls, banana flower salad and a rice noodle dish with scrumptious prawns and chicken covered with an aromatic broth.

If it doesn't involve food or being horizontal though, Mrs Smith and I find it hard to muster much enthusiasm. We are here to relax, so opt for gentle yoga, much reading time, mojitos by the pool and as many spa treatments as the missus can squeeze into her busy schedule. In our more energetic moments we trundle into the beautiful nearby town of Hoi An, a Unesco World Heritage site. It's the most charming place, packed with hawkers touting handmade shoes, clothing and jewellery. We visit delightful eateries or simply drink the locally brewed Biere Larue and watch the world go by.

When the end of our stay draws near we try to sum up our time here and wonder how we can ever describe this place to our family and friends. Mrs Smith says it reminds her of a movie setting that you can't imagine could be anywhere near as amazing in real life. But Nam Hai is. From the beauty of the natural surrounds to the luxury of our room and the allure of the hotel itself, every detail of our time here has been meticulously considered by someone intent on making sure we have the most relaxing time of our lives. And to whomever that is, Mrs Smith and I say a big *cam on* (that's Vietnamese for thank you).

Reviewed by Trevor Hannam

NEED TO KNOW

Rooms 100 villas, including 60 one-bedroom villas and 40 pool villas each with one to five bedrooms.
Rates US$750–US$3,800, excluding 10 per cent tax and five per cent service charge. Breakfast is extra at US$28 for adults or US$14 for children under 12.
Check-out Noon, but flexible subject to availability. Earliest check-in, 2pm, unless rooms become free earlier.
Facilities Spa, gym, health centre, yoga pavilion, tennis courts, free WiFi throughout. In rooms: flatscreen cable TV, Bose sound system, multimedia player with preloaded movies, iPod dock, Panpuri toiletries, minibar, espresso machine.
Poolside The temperature-controlled upper pool features artsy ceramic urns on plinths. Dropping down a level is a long, narrow lap pool for serious swimmers. Finally comes the definitive infinity pool blending into the ocean horizon.
Children Kids are welcome; baby cots are free; extra beds for older children cost US$35 a night. You can also convert the sofa to a bed for US$70 in a Villa or US$120 in a Pool Villa. Babysitting costs US$20 an hour, with 24 hours' notice, and the Children's Club will keep junior Smiths amused with kite flying, tug-of-war, art and baking classes.
Also Guests staying in any of the Pool Villas enjoy Club Benefits, including free airport and local town transfers, butler service, free minibar items, daily breakfast, in-room afternoon tea and complimentary pre-dinner drinks and snacks.

IN THE KNOW

Our favourite rooms All designer dens are truly Zenic with romantic net-canopied platform beds flanked by divans and freestanding eggshell-lacquered baths opening up to private gardens and outdoor rain showers. The Beachfront Villas are particularly alluring thanks to instant access to China Beach and sexy sea views. 4010 and 4020 are closest to the infinity pool; 4030 is just one villa back from the waves, so is a cheap Charlie answer to the Beachfront Villa.
Hotel bar The Bar sits atop the restaurant and the outdoor terrace offers panoramic views over the pools. A sneaky insider trick is to order food at the bar terrace, as bar table E3 has the best views in the house.
Hotel restaurant The Restaurant is another style icon. Mod international cuisine complements the delicious artistically presented Vietnamese dishes. The Beach Restaurant is perfect for a lazy lunch by the pool.
Top table Settle outdoors on a balmy night and try to score E4, a table with both pool and beach views. On honeymoon? Request a private gazebo for a beach barbecue. It'll work wonders for proposals, too.
Room service Available from 6am to 10.30pm, with a more limited night menu from 11pm to 6am.
Dress code Don't forget the designer wear as this place is mode to the max.
Local knowledge Heaven for sun lizards, the Nam Hai languishes on a pristine stretch of sand on China Beach. Just 8km down the road awaits the seductive charms of Hoi An. Wander the streets and spot kaleidoscopic influences from global traders who have made their home here. Gold fans can tee off at two-star courses nearby, too.

LOCAL EATING AND DRINKING

Owner Duc Tran whips up some of Central Vietnam's most exciting contemporary cuisine at the Mango Rooms (+84 (0)510 391 0839) at 111 Nguyen Thai Hoc Street. Just across the road, Tam Tam (+84 (0)510 386 2212), is Hoi An's longest-running bar, set in an imposing French colonial trading house. Completing a trio of neighbourhood joints, Cargo Club (+84 (0)510 391 0489), at number 107, is a five-star patisserie at one-star prices.

GET A ROOM!

For more information, or to book this hotel, go to www.mrandmrssmith.com – our expert team can take care of all your travel arrangements. Register your Smith membership card to enjoy exclusive offers and privileges.

 SMITH MEMBER OFFER
A bottle of sparkling wine on arrival.

The Nam Hai Hamlet 1, Dien Duong Village, Dien Ban District, Quang Nam Province, Vietnam (+84 (0)510 394 0000; www.ghmhotels.com)

NHA TRANG

COASTLINE Mountain-backed bays
CITY LIFE Fluttering *ao dais*, spluttering cyclos

There's more to Vietnam's leading seaside resort than a sweeping stretch of sand. Nha Trang, on the south-central coast, is a buzzing town that offers a compact window on the country for those overwhelmed by the scale of nearby Ho Chi Minh City or Hanoi. Boasting a beautiful backdrop, hemmed in by jagged peaks and ringed by tropical islands, it is also one of Vietnam's top dive destinations. Some fear that Nha Trang is on its way to becoming the next Pattaya. There are several high-rise hotels springing up along the beachfront and the nightlife is more raucous than Hoi An or Hué, but it still retains a unique individual charm. It's not hard to escape by boat to a secluded bay if it all gets too much.

GETTING THERE

Planes Cam Ranh International Airport, 35km to the south, is the jumping-off point for Nha Trang with connections from major hubs in Vietnam, including Ho Chi Minh City, Hanoi and Danang. With its newfound international status, direct flights are being planned for travel to and from neighbouring capitals, but for the time being there are only domestic links.

Trains The Reunification Express (www.vr.com.vn) connects the north and south of the country with Nha Trang en route. Nightly sleeper berths are available to and from Ho Chi Minh City, Danang and Hanoi — first class with air-con is really the only way to go.

Automobiles Witnessing the traffic on the coastal highway, you'll be relieved that self-drive is unavailable for visitors. Organising a car with a driver through your hotel or travel company from Ho Chi Minh City is a more relaxing option (stop off at surfing village Mui Ne, famous for its enormous red and white sand dunes, or at the ancient Cham Towers of Phan Rang).

LOCAL KNOWLEDGE

Taxis From the airport taxis cost about US$16, although it's less than US$10 in the other direction. Once in Nha Trang they, along with cyclos (three-wheeled pedicabs) and xe oms (motorbike taxis) are plentiful, but ask the driver to turn on the meter or at least negotiate the fare before you head off.

Siesta and fiesta Banks and government agencies take a little break during the day, so tend to ply their trade 8am to 11.30am and 1pm to 4pm, plus Saturday mornings. Shops usually keep longer hours 8am to 8pm. Restaurants are open until around 10pm. A handful of bars will stagger beyond the midnight hour.

Do go/don't go Nha Trang has some of the best weather to be found along Vietnam's coastline. Officially the rains dampen the party from October to December, but in recent years they have been fairly light.

Packing tips Mrs Smith, you need to bring lots of flowing dresses to compete with the *ao dais* on show in Nha Trang. The Vietnamese have a proverb that their female national dress covers everything but hides nothing, so don't be afraid to be a little provocative. Mr Smith, no such worries for you — pack your Gap slacks and relax.

Recommended reads *A Rumor of War* by Philip Caputo is one of the best-written memoirs to emerge from the American War in Vietnam. For something to make you laugh, seek out a copy of *Phaic Tan: Sunstroke on a Shoestring* by Santo Cilauro, Tom Gleisner and Rob Sitch. A spoof guidebook to a composite country in south-east Asia — read it and weep with mirth.

Local specialities Nha Trang is the seafood capital of Vietnam, with a huge fishing fleet visible in the river estuary nestled beneath the Po Nagar Cham Towers. Lobster farms provide fresh tails daily. Whether bubbling in a hotpot or grilled on the beach, *fruits de mer* should top your list of indulgences.

Also Mud, glorious mud. If your spa treatment habit is breaking the bank, get down and dirty with a traditional mud bath. Thap Ba Hot Spring Centre (+84 (0)58 383 4939; www.thapbahotspring.com.vn) offers toasty thermal mud baths for less than US$10 or, to save even more dollars, you can join the crowd in a communal slop.

WORTH GETTING OUT OF BED FOR

Viewpoint Facing due east – next stop, the Philippines – Nha Trang Beach is the prime spot for soaking up the infinite horizon, ideally from a horizontal position. Get up early to experience the sunrise, when the rosy dawn light washes across the lapping waves and the bay's verdant islands. Sunset is no slouch either.

Arts and culture The Chams controlled this area of Vietnam long before the Viets came to town, with the Kingdom of Champa stretching from Central Vietnam to the borders of the Khmer Empire near the Mekong Delta. Dedicated followers of Hinduism, they built delicate brick temples honouring their pantheon of gods and it is worth visiting the Po Nagar Cham Towers in Nha Trang. Constructed between the 7th and 12th centuries, this group of towers is a gentle introduction to Cham art and architecture.

Activities Nha Trang is rightly considered the diving capital of Vietnam. Underwater Smiths will be eager to earn their Vietnamese stripes with some offshore dives in the warm tropical waters of the South China Sea around the islands of the Hon Mun Marine Park. While the aquatic life might not be the biggest you've ever seen, there is an amazing array of coral species – around 350 different types. Rainbow Divers has been exploring the waters longer than anyone else in the region, and can whisk you out to most dive sites within 15 minutes by speedboat (www.divevietnam.com).

Best beach It couldn't be easier. Nha Trang Beach, sweeping for 6km along the town's seafront, has sparkling waters and an enviable stretch of sand dotted with beach chairs for hire. If you get thirsty, or peckish, Louisiane Brewhouse and the Sailing Club (29 and 72 Tran Phu Boulevard) are the go-to hang-outs.

Daytripper More than 70 islands beckon just offshore. Your hotel can hook you up with one of the popular boat trips, which usually include visits to an aquarium, a lobster farm and a local fishing village, along with a spot of snorkelling. Sumptuous seafood feasts are often part of the deal, so plan for a light dinner.

Children Apologies in advance for dropping you in it, but we have to mention the V-word. Vinpearl Amusement Park (www.vinpearlland.com) is kitsch and cheesy, but the kids will have a ball. Take the cable car to Hon Tre Island's oversized funfair, where the huge water park boasts dozens of wild slides and rides.

Walks Stroll along the extensive beachfront, which now has a promenade running most of its length. Start early to catch the Vietnamese practising t'ai chi at dawn or playing badminton. As the day wears on, weave in and out of the city streets as the mood takes you.

Perfect picnic Hire a motorbike and follow the coastal road north as it hugs the dramatic coastline. Your destination is Doc Let Beach, 40km away. This is one of the less-developed beach strips in the Nha Trang area, so it's still possible to find a secluded enclave.

Shopping Compared with Hanoi or Hoi An, this isn't exactly the town for spending your dosh. Make for Cho Dam Market to pick up fish, fruit and other tasty food as well as textiles, clothing and trinkets. Tran Phu Street offers a tempting selection of handicrafts: Kim Quang hand-paints T-shirts at his small shop near the Sailing Club.

Something for nothing Make a pilgrimage to the Long Son Pagoda, with its mosaic dragons, perched on a hilltop above town. Beyond the pavillion is the Big Buddha, a giant white statue visible from all over Nha Trang. Just as you can see him, he can see you, so the views over the coast are spectacular.

Don't go home without... checking out Studio & Gallery Long Thanh Art at 126 Hoang Van Thu Street (www.longthanhart.com), owned by the country's most celebrated photographer, Long Thanh. Eschewing modern technology, he concentrates on haunting black-and-white images that capture the spirit of Vietnam.

NATURALLY NHA TRANG
Nha Trang Beach is one of the few stretches of sand in Vietnam to be located in the city centre, offering the best of both worlds. Mr and Mrs Smith can laze away the day from the comfort of their loungers, then prowl the urban jungle by night, browsing restaurants and hopping bars. Live the quiet life in your resort, and the high life in town.

DIARY
January/February Vietnamese New Year, known as Tet, falls on the same lunar calendar dates as Chinese New Year, with much of the country on the move for holidays or family visits. **March** Held across four days during the third lunar month, the Thap Ba Festival celebrates the Holy Mother at Nha Trang's Po Nagar Cham Towers, with religious rituals and traditional dances. **June** The city's upbeat Sea Festival, including street and fashion parades, cultural performances and kite flying, takes place every two years on odd-numbered years.

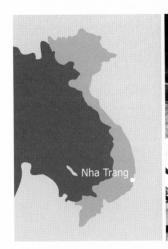

Nha Trang

Six Senses Ninh Van Bay

STYLE Eco-chic castaway
SETTING Private peninsula

'Our weekend getaway first reveals itself as a long crescent of white sand backed by towering mountains with dramatic rock formations'

To the Vietnamese, geckos are considered symbols of good luck. A small white one welcomes us at the front door of our villa and already this weekend away feels auspicious. Our two-storey lodgings at Six Senses Ninh Van Bay is an inspiring example of eco-serenity. Wooden features throughout, bamboo railings and whitewashed walls are just the start. Lashings of natural light stream in from all sides. The bay window overlooking our own secluded infinity pool and the beach beyond is most impressive, although Mr Smith is having all sorts of problems dragging himself away from another arresting sight – the fridge, which is stocked with 16 bottles of wine as well as Taittinger Champagne.

It's all a far cry from the scene that welcomed us – thankfully, from the comfort of an air-conditioned car – as we left Nha Trang's Cam Ranh airport. The city's scooter mob is a remarkable sight; hundreds of mopeds zip along the streets, and almost anything goes, from a tradesman carrying a long ladder to a family of four on a single motorbike. Although driving Vietnam-style resembles out-and-out chaos, you quickly realise there is some vague logic shaped largely by horn etiquette. Basically, you honk when you start, stop, overtake or at will any time in between.

Finally we arrive, happy and safe, at the Six Senses Lounge. Although not on an island, as many think, the resort isn't accessible by road, so we take a short trip north by speedboat – very James Bond – to Ninh Van Bay. Each time we experience a surprise bout of South China Sea spray, Mr Smith and I exchange smiles.

Our weekend getaway first reveals itself as a long crescent of white sand backed by towering mountains with dramatic rock formations closer to shore. Arriving on the private jetty we're met by our butler, who escorts us to our villa. During the buggy ride An informs us that Ninh Van Bay is one hour ahead of Hanoi. Not because of an officially different time zone, mind, but purely to give holidaymakers an extra hour of daylight. Here, time seems to be on our side.

Dragging Mr Smith away from the fully laden fridge, we explore our Hill Top Villa, a mod Robinson Crusoe abode. We have a choice of sleeping either upstairs beneath a mosquito net that splays over a giant day-bed on an open balcony, or in the air-conditioned comfort of the downstairs room. The bathroom blends perfectly with the subtropical outdoors courtesy of an open-air shower and a wooden bath tub for two – it looks a bit like a huge, misshapen wine barrel – that Mr Smith suggests we try out later. Small details – herb-filled linen pouches to scent the room, soaps wrapped in recycled paper and ceramic jars filled with Six Senses bath products – add an eco-friendly, at-one-with-nature feel and help distinguish this retreat from so many others. An leaves us to enjoy the welcome platter of exotic fruits and champagne, and to explore two very large beds plumped with dream-inducing pillows.

Dinnertime finally arrives, so we amble to the grand wooden pavilion of Dining by the Bay. It's a balmy evening and the view of the bay as the sun sinks is sublime. Mr Smith enjoys a local Vietnamese beef stew, but since we're on holiday I don't hesitate before ordering lobster. Freshly caught this morning, it's barbecued before my eyes and served with just a wedge of lime and salt and pepper. It's simple but sensational. Once the last of our feast has been devoured we head back to the villa, take a dip under the stars and then luxuriate with a long, relaxing herbal soak in the tub, glass of red in hand.

Waking mid-morning to the sound of a fishing boat puttering past, we decide on the day's plans while helping ourselves to a breakfast spread worthy of royalty. First stop: the spa. When you opt for a Six Senses Spa experience, the pampering starts the moment you step into its sanctuary. Here, the entrance features enormous white stepping stones suspended over a small lake. We're seated for our consultation with the spa manager and given ginger-infused tea and cool towels. Pardon the cliché, but there is a plethora of treatments on offer. However, I'm smitten by the sound of the Escape Journey – exfoliation, massage and facial. Mr Smith, meanwhile, has set his heart on the Oriental Massage, which is meant to uplift and enhance vitality. We peel off to our respective women's and men's sauna and steam rooms before rejoining for two blissful hours in the couple's treatment room.

For more energetic holidaymakers there are all sorts of daytime activities and excursions – from diving and fishing trips to cultural visits to local villages – but this place, to us, is all about rest and relaxation in the comfort of our private villa. On our final evening, we organise an intimate meal in the romantically lit Wine Cave. It's just Mr Smith and me, rows and rows of fabulous wines, and a few lucky geckos.

Reviewed by Carrie Choo

NEED TO KNOW

Rooms 58 villas, including one suite.

Rates US$675–US$2,980, excluding breakfast (US$25), 10 per cent tax and five per cent service charge.

Check-out Noon; earliest check-in, 1pm, but both are flexible subject to availability.

Facilities Six Senses Spa, gym, yoga pavilion, excursions/watersports centre, golf buggies and bicycles, free WiFi in lobby, free broadband in public areas. In rooms: TV, CD/DVD player, iPod dock, minibar, mini wine cellar, free bottled water, free broadband (free WiFi by request only).

Poolside Every villa has its own pool. The main pool is spacious and quiet, with a beachside location.

Children Very welcome. There's a children's club with organised activities. Cots are free for infants. All villas include double day-beds, which can be converted into beds for older kids. Babysitters are available for US$10 an hour.

Also The resort is accessed by boat. Staff will pick you up from the airport and organise your water taxi from the Six Senses Lounge in Nha Trang. Presidential Suite guests get a private boat transfer. Butler service is available.

IN THE KNOW

Our favourite rooms For those who prefer jungle seclusion, request Spa Suite Villas 4 or 5. Beach Pool Villas are inspirationally set over two levels near the beach. Oh, but the Water Villas: with a private plunge pool perched amid boulders, and a ladder directly into the sea, this is special – Water Villa 5 is the pick.

Hotel bar Poolside drinks are on offer throughout the day, but towards evening, make a beeline for Drinks by the Bay. During 'no rush hour', from 4pm until 7pm, drinks are two for one.

Hotel restaurant Dining by the Bay offers informal dining with expansive views over the twinkling resort by night. The menu includes Vietnam's finest such as *banh xeo* (stuffed savoury pancakes) and seafood hotpot. Dining by the Pool is ideal for a light lunch such as papaya and seafood salad. Dining by the Rocks is the resort's special-occasion eatery, high on the cliffs and only available by reservation. You can also dine à deux in the romantic Wine Cave.

Top table The best views are to be had at Dining by the Rocks. For a more intimate affair, request a villa barbecue.

Room service Available from 7am–10.30pm, featuring a hearty selection from the restaurant menu. A more limited after-hours menu is on offer through the night, including pizzas, salads and ice cream.

Dress code Walking boots for Dining by the Rocks (only teasing, it's not a major climb); swimwear and sarongs for Dining by the Pool; and anything goes at Dining by the Bay.

Local knowledge The resort's excursion centre offers watersports and land-based adventures such as picnics at local waterfalls, and hilltop hikes to hidden coves. All itineraries are available in combination with Spa Escape packages.

LOCAL EATING AND DRINKING

So many dining options on your castaway peninsula, so little reason to leave. If you must, take a sunset cruise, and quaff champagne and canapés as the sun melts into the horizon. For a slice of local life, it's back to Nha Trang: Truc Linh 1 (+84 (0)583 526 742), on Biet Thu, is a popular open-sided restaurant serving succulent seafood. Beachfront the Sailing Club (+84 (0)583 826 528), at 72 Tran Phu Boulevard, also excels at shellfish, alongside a varied menu of Vietnamese, French, Italian, Indian and more. A Vietnamese beach resort seems an unlikely spot for a microbrewery – all the more reason to sup for yourself at the Louisiane Brewhouse (+84 (0)583 521 948) on 29 Tran Phu Boulevard.

GET A ROOM!

For more information, or to book this hotel, go to www.mrandmrssmith.com – our expert team can take care of all your travel arrangements. Register your Smith membership card to enjoy exclusive offers and privileges.

 SMITH MEMBER OFFER A 30-minute body scrub massage for two.

Six Senses Ninh Van Bay Ninh Hoa, Khanh Hoa, 5700 Vietnam (+84 (0)58 372 8222; www.sixsenses.com)

(something on the house)

 Look out for this Smith member offer icon at the end of each hotel review.

As a BlackSmith member, you're automatically entitled to exclusive added extras: it's our way of saying thank you, and ensuring your stay is as enjoyable as possible. Activate your free membership now (see pages 4–5) to take advantage of the offers listed below when you book one of these hotels with us. For more information, or to make a reservation, visit www.mrandmrssmith.com or talk to our expert travel team.

ABACA BOUTIQUE RESORT
Cebu & Mactan Island, Philippines
A bottle of sparkling wine and 10 per cent off spa treatments.

ALEENTA HUA HIN
Hua Hin, Thailand
A bottle of Aleenta label wine and a gift set from the Galleria Aleenta Luxury collection; a bottle of champagne for five-night stays; a three-course meal for 10-night stays.

ALEENTA PHUKET–PHANG NGA
Phang Nga, Thailand
A romantic breakfast with bubbles and a red rose; a magical bath experience for five-night stays; a candlelit dinner for two for seven-night stays.

ALILA CHA-AM
Hua Hin, Thailand
A mixology class for two.

ALILA VILLAS SOORI
Seminyak & Tabanan, Bali, Indonesia
A 90-minute spa treatment for two; and, if you stay for two nights or more, dinner for two at Cotta restaurant.

ALILA VILLAS ULUWATU
Bukit Peninsula, Bali, Indonesia
A 90-minute Balinese massage for each guest.

THE AMALA
Seminyak & Tabanan, Bali, Indonesia
Healthy canapés and a fruit platter on arrival; and a romantic candlelit bath experience set up in your room.

AMANTAKA
Luang Prabang, Laos
An Asian Blend Massage for two.

ANANTARA PHUKET RESORT & SPA
Phuket, Thailand
An hour's unlimited Anantara signature cocktails for two.

THE APSARA RIVE DROITE
Luang Prabang, Laos
Dinner for two at the hotel's restaurant, excluding drinks.

THE BALE Bukit Peninsula, Bali, Indonesia
A bottle of wine and canapés on arrival and late check-out at 3pm.

BON TON RESTAURANT & RESORT
Langkawi, Malaysia
A welcome drink and a lime margarita each.

CAPELLA SINGAPORE
Singapore, Singapore
English High Tea for two at the Knolls.

COMO SHAMBHALA ESTATE
Ubud, Bali, Indonesia
A Como Shambhala aromatherapy gift; a
60-minute massage for two for five-night stays;
or for seven-night stays, a two-hour bath body
treatment for two.

HERITAGE SUITES HOTEL Siem Reap, Cambodia
A tour of the Angkor Wat temples in the hotel's
vintage Mercedes.

KARMA KANDARA
Bukit Peninsula, Bali, Indonesia
A wine appreciation session for two.

KIRIMAYA GOLF RESORT SPA Khao Yai, Thailand
A bottle of wine; 20 per cent off all food,
drink and spa treatments; and 50 per cent off
green fees.

KNAI BANG CHATT Kep, Cambodia
A 30-minute massage or a discovery hour
on a sailing boat for each guest.

THE LEGIAN & THE CLUB
Seminyak & Tabanan, Bali, Indonesia
A 30-minute neck and shoulder massage each.

THE LIBRARY Koh Samui, Thailand
A bottle of sparkling wine on arrival. Members
booking a suite will get free airport transfers,
members staying five nights will be treated to
a romantic dinner for two at the Page.

MA DU ZI HOTEL Bangkok, Thailand
A bottle of red, white or sparkling wine on arrival.

MAISON D'HANOI HANOVA HOTEL
Hanoi, Vietnam
A margarita cocktail for each guest.

THE NAM HAI Hoi An, Vietnam
A bottle of sparkling wine on arrival.

NAUMI Singapore, Singapore
Breakfast for two served in your room.

PURIPUNN Chiang Mai, Thailand
A choice of either a Puripunn Chill or Puripunn
Lovely cocktail, and 15 per cent off your first
spa treatment.

THE PURIST VILLAS & SPA Ubud, Bali, Indonesia
An Anti-Jetlag package for two, including a
30-minute neck and shoulder massage on
arrival, healthy mocktail and Balinese offering box.

THE RACHA Phuket, Thailand
A bottle of wine and a fruit basket.

RACHAMANKHA Chiang Mai, Thailand
A bottle of chilled sparkling wine on arrival.

SATRI HOUSE Luang Prabang, Laos
A Jet Lag massage for two in Satri House Spa.

SIX SENSES NINH VAN BAY Nha Trang, Vietnam
A 30-minute body scrub massage for two.

THE SUKHOTHAI Bangkok, Thailand
A bottle of sparkling wine on arrival.

TRISARA Phuket, Thailand
An exclusive gift of handmade chocolates and
fruit, plus 25 per cent off all massages in the spa.

VIROTH'S HOTEL Siem Reap, Cambodia
A hand-woven cotton scarf for each room.

YL RESIDENCE NO. 17 Koh Samui, Thailand
A cocktail and a Thai tapas party, and an Urb
spa gift for all guests.

To browse all offers available
at each of the 700+ hotels in
the Mr & Mrs Smith collection, go to
www.mrandmrssmith.com/smith-card-offers.

(useful contacts)

PLANES (REGIONAL)

China China Airlines (+886 (0)2 2715 1212; www.china-airlines.com); China Southern Airlines (+86 (0)20 95539; www.flychinasouthern.com)
Hong Kong Dragonair (+852 3193 3888; www.dragonair.com)
Indonesia Merpati Nusantara Airlines (+62 (0)21 654 6789; www.merpati.co.id)
Laos Lao Airlines (+856 (0)21 212057; www.laoairlines.com)
Malaysia Air Asia (+60 (0)3 2171 9333; AUS: 1300 760 330; UK: 0845 605 3333; www.airasia.com); Firefly (+60 (0)3 7845 4543; www.firefl yz.com.my)
Philippines Cebu Pacific Air (+63 (0)32 230 8888; www.cebupacificair.com)
Singapore Silk Air (+65 6223 8888; www.silkair.com); Tiger Airways (+65 6808 4437; AUS: +61 (0)3 9335 3033; www.tigerairways.com)
Thailand Bangkok Airways (+66 (0)2 270 6699; www.bangkokair.com)
Vietnam Vietnam Airlines (+84 8 3832 0320; AUS: +61 (0)2 9283 1355; US: +1 415 677 8909; www.vietnamairlines.com)

PLANES (INTERNATIONAL)

Air France (AUS: 1300 390 190; UK: 0871 663 3777; US: 1 800 992 3932; www.airfrance.com)
Air India (AUS: 1800 227722; UK: 0800 635 0041; US: 1 800 223 7776; www.airindia.com)
Air New Zealand (0800 737 000; AUS: 132 476; UK: 0800 028 4149; US: 1 800 262 1234; www.airnewzealand.com)
British Airways (0844 493 0787; AUS: 1300 767 177; www.britishairways.com)
Cathay Pacific (+852 2747 1888; AUS: 131 747; UK: +44 206 634 8888; US: 1 800 233 2742; www.cathaypacific.com)
Emirates (+971 (0)4 214 4444; AUS: 1300 303 777; UK: 0844 800 2777; US: 1 800 777 3999; www.emirates.com)

Garuda Indonesia (+62 (0)21 2351 9999; www.garuda-indonesia.com)
Japan Airlines (+81 (0)3 5460 0511; AUS: 1300 525 287; UK: 0844 856 9700; US: 1 800 525 3663; www.jal.com)
Jetstar (+61 (0)3 9347 0091; US: 1 866 397 8170; AUS: 1300 392 192; www.jetstar.com)
Lufthansa (+49 (0)1 805 805 805; AUS: 1300 655 727; UK: 0871 945 9747; www.lufthansa.com)
Malaysia Airlines (+60 (0)3 7843 3000; AUS: +61 (0)2 9364 3500; UK: +44 (0)20 7341 2000; US: 1 800 5529 264; www.malaysiaairlines.com)
Philippine Airlines (+63 855 8888; AUS: 1300 888 725; US: 1 800 435 9725; www.philippineairlines.com)
Qantas (AUS: 131 313; UK: 0845 774 7767; US: 1 800 227 4500; www.qantas.com)
Singapore Airlines (+65 6223 8888; AUS: 131 011; UK: 0844 800 2380; US: 1 800 742 3333; www.singaporeair.com)
Thai Airways (+66 (0)7 636 0444; AUS: 1300 651 960; UK: 0844 561 0911; www.thaiairways.com)
United Airlines (US: 1 800 538 2929; AUS: 131 777; UK: 0845 844 4777; www.united.com)
Virgin Atlantic (UK: 0844 874 7747; US: 1 800 821 5438; AUS: 1300 727 340; www.virgin-atlantic.com)

AIRPORTS

Cambodia Phnom Penh International Airport (www.cambodia-airports.com); Siem Reap International Airport (www.cambodia-airports.com)
Indonesia Bali: Ngurah Rai International Airport, Denpasar (www.baliairport.com); Java: Soekarno-Hatta International Airport, Jakarta (www.airport-jakarta.com)
Laos Luang Prabang International Airport (www.luangprabangairport.com); Vientiane (Wattay) International Airport (www.vientianeairport.com)
Malaysia Kuala Lumpur International Airport; Langkawi International Airport (www.malaysiaairports.com)
Philippines Mactan-Cebu International Airport (www.mactan-cebuairport.com.ph); Manila Ninoy Aquino International Airport (www.manila-airport.net)

Singapore Changi Airport (www.changiairport.com)
Thailand Bangkok Suvarnabhumi International Airport
(www.bangkokairportonline.com); Krabi International
Airport (www.krabiairportonline.com); Phuket
International Airport (www.phuketairportonline.com);
Koh Samui Airport (www.samuiairportonline.com); Surat
Thani International Airport (www.suratthaniairport.com)
Vietnam Hanoi: Noi Bai International Airport (www.
hanoiairportonline.com); Ho Chi Minh City International
Airport (www.hochiminhcityairport.com)

TRAINS

Thailand The SkyTrain (or Bangkok Mass Transit System)
connects visitors to the Thai capital to the CBD and the
main shopping hubs (www.bts.co.th). Head from the
main State Railway of Thailand terminus at Krungthep
Station to other destinations (www.railway.co.th).
Thailand, Malaysia and Singapore Eastern & Oriental
Express trains offer a luxury service through these
countries (www.orient-express.com).
Singapore The Mass Rapid Transit connects the entire
city-state via 79 stations (www.smrt.com.sg).
Malaysia The Keretapi Tanah Malayu Berhad offers
a reasonable if infrequent service along the peninsula
(www.ktmb.com.my).
Vietnam The Vietnam North-South Railway aka the
Reunification Express snakes along the coastline from
Hanoi to Ho Chi Minh City (www.vr.com.vn).

AUTOMOBILES

Avis (www.avis.com) and Hertz (www.hertz.com)
offer standard car hire from many hubs and
Globalcars.com.au and CarRentals.co.uk source you
wheels in Malaysia, Singapore and Thailand. Self-drive
is not possible in many parts of south-east Asia, so
speak to your hotel about booking a local driver.

BOATS

Cambodia Sailing Club, Kep (www.knaibangchatt.com)
Indonesia Bali Hai Cruises, Benoa Harbour
(www.balihaicruises.com)
Laos Luang Say Cruise, Mekong (www.luangsay.com)
Malaysia Langkawi: Crystal Yacht Holidays
(www.crystalyacht.com); Langkawi Ferry
(www.langkawi-ferry.com)

Philippines Cebu: OceanJet (www.oceanjet.net) and
SuperCat (www.supercat.com.ph); Mactan Island:
Islands Banca Cruises (www.islandsbanca.com)
Singapore SAF Yacht Club (www.safyc.org.sg) and
Watertours (www.watertours.com.sg)
Thailand Bangkok: Chao Phraya Expressboat
(www.chaoprayaboat.co.th); Phuket: Phi Phi Ferry
(www.phiphiferry.com)
Vietnam Bhaya Cruises, Halong Bay
(www.bhayacruises.com)

ECO RESOURCES AND OTHER EXPERTS

CheckMeIn.eu allows you to check-in online as soon
as you have tickets, so you don't have to get up at dawn
to reserve the best seats.
ClimateCare.org offers advice on reducing your footprint,
and can help offset CO^2 emissions from your journeys
with its carbon calculator.
Greenspotter.org locates ethical businesses near you;
find eco-chic beachwear, green gifts and travel gadgets
using its online search.
JiWire.com flags up WiFi hotspots around the world.
SeatGuru.com has handy plans of the best seats to book.
Timeanddate.com gives you international dialling codes
and time zones, so you can plan the perfect time to
make your call, and punch all the right digits.

HOLIDAY HOUSES

Smith & Friends (www.smithandfriends.com) lists hip
holiday rentals, serviced apartments, private villas and
cherry-picked country cottages in Australia, France, Italy,
Spain, the UK and beyond.
Smith Ski (www.mrandmrssmith.com/ski) lets you find
and book super-stylish ski chalets.

(who are Mr & Mrs Smith?)

Our reviewers are a hand-picked panel of people we admire and respect, all of whom have impeccable taste, of course, and can be trusted to report back to us on Smith hotels with total honesty. The only thing we ask of them is that they visit each hotel anonymously with a partner, and on their return, give us the kind of insider lowdown you'd expect to hear from a close friend.

REVIEWERS' WHO'S WHO

Tony Ayres FREEWHEELING FILMMAKER
Tony is a filmmaker and sporadic nomad. As an old leftie, he has pangs of guilt about travelling in luxury, although his experience reviewing for Mr & Mrs Smith has helped him to work through that. Born in Macau, Tony has lived in Australia since he was a small child. As writer, director and producer he's been responsible for a clutch of award-winning productions, including *Walking on Water*, his feature film debut, and *The Home Song Stories*. He and Mr Smith live in Melbourne; he doesn't think of himself as Mrs Smith.

Helen Bodycomb MASTER MOSAICIST
Her work has taken Helen everywhere, from the north of Italy to central Malaysia, as both a teacher and student of the delicate art of mosaics. Often found concentrating on a small area of a design, this artist is clearly a believer in the old adage 'the devil's in the detail', something that should make hotel owners quake with fear. When not travelling the globe, Helen can be found practising her craft in a studio in Central Victoria, Australia.

Ellie Brannan ARTISTIC ALL-ROUNDER
After starting out in editorial on UK *InStyle*, Ellie was attracted to the more visual side of magazines and jumped to the art department. As her career advanced in leaps and bounds, she and her boyfriend (now Mr Smith) decided to see more of the world and made the move to Bangkok. After a few glitzy years attending perfume launches and interviewing fashion designers as the deputy editor on the *Bangkok Post*'s *the magazine*, Ellie worked on the launch of the south-east Asian edition of *Travel+Leisure*. Five years of expat adventures later, after the arrival of Smith Junior, she has returned to Brighton, England, where Ellie now plies her trade as a freelance writer and graphic designer.

Evelyn Chen COSMOPOLITAN CRITIC
Singapore-based Eveyln Chen traded her near-Solitaire frequent flyer miles from her jet-setting corporate days for a critic's pen, and has been eating, drinking and sleeping on the job ever since. In between reviewing the latest cool hotels for *Condé Nast Traveller*, *DestinAsian* and *The Independent*, she writes about food and travel. Evelyn also sits on the south-east Asian judging panel of the coveted S Pellegrino World's 50 Best Restaurants awards.

André Chiang GLOBE-TROTTING FOOD GURU
There's not much time for holidays when you're travelling from home in Singapore to international culinary events such as Madrid Fusion or the announcement of the S Pellegrino World's 50 Best Restaurants awards in London (where André's former eatery Jaan par André came in at a prestigious number 39). It does, however, give you the opportunity to do some rather interesting exploratory work, as chef André will attest. Dining out at the best places wherever he goes, as well as sussing out stylish trends that catch his eye, provides inspiration for dishes at his acclaimed new French nouvelle cuisine restaurant in Singapore, Par André.

Sudarampai Chiang THAI HIGH STYLISTA
Splitting her time between Bangkok, where she works, and Singapore, where Mr Smith works as a talented chef, has allowed Sudarampai (or Pam, as her friends know her) to rack up some serious frequent flyer miles. The former ballet dancer and yoga buff studied fashion and interior design in the US before working in public relations. It may come as no surprise that she loves to travel and has a keen eye for style, a trait that is invaluable in her latest role as editor-in-chief of *Grazia*'s Thai edition.

Carrie Choo ON-THE-PULSE BLOGGER
Life hasn't been the same for Carrie since she founded her website (www.dailyaddict.com.au), a style-savvy guide to what's hot in Sydney, at the start of 2008. Inspired by her constant quest for entertainment and enlightenment, she has put her love of writing, 10 years in corporate marketing and a fascination with people to good use, lifting the lid on the best the city has to offer – recently expanding the site to cover Melbourne's inside track too. She travels extensively and is addicted to caffeine, fashion, French films, Adriano Zumbo cakes, playing poker and exploring the worldwide web.

Krissada Clapp ACTOR, SINGER, SUPERSTAR
The love of luxury hotels runs in Kriss's veins: his mother, Kamala Sukosol, is both a jazz singer and owner of a boutique hotel and resort collection. It

was a passion for music, however, that set him on his current path. He was a member of a Thai pop band Pru (his brother Sukie was also a band member), and his debut solo album launches at the end of 2010. He has starred in films including *Bangkok Loco* and *13 Beloved*, winning a string of best actor awards for the latter. Next up he's playing a monk in the Thai comedy *Uncle Teng*. Kriss lives in Bangkok with Mrs Smith and their two children.

Bill Condie ASIA ADVENTURER
After half a lifetime on Fleet Street, Bill Condie heard about the Global Village and decided to make it his own by becoming the *Evening Standard*'s night editor in Bangkok. He travels extensively through Asia and beyond and has learnt many useful things, the most important being that he must never, ever discuss the weather with the London newsdesk in February.

Amy Cooper SEEN-IT-DONE-IT SCRIBE
Brit-born Sydneysider Amy's fascination with hotel minutiae comes as no surprise to her parents, who recall a child curiously obsessed with ice machines, shoe polishers and the housekeeper's cupboard during family holidays. UK tabloid journalism and its long hours spent lurking in hotels in pursuit of celebrities suited her well, but after editing women's magazines, writing dating columns in Australia and co-authoring a book about bad movies, Amy found her true calling writing about bars, parties and travel for *The Sun-Herald*. She remains at heart a frustrated hotelier. To this end, she recently mastered the art of towel sculpture and is particularly good at elephants and lobsters. Mr Smith is a tolerant man.

Sophie Dening ELOQUENT EDITOR
Originally one of Mr & Mrs Smith's founding editors, Sophie is now a freelance journalist and specialises in UK travel and restaurants, contributing to *High Life*, *Square Meal*, *Country & Town House* and *The Daily Telegraph*, for whom she seeks out the best new eateries, gastropubs, beach cafés and hotel dining rooms. When she isn't asking chefs for their foraging secrets or ordering another half of bitter shandy somewhere off the A49, Sophie likes eating figs in the south of France and rambling in East London, where she lives and works.

Stuart Gregor PR AND WINE WIZARD
Stuart takes the taste out of tastemaker. He is a slightly overweight, balding man who has a wardrobe full of brown shoes, jeans and golf shirts. He does, however, have a monumental wine cellar, which makes him popular at parties. He runs a luxury and lifestyle PR firm called Liquid Ideas, working with many of the smartest brands in the market. Before he ran out of adjectives, Stuart used to write about wine, penning six books and Australia's most widely read wine column for five years. He eats, he drinks, he shoots, he scores. He lives with Mrs Smith, his two children and a dog in Sydney.

Fiona Gruber WANDERING WORDSMITH
Hailing originally from the UK, Fiona is a journalist, broadcaster and writer based in Melbourne. She is struggling to finish a biography of Australia's first female gold miner and, for relaxation, runs Gert's Sunday Salon, a monthly cabaret club for trashy bohemians and serious wage-earners. Fiona's dream holiday involves a rocky Mediterranean cove, a classical ruin or two and a classy companion with lots of energy. Her favourite Australian destination is a small hut called Coolumbooka, a hide-out beside the rushing Buffalo River in upstate Victoria. She manages several holidays a year, although often disingenuously refers to them as work or retreats.

Trevor Hannam LUXURY MARKETING WHIZZ
Sydney-based Trevor has spent more hours than he'd care to confess searching the world for the perfect Negroni. As a drinks connoisseur working for more than a decade with a collection of the world's finest spirit and champagne houses, he has travelled extensively, researching what it takes to create the ultimate drinking experience. Trevor can be found sipping the finest martinis in near-impossible to find speak-easies, dining in Michelin-star restaurants or preferably spending long weekends with his very own Mrs Smith in exquisite spaces, enveloped in luxury. Give him a warm welcome with a big smile, a bed with beautifully soft pillows – oh, and that just-so Negroni – and he's in heaven.

Nadya Hutagalung ECO STAR
She made her name as one of Asian MTV's pioneering VJs, beamed into more than 70 million households around the continent, but former model turned entrepreneur Nadya's real passion is green issues.

She's an ambassador for the World Wildlife Fund's Earth Hour, runs a website called Green Kampong, has started her own sustainable jewellery line Osel and sold her paintings to aid the Tsunami Relief Fund. Her eco-friendly house in Singapore – filled to the brim with Mr Smith, three smaller Smiths, three cats and an edible garden – is like a holiday home at home. When she does travel, Nadya draws inspiration from her foodie-family upbringing and seeks out exquisite culinary experiences.

Rick Jordan RESTLESS WRITER
At the age of four months, Rick Jordan set sail for Sierra Leone with his parents, an epic voyage he has no memory of but has struggled to match ever since. He has written and sub-edited for *Wallpaper**, *Esquire* and *The Guardian*, and is currently chief sub-editor on *Condé Nast Traveller*. During his time at *Vogue House* in London he stayed in hotels from Bangkok to Kerala, although his favourite hotel experience was in a rooftop hot tub in Manchester, overlooking Coronation Street. He wonders why 'tea and coffee-making facilities' is still a selling point in this day and age.

Aun Koh MARKETING MEDIA MAN
This fast-talking world traveller grew up in New York and worked as a journalist in Manhattan, Paris and Hong Kong, before settling in Singapore. There Aun edited one of the region's first lifestyle magazines and dabbled in arts administration for the National Arts Council Singapore. Aun eventually left to start his own communications firm Ate, a dynamic mix of PR, marketing, event management and custom publishing. The author of several lifestyle, travel and food books, including *SingaporeChic*, *The Six Senses Cookbook* and *French Classics Modern Kitchen*, Aun also pens food blog Chubby Hubby.

Lee Manton CARD SHARP
A love of property has meant Lee's trips abroad are spent gazing in real estate windows and pretending, to over-eager agents, that she is interested – really – in buying a holiday home. Clued up on her habit, Mr Smith and the juniors now insist on a five-star hotel stay where they can relax by the pool while Mum goes a-viewing. When not gazing at luxe overseas apartments, school fees and shopping binges are funded via corporate life, creating premium card benefits for the masses. Lee's dream is to merge her professional and personal obsessions by using a premium card to access sensational properties throughout the world.

Jo Soh HIGH-FLYING FASHIONISTA
At age 12, Jo decided she wanted to be a fashion designer, so later in life she studied in the UK, worked in Italy and the US, and finally set up her whimsical womenswear label Hansel – named after her beloved pet Jack Russell terrier – in Singapore in 2003. Since then, her designs have graced the likes of Emily Barclay and Rose Byrne, she's launched a shop and she keeps in touch with fans via her popular blog. How different things could have been. Her first ambition was to be a pilot, but now she satisfies travel urges by sailing and getting close to the ocean.

Lyndsey Steven JET-SET EDITOR
Her first venture overseas from her native South Africa saw Lyndsey returning with a bald spot, courtesy of her two elder brothers, and disenchanted by the lack of leprechauns in Ireland. When Lyndsey was 13 her mum took her backpacking across Europe and America for six months, an eye-popping experience that would shape her future as a travel writer. She relocated from London to Dubai in 2005 to launch the *Time Out Middle East* guides in Qatar, Muscat and Bahrain, before moving on to edit in-flight and luxury hotel magazines.

Sofia Suarez JAUNTING JOURNO
When not posing as Mrs Smith in exotic locales, challenging conventional notions of disco dancing or trying to explain her eclectic background, Sofia writes for a variety of travel guides, luxury brands and magazines. She was born in Hong Kong to her Italian mother and Filipino father. Adding to the cultural confusion, she went to high school and university in the US. Sofia can usually be found exploring the streets of Hong Kong, researching for 'The Dictator' (her acerbic weekly style advice column in the *South China Morning Post*), enthusiastically guiding visitors and personal shopping clients around her hometown, or plotting her next escape.

David Thompson MASTER CHEF
David knows what he's talking about when it comes to south-east Asia. The Australian chef is considered an authority on Thai cuisine: he opened Darley Street Thai

and Sailors Thai in Sydney, before taking London by storm with his Michelin-starred restaurant Nahm. In the midst of opening his latest venture – a second branch of Nahm at the Metropolitan Bangkok – the Smiths sent him off on a stress-relieving break to Siem Reap. David is also the author of two comprehensive tomes, *Thai Food* and *Thai Street Food*, neither of which you'd ever want to have to carry in your luggage.

Liz Weselby ASIA-HOPPING EDITOR
When she arrived in Bangkok in 2003, little did Liz Weselby know that the hectic, steamy city would become her home for the next seven years. As she soon discovered, one of the best aspects of life in the Thai capital is the ease of escape from it: Liz uses the city as a base from which to explore south-east Asia, staying in tents, tree houses and boutique hotels along the way. After launching a lifestyle magazine supplement for Thailand's *Bangkok Post*, Liz set up a successful custom publishing business. She recently relocated to Singapore as editorial director at Ink Publishing.

MR & MRS SMITH TEAM

CEO James Lohan is one half of the couple behind Mr & Mrs Smith. James' first company, Atomic, created the infamous Come Dancing parties and club promotions. He built on this success by designing and producing events for clients such as Finlandia vodka and Wonderbra, then went on to co-found the White House bar, restaurant and members' club in London. Since publishing Mr & Mrs Smith's first book, James has visited almost 1,000 hotels and, now a father of two, he's become a keen advocate of our child-friendly hotel collection, Smith & Kids.

Chief technical officer Tamara Heber-Percy, co-founder of Mr & Mrs Smith, graduated from Oxford with a degree in languages, then left the UK for Brazil, where she launched an energy drink. She went on to work at one of the UK's top marketing agencies as a consultant for brands such as Ericsson and Honda and in business development for Europe, the Middle East and Africa. She left in 2002 to run her own company, the County Register – an exclusive introductions agency – and to launch Mr & Mrs Smith.

Asia-Pacific co-founder and managing director Simon Westcott grew up in London, but has called Melbourne home for more than 10 years. A graduate of Oxford and Indiana universities, he is a former global publisher and director of *Lonely Planet*, and has been a contributing editor for *Travel+Leisure* Australia/New Zealand. He has travelled extensively in Australia, NZ, Asia, Europe and North America, always and only with a single soft leather holdall from Gurkha.

Chief financial officer Edward Orr has worked in investment banking and managed companies in their early stages for more than a decade. As a result, he has stayed in hotels on every continent – and, generally, he doesn't like them. This makes him qualified not only to look after Mr & Mrs Smith's finances, but also to have penned the odd review. He can confirm that Smith hotels really are special enough to be a treat, even for the most jaded corporate traveller.

Publishing director Andrew Grahame launched the UK's first corporate-fashion magazine in 1990. After moving into catwalk shows and events, he transferred his talents from fashion to finance, launching *Small Company Investor* magazine. He started a promotions company in 1993 and, after a spell as a restaurant/bar owner in Chelsea, turned his hand to tourism in 1997, creating the award-winning London Pass and New York Pass, which give visitors access to the cities' attractions. With Juliet Kinsman, Andrew co-produced and co-presented our TV series *The Smiths' Hotels for 2* for the Discovery network.

MR & MRS SMITH IN LONDON

Associate director Laura Mizon spent her younger years in Spain and, after graduating from Manchester University, returned to her childhood home to work for four years at an independent record label in Madrid, promoting the emerging Spanish hip-hop movement. When she joined Mr & Mrs Smith as a freelancer in 2004, it soon became clear that Laura was to play a key role. She is now responsible for building relationships with like-minded brands, and all things operational.

Editor-in-chief Juliet Kinsman, part of the original team, helped create Mr & Mrs Smith's distinctive voice and can be caught leaking travel secrets in numerous publications, from *Elle Decoration* to the *New York Times*, as well as radio and TV. Juliet also presented *The Smiths' Hotels for 2* for the Discovery network, which has allowed her to visit just about every continent except Antarctica. Juliet's woken up in more stylish bedrooms than a high-class harlot, and reviewed more hip hotels and holiday houses than most people have sent postcards.

Managing editor Anthony Leyton joined Smith in 2007 to provide short-term help launching a handful of hotels in Asia, and has been an editorial fixture ever since. Before being embraced by the Smith family, he worked for *The Independent* and has penned pieces for publications both top-drawer (*The Daily Telegraph*) and top-shelf (*Fiesta*). He has had a love of travel ever since he found bullet holes in the walls of a hotel room in New Orleans.

Associate editor Lucy Fennings cut her travel teeth early; as daughter of a hotel PR, she visited far-flung flophouses from French châteaux to Ethiopian tukuls. After a year in Dubai (working on *Emirates Woman* magazine and enjoying the kind of dives that require a wetsuit), Lucy honed her production skills at Legalease in London, before exploring Asia. Mr & Mrs Smith found her

at *Harper's Bazaar*, keeping her finger on fashion's pulse and sharpening her editorial knife on hapless hotel PR copy. She has been a driving force in making the Smith Travel Blog an award winner.

Production executive Jasmine Darby has been with Smith since she graduated from Manchester University with an art history degree in 2006. Our reviewers know her as the reassuring voice on the end of the phone when they're in a crisis (whether it's lost passports or unexpected stomach bugs), but her areas of expertise are far more wide-ranging. Jasmine ensures that the process of introducing new hotels into the Smith collection runs smoothly, dispatching our reviewers across the world, and helping with every aspect of the book production process.

Designer Gareth Thomas joined Mr & Mrs Smith in 2009 to become the visual mastermind behind all things Smith-branded. Previously, he worked at London design agency Boston Studio, bringing his graphical flair to luxury brands such as Daylesford Organic, Bamford and Soane. Today, he alternates between creating beautiful layouts for Smith's books and website, and hanging out in the kitchen creating freshly baked surprises for the Smith team.

Head of hotel collections Katy McCann grew up in the south of Spain and later became editor of *InMadrid*, the largest English-language publication in the city. She was tracked down by Mr & Mrs Smith in 2004 to develop and expand our hotel collections, which fitted in perfectly with her love of travel and her multilingual skills. Having seen more than 2,000 hotels in the past six years, Katy is probably the world's most qualified person to ensure each property is the perfect addition to the Smith collection.

Head of hotel relations Peggy Picano-Nacci was born in Indonesia and grew up in France. The past 15 years have seen her earn an unrivalled understanding of what makes a great boutique hotel tick. A former sales manager at the Dorchester and an alumnus of Small Luxury Hotels of the World, where she was responsible for the French, Spanish and Portuguese territories, she also makes use of an alarming array of languages when working closely with our member hotels.

Head of PR and marketing Aline Keuroghlian has worked in travel for 15 years. Stints at Armani and London's quirky Sir John Soane's Museum helped cultivate her love of stylish things. After university came several years of guiding professionals across Italy for niche tour operator ATG Oxford, which made use of her maternal heritage. Nowadays, she puts both her sense and sensibility to work by dealing with some of the most beautiful hotels in the world, as featured in Mr & Mrs Smith's collections.

Head of relationship marketing Amber Spencer-Holmes may be a Londoner, but she has cosmopolitan credentials, having lived in Sydney and Paris before reading French and English at King's College London. Before joining Mr & Mrs Smith, Amber made waves in the music industry, running a number of well-respected record labels. She is married to our TuneSmith columnist Rob Wood.

Smith & Friends manager Natasha Shafi acquired an encyclopaedic travel knowledge working at Notting Hill's famed Travel Bookshop and a disarming charm from her role as marketing manager for a Middle Eastern publishing house. Although she came to Mr & Mrs Smith to take charge of office management, she quickly showed she was capable of much more, and now looks after our collection of stylish self-catering properties Smith & Friends.

Online manager Patsie Muan-ngiew left academia with a post-grad marketing diploma under her arm and went straight into the world of advertising and media buying. When she's not maintaining and improving the Smith website, she can be found in front of a sewing machine creating her latest fashion masterpiece. However, we still think that Patsie's greatest achievement is her turn as a Thai jailbird in Bridget Jones: The Edge of Reason.

Analyst, PPC and affiliate manager Andrew Leung was born in the cosmopolitan city of Hong Kong. Early exposure to varied cultures inspired his interest in travel, leading him to Switzerland where he studied international hospitality management at the Ecole Hôtelière de Lausanne. Working with Mandarin Oriental, Design Hotels and the ilk gave Andrew a taste of boutique hotel life, making him perfect to work on Smith's US expansion. The team quickly realised

Andrew had become indispensable, et voilà: he now plays an essential part in shaping Smith's web strategy.

Head of the Smith Travel Team, Rebecca Martin has worked in travel for more than a decade, and now uses skills she learnt from her psychology degree to motivate Smith's 21-strong team of consultants. Rebecca has worked as head of global account management for Small Luxury Hotels of the World, and spent eight years at Kuoni, managing the luxury World Class department, where she became a bona fide globetrotter, road-testing luxurious holidays ranging from idyllic Indian Ocean beach retreats to action-packed African safaris.

MR & MRS SMITH IN MELBOURNE

VP of hotel relations Debra McKenzie has lived and breathed hospitality throughout her working life, with time spent in front-of-house and managerial roles at the Ritz-Carlton and Hayman Island Resort. After refining her palate in the Sydney restaurant world, Debra went on to globetrot for Kiwi Collection from Australia to Europe – perfect training for her role as head hotel-hunter in Mr & Mrs Smith's Asia–Pacific office. She also moonlights as a photographer and stylist, working in Vancouver and Sydney with blue-chip clients.

Editorial manager Sophie Davies grew up in Turkey, Indonesia and Iran, exiting stage left during the revolution. After studying at Oxford, she worked as a researcher for Japanese TV, before swapping bento for boy bands with a features gig at Just Seventeen. Having freelanced for everyone from Time Out to The Telegraph, she spent six years at Elle Decoration, where, as assistant editor, Sophie learnt how to spot a good table at 20 paces, and honed her hotel-appreciation skills. When Smith's Melbourne office beckoned, it was time to leave London (and her beloved Arsenal) for pastures new.

Asia-Pacific hotel relations manager Samantha Anderson's career has taken her from Sheraton Hotels to Atomic Events, where she organised parties under the guidance of James Lohan, and was delighted to be there to see the birth of Mr & Mrs Smith. After a stretch as a chef at a hotel restaurant in Tuscany, Sam was lured back to Smith to research hotels Down Under for our Australia/

New Zealand collection and to join the new team in her home town of Melbourne.

Head of Asia-Pacific marketing & business development Amira Morgan forged her travel credentials early, attending an exotic mix of schools across Russia, Tunisia, Qatar, Austria and Australia. After graduating in foreign languages in Moscow, she swapped fur hats for flip-flops, going on to study marketing and advertising in Melbourne, the city she now calls home. Amira's professional savvy comes from her equally diverse background in both corporate marketing and creative ad agency roles. With her love for all things globe-encompassing, it's no surprise that Amira was thrilled to join Mr & Mrs Smith in 2010.

PR manager Rowena Fitzgerald was integral to launching Mr & Mrs Smith to the southern hemisphere as a senior account manager at Sydney PR firm Liquid Ideas. After four years of luxe parties, chic sports events and delectable food and wine, Rowena jumped ship to push the pleasures of Smith full time. Former journo and copywriter Ro is no stranger to drink, having promoted global brands such as Chivas Regal, Jameson Irish Whiskey and Wyborowa Vodka, although she prefers not to be pressed on the time she had to don a dirndl in the name of Bavarian Bier.

Partnership and events manager Sabine Zetteler, having been born to Finnish and Dutch parents, was always destined to work in a cosmopolitan setting. Her first job was international sales manager at London fashion house Belle & Bunty, jetting between fashion weeks in Milan, Paris, London and Los Angeles. She then worked for the BBC, before emailing her CV to us while on a trip around India. A few days after her return, she found herself sitting at a new desk contemplating her next adventure: promoting Mr & Mrs Smith around the world and curating unmissable Smith events Down Under.

GoldSmith Travel Consultant and Smith's antipodean office manager Tamara Ryan swapped an arts degree for globetrotting in true Australian rite-of-passage style – backpacking, pint-pulling and nannying her way around Europe. Catching a bad case of wanderlust en route, she returned to Melbourne to forge a career in travel. Her time in the international corporate travel market saw her canoeing the Zambezi, diving the Great Barrier Reef and getting lost in souks of Marrakech. Now, she's the lynchpin of Smith's Melbourne team, where she not only handles bookings, but also helps coordinate review stays for our anonymous tastemakers and keeps the office shipshape.

MR & MRS SMITH IN NEW YORK

Associate director Rodrigo Calvo grew up in Bolivia and hit the road days after his 18th birthday to study marketing in Austin, work as an ad man in Boston, and enjoy island seclusion in Elba, before heading back to South America to launch a marketing consultancy. Rodrigo crossed paths with Mr & Mrs Smith while he was doing an MBA in London, and he set to work expanding the brand in the US. Luckily for Smith, his next attack of wanderlust coincided with the opening of our Melbourne office, and he hotfooted it over to Australia to be part of the Asia–Pacific launch. When we founded our New York bureau in 2010, Rod was the natural candidate to head up the team.

US operations executive Chloe Smith developed a hunger for travel long before she finished her law degree. Having explored various corners of the world – highlights include living and working in Phnom Penh, discovering the jungles of Sabah and beach-hopping down Mexico's Pacific surf coast – she is now concentrating her efforts on bringing Smith's boutique-hotel expertise to North and South America. During her downtime, she plots her dream trip: conquering the Silk Road overland from Istanbul to Beijing.

(where in the world)

THE GLOBAL MR & MRS SMITH HOTEL COLLECTION

ICELAND

UNITED KINGDOM

SWEDEN

ESTONIA

CANADA

DENMARK

IRELAND

NETHERLANDS

GERMANY CZECH REPUBLIC

BELGIUM AUSTRIA

SWITZERLAND

FRANCE

UNITED STATES

SPAIN MONACO

ITALY

GREECE

PORTUGAL

TURKEY

CYPRUS

MOROCCO

BHUTAN

CHINA

MEXICO

CARIBBEAN

BELIZE

UNITED ARAB EMIRATES

INDIA

LAOS

THAILAND

GUATEMALA

CAMBODIA

VIETNAM

PHILIPPINES

SINGAPORE

MALAYSIA

BRAZIL

ZAMBIA

SOUTH AFRICA

INDIAN OCEAN

INDONESIA

AUSTRALIA

URUGUAY

ARGENTINA

NEW ZEAL

ASIA

Bhutan Paro, Thimphu
Cambodia Kep, Siem Reap
China Beijing, Hong Kong, Shanghai, Yangshuo
India Karnataka, Kerala
Indian Ocean Maldives, Mauritius, Seychelles
Indonesia Bali (Bukit Peninsula, Seminyak & Tabanan, Ubud), Jakarta, Lombok, Moyo Island, Sumba, Yogyakarta
Laos Luang Prabang
Malaysia Langkawi
Philippines Cebu & Mactan Island
Singapore Singapore
Thailand Bangkok, Chiang Mai, Chiang Rai, Hua Hin, Khao Yai, Koh Phi Phi, Koh Samui, Krabi, Phang Nga, Phuket
Vietnam Hanoi, Hoi An, Nha Trang

AUSTRALASIA

Australia Adelaide, Barossa Valley, Bay of Fires, Beechworth, Blue Mountains, Brisbane, Byron Bay, Canberra, Central Coast, Central Highlands, Clare Valley, Daylesford, the Grampians, Great Barrier Reef, Great Ocean Road, Hobart, Hunter Valley, Kangaroo Island, the Kimberley, Launceston, Lord Howe Island, Margaret River, Melbourne, Ningaloo Reef, Northern Beaches, Port Douglas, Red Centre, Southern Forests, Sydney, Top End
New Zealand Auckland, Bay of Islands, Christchurch, Hawke's Bay, Kaikoura, Lake Taupo, Queenstown, Wairarapa, Wellington

EUROPE

Austria Vienna, Zell am See
Belgium Antwerp, Brussels
Cyprus Limassol
Czech Republic Prague, Tábor
Denmark Copenhagen
Estonia Tallinn
France Aquitaine, Beaujolais, Bordeaux, Brittany, Burgundy, Cannes, Chamonix, Champagne-Ardenne, Côte d'Azur, Courchevel, Dordogne, Gers, Languedoc-Roussillon, Lyon, Normandy, Paris, Pays Basque, Poitou-Charentes, Provence, Rhône-Alpes, St Tropez, Tarn, Tignes Les Brévières, Vaucluse
Germany Berlin, Munich
Greece Athens, Crete, Kefalonia & Ithaca, Mykonos, Santorini
Iceland Reykjavík
Ireland County Carlow, County Meath, Dublin

Italy Abruzzo, Aeolian Islands, Amalfi Coast, Basilicata, Capri, Florence, Lake Como, Milan, Piedmont, Puglia, Rome, Sardinia, Sicily, Sorrento, South Tyrol, Treviso, Tuscany, Umbria, Venice
Monaco Monte Carlo
Netherlands Amsterdam
Portugal Cascais, Douro Valley, Lisbon
Spain Barcelona, Basque Country, Cadiz Province, Córdoba, Costa de la Luz, Empordà, Granada, Ibiza, Madrid, Mallorca, Marbella, Ronda, San Sebastián, Seville Province, Valencia
Sweden Stockholm
Switzerland Adelboden, Verbier
Turkey Istanbul
United Kingdom Argyll, Bath, Belfast, Berkshire, Birmingham, Brecon Beacons, Brighton, Cardigan Bay, Carmarthen Bay, Chilterns, Cornwall, Cotswolds, County Durham, Devon, Dorset, East Sussex, Edinburgh, Glasgow, Gloucestershire, Hampshire, Harrogate, Kent, Lake District, Liverpool, London, Manchester, Norfolk, Northamptonshire, North Yorkshire, Oxfordshire, Peak District, Pembrokeshire, Perthshire, Powys, Snowdonia, Somerset, Suffolk, Vale of Glamorgan, West Sussex, Wester Ross, Wiltshire, Worcestershire

REST OF THE WORLD

Argentina Buenos Aires, Salta
Belize Ambergris Caye, Cayo, Placencia
Brazil Bahia, Rio de Janeiro, Santa Catarina
Canada Montreal, Toronto
Caribbean Antigua & Barbuda, Barbados, Grenada, Jamaica, Mustique, St Barths, St Lucia, Turks & Caicos
Guatemala Flores
Mexico Colima, Jalisco, Mexico City, Puebla, Riviera Maya, Yucatán
Morocco Atlas Mountains, Essaouira, Marrakech, Ouarzazate
South Africa Cape Town, Garden Route & Winelands, Hermanus, Johannesburg, Kruger National Park, Madikwe, North West Province, Western Limpopo
United Arab Emirates Dubai
United States Austin, Berkshires, Big Sur, Boston, Hamptons, Litchfield Hills, Los Angeles, Miami, Napa Valley, New York, Palm Springs, Portland, San Antonio, San Diego, San Francisco, Smoky Mountains, Sonoma County, Washington DC
Uruguay Punta del Este
Zambia Lower Zambezi

(bit on the side)

Visit our online shop and you'll find all you need to complete your escapes – or remember them by. We don't just create boutique-hotel bibles: our sexy music compilations will soundtrack your weekends; a little black-leather luxury will enhance your passports and luggage. At Mr & Mrs Smith, we're all about making the very most of your time away...

JOIN THE CLUB

With this book, you're already a BlackSmith member for six months, and entitled to all sorts of benefits (see pages 4–5 for details). Treat yourself to even more with an upgrade: SilverSmith gets you four per cent back from each booking towards your next hotel stay. You also get half-price deals at new Smith hotels, and Last-Minute Club discounts of over 40 per cent. Upgrade to a GoldSmith, and we'll handle hotel, flight, theatre and restaurant bookings – we'll even arrange someone to feed your pets while you're away. You'll get automatic room upgrades at Smith hotels whenever available, free airport lounge access and exclusive brand partner discounts, as well as five per cent back in loyalty credits. Plus much more, including – ahem – essential black leather extras...

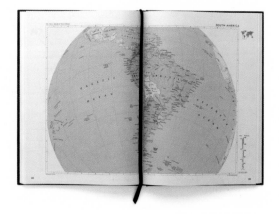

NOT JUST ABOUT PRETTY PLACES

Browse our online boutique and discover elegant travel essentials for globetrotting sybarites:

• Whet your wanderlust with an oversized, sleekly bound, special Smith edition of the prestigious and authoritative *The Times Reference Atlas of the World*.

• How's about a heavyweight black brushed-cotton bathrobe embroidered in gold? Hugh Hefner, we're standing by for your order.

• A pair of leather luggage tags or a passport holder, designed exclusively for Mr & Mrs Smith by Bill Amberg, ensures your packing has panache.

SIX BOOKS, HUNDREDS OF STYLISH HOTELS, ENDLESS INSPIRATION

Whether you're looking for a romantic spa retreat, a cosy inn or a blow-out beach hideaway, Smith's hotel guides signpost you to the most ravishing stays around the world. Each is, as ever, a capsule kit for an effortless escape, beginning with that all-important BlackSmith membership card. Other guidebooks (as pictured above), include:

- *European Cities*
- *Australia/New Zealand*
- *European Coast & Country*
- *France*
- *UK/Ireland Volume 2*

TUNE IN AND SWITCH OFF

Essential accessories whether you're lounging in a sumptuous suite or hitting the road, Smith CDs make the ideal aural aphrodisiac. Our four *Something for the Weekend* albums move from jazz-funk to soul via sexy rock riffs. The brand new *In Bed With...* is an inspired romp through a genre-hopping array of the classic and the contemporary, with 16 tracks personally picked by art, fashion, media and music luminaries. This album also supports Shelter, the UK housing and homelessness charity.

THE GIFT THAT KEEPS ON GIVING

Gift vouchers have never been more seductive: treat someone to a stay at any hotel in our collection, with a Mr & Mrs Smith *Get a Room!* gift card. In a slender black box this gift voucher is the perfect way to surprise your partner, family or friends – they might even invite you along.

shop.mrandmrssmith.com

BlackSmith, SilverSmith and GoldSmith members get exclusive discounts when purchasing anything from the Mr & Mrs Smith shop. Retail therapy, indeed.

(applause)

thank you

Earl Carter and his assistant Fraser Marsden for the lion's share of our gorgeous photography; Lauryn Ishak and Jason Lang for inspiring additions; editorial whizzes, the all-knowing Sophie Davies, Lucy Fennings, Carrie Hutchinson, Juliet Kinsman, Anthony Leyton and Kate Pettifer for their wondrous wordsmithing; star interns Chloe Gardner and Liarna La Porta for their help along the way; Smith Asia hounds Jerome Bouchaud, Graeme Green, Nick Ray, Cynthia Rosenfeld, Andrew Spooner, Liz Weselby and Daven Wu for their on-the-ground, insider smarts; heroic project manager and editor Jacqueline Blanchard for keeping us on track and Laura Mizon and Jasmine Darby for their unflustered support and wisdom. Not all our good looks are genetic – thanks are due to: designers Gareth Thomas and Nikki Paff for making it all look so beautiful, and to Bloom for the original creative Big Bang; picture editor Lisa Steer for her keen eye; Warren Smith at Splitting Image and Lena Frew at C and C for first-class repro and printing; Sandy Grant, Keiran Rogers and the sales team at Hardie Grant for bookstore brilliance; all our stockists; Lynn Yeow and Dennis She at Ate Media in Singapore for shouting about us in south-east Asia; and to all of our tastemakers and 'other halves' who so ably shared the stories of their stays. And finally, the ever-extending Smith family Down Under, who live the dream daily and made this book possible; in Asia-Pacific, Debra McKenzie for relentless hotel-hunting; and in the UK Mary Garvin and Katy McCann for their global getaway-gathering missions; Aun Koh and Daphne Tan for original Eastern adventures; Tamara Ryan and Gabriella Higham for travel planning and booking; Samantha Anderson for hotel liaison; Rowena Fitzgerald for in-house spruiking; Rodrigo Calvo and Erin Morris for marketing marvels; and newest recruits Amira Morgan and Sabine Zetteler. Stars one and all.

Smith

Mr & Mrs Smith

(index)

To book any of the hotels featured, visit www.mrandmrssmith.com

(the small print)

Editorial Sophie Davies, Juliet Kinsman, Carrie Hutchinson, Lucy Fennings, Kate Pettifer
Design Gareth Thomas and Nikki Paff
Art direction Bloom (www.bloom-design.com)
Project management Jacqueline Blanchard
Photography Earl Carter, except as indicated below
Picture editor Lisa Steers
Cover Six Senses Ninh Van Bay, Vietnam, shot by Earl Carter
Font designer Charles Stewart and Co
Wallpaper istockphoto
Printed and bound in China by C and C Printing. This book is printed on paper from a sustainable source.
ISBN 978-0-9565347-0-5

Photography Cover (Six Senses Ninh Van Bay) and all hotel images shot by Earl Carter, except: 160–170 and 135–139 shot by Lauryn Ishak; 149 (bottom left) shot by Jason Lang; 146, 147, 148, 149 (top right), 150 Abacá Boutique Resort; 82–83 The Legian & The Club; 92, 94 Como Shambhala Estate; 134 Bon Ton Restaurant & Resort; 236 The Library; 13, 15, 22, 25, 43, 45, 64–66, 86, 88, 108–109, 130, 134, 157, 159, 207, 286, 295 Lonely Planet Images; 14, 23, 107, 142, 156, 158, 174, 176, 193, 225, 233, 235, 248, 250, 259, 261, 284, 285, 287, 294, 305, 307 Getty; 24, 87, 131, 175, 177, 192, 206, 208, 234, 258, 296–297 istockphoto; 44, 145, 306 Corbis; 67, 89, 144, 224, 304 Alamy; 133, 190–191, 209, 222 Dreanstime; 232, 249 4Corners; 251, 260 Thinkstock; 143 Grahame Green; 223 Khao Yai Winery.

First published in 2010 by Mr & Mrs Smith Pty Ltd
© Mr & Mrs Smith Pty Ltd

British Library Cataloguing-In-Publication data. A catalogue record of this book is available from the British Library.

Mr & Mrs Smith
2nd floor, 334 Chiswick High Road
London W4 5TA
Telephone: +44 (0)20 8987 6970
Fax: +44 (0)20 8987 4300
Email: info@mrandmrssmith.com

Mr & Mrs Smith (Asia-Pacific)
Suite 1-C, 205–207 Johnston Street, Fitzroy
Melbourne, VIC 3065, Australia
Telephone: +61 (0)3 9419 6671
Fax: +61 (0)3 9419 6673
Email: info@mrandmrssmith.com.au